Governance and Sustainability

New Challenges for States, Companies and Civil Society

Governance and Sustainability

NEW CHALLENGES FOR STATES, COMPANIES AND CIVIL SOCIETY

BUSINESS LIBRARY

EDITED BY ULRICH PETSCHOW, JAMES ROSENAU
AND ERNST ULRICH VON WEIZSÄCKER

Greenleaf
PUBLISHING

2 0 0 5

1005072710

© 2005 Greenleaf Publishing Ltd, unless otherwise stated

Published by Greenleaf Publishing Limited
Aizlewood's Mill
Nursery Street
Sheffield S3 8GG
UK
www.greenleaf-publishing.com

Printed on paper made from at least 75% post-consumer waste
using TCF and ECF bleaching.
Printed in Great Britain by William Clowes Ltd, Beccles, Suffolk.
Cover by LaliAbril.com.

British Library Cataloguing in Publication Data:
    A catalogue record for this book is available from the British Library.

ISBN 1874719799

Contents

Preface

The processes of economic and cultural globalisation, the modification of 'stateness', along with tendencies towards individualisation, have all led to the wide use of the term 'governance' but without any standard definition. 'Governance' is often regarded as a 'system of rule' in the absence of a central assertion of authority. This is not to say, however, that a continuous diminution of authority can be observed; rather, it concerns a diffusion or redistribution of authority. In future, national states will play an important, if changed, role. The significance of players from companies and civil society will, however, increase.

Sustainable development, often interpreted as a regulative concept, cannot be viewed as a top-down approach, but rather requires the inclusion of all players. The focus of sustainable development lies in the relationships, often pre-structured owing to power balances, between social players, and thus exerts influence on socially (self-)controlling structures.

Sustainable development is thus closely connected to governance structures and requires the investigation of new forms of social co-operation and confrontation. In this, we must take into consideration different levels (global to local), players (state, company and civil society), control structures (hierarchy, market, joint) and also fields of action. Governance structures for sustainable development must especially enable individual and social learning processes and create options for design. This applies particularly against the background of the intra- and inter-generational justice precepts of the sustainability concept.

Some of these subjects have been focal points of the conference 'Governance and Sustainability: New Challenges for the State, Business and Civil Society' which took place in Berlin shortly after the World Summit for Sustainable Development in Johannesburg in 2002. The editors are happy to present some results of this conference in this volume.

The editors also wish to express their gratitude for the funding of the conference as well as the book by the German Federal Ministry for Education and Research (BMBF), Bonn, within the framework of Socio-ecological Research (SÖF), and for the co-operation of the Friedrich Ebert Foundation Berlin in preparing and managing the conference which took place in the Foundation's premises in Berlin.

They further wish to express their gratitude towards the contributors, who have drafted and redrafted their contributions and shown considerable patience during the long process of completing the book.

James Rosenau, Ernst Ulrich von Weizsäcker and Ulrich Petschow

Introduction

Ulrich Petschow, James Rosenau and Ernst Ulrich von Weizsäcker

As the title *Governance and Sustainability* indicates, the main goal of this book is to link two debates that rank rather highly on the scientific and political agenda. At the same time, these two key concepts point to relevant societal problems at the beginning of the 21st century. The combination of the terms **governance** and **sustainability** refers to the question of steering societies towards sustainability. This combination of concepts/terms brings analytical as well as normative aspects into focus. It is our hope that the linkage may provide some innovative insights and direction for further debate, as well as steps towards sustainability.

At first sight political steering in general as well as discussions about sustainability are seen as the main issues within global development processes. Discussions about the limits to the steering capacity of nation-states are entwined with processes of economic globalisation (compare the contributions of Petschow and von Weizsäcker in this volume). The ongoing processes of globalisation are changing the possibilities for political influence. This holds true at the political level, where multi-level governance becomes increasingly important, and at the market level, where an increasing transnationalisation of economic relations is to be observed. As one consequence market actors may use their 'exit option', forcing nation-states into adjustment processes, and putting the regulatory power of states into perspective directly or indirectly. But these adjustment processes are driven, too, by processes of societal differentiation. Intensive discussion processes are being conducted about steering capabilities against the background of economic and societal processes of differentiation. This process is tightly knit to the governance concept. Despite variations in detail, the common core of most governance approaches is to include other actors, and not just governments, and their contribution to steering structures (compare the contributions of Rosenau and Petschow).

At the same time, awareness-raising processes concerning environmental protection have arisen, pointing out that certain types of environmental problems have not been solved even in a rudimentary fashion, and that simple solutions especially at the global level are not in sight. The global dimension of the debate about sustainability is witness to this increased awareness. At the beginning the main reasons for this debate were not the limits of steering capacities of nation-states but rather the globalisation of environmental problems. These problems are increasingly not only concentrated at the regional or national level but at the global level, either by shifting from one medium to another or by cumulative effects. In sum global environmental problems are the outcome of myriads of individual actions. Traditional approaches of environmental policies, often hierarchic and focused on end-of-pipe solutions, fail, not least because of these developments. As a result instruments and governance approaches become more differentiated and there is an increasing need for new governance mechanisms, which have to be embedded into changing economic and societal structures. Problems of sustainability prove to be intractable because of their spatio-temporal structures and interconnectedness, representing complex social–ecological problems. This is especially true concerning the global commons, and the global dimension and the interaction with national or regional levels might be one main theme of the general problems of governance. This holds true all the more as questions are raised not only about global governance but also about very different governance scales.

Linking two separate debates

Against this background there is a sound argument for the analytical connection of the concepts of governance and sustainability although they are often characterised by different scientific traditions. As common ground, both concepts point towards the fading opportunities of nation-states to steer by their traditional means; nevertheless they remain significant. Furthermore both issue areas increasingly demand new models of regulation, including self-regulation mechanisms. Within the debate about sustainability (not only at the international level) quite different normative approaches meet each other, whereby the discourse about norms becomes increasingly important.

Furthermore both debates are focused on diffusion and fragmentation. Within the governance debate it is pointed out that centres of power are fading. They are replaced by emerging layers of influence shaped by multi-level governance on the one side and on the other side by the increasing importance of private actors. In the context of the sustainability debate there are similar developments to be observed. The so-called 'low-hanging fruit' in the form of emissions reductions via point source measures are reaped; however, some fundamental changes in development are needed. One main approach, especially within the European Union, is the integration of environmental protection into other policy fields or into economic and social relationships. Therewith environmental protection is a main part of sustainable development and goes further than traditional approaches of environmental policy. The fragmentation of problem-solving approaches in environmental policy as well as of general development problems becomes one main issue of the debate about governance.

One of the starting theses of this book is that coping with the challenges of sustainable development requires a change of steering processes and these changes have to include the challenges of globalisation. Therefore there is the need for modification of governance mechanisms. The processes of globalisation lead to changes of power between different actors; some actors lose influence while others, especially mobile actors, win. Sustainability requirements are often mainly connected with actors that have only limited influence and therefore only one main source of power, that of discourse. Eventually discourses might become powerful and might change problem awareness and, furthermore, initiate learning, which in the long run might have important effects on steering

Opportunities for governance for sustainability

Governance for sustainability under contemporary conditions is confronted with challenges that exceed the capacity of traditional governance solutions for local or regional commons in which sustainability could be sustained over long time periods. In these cases governance is marked by the coherence of economic, social and environmental developments. Therefore one of the main challenges is to identify solutions that might be appropriate for the governance of the global commons. Environment has increasingly to be regarded as a limiting production factor, deterioration of which leads to more or less direct feedback effects. The new and globalised environmental problems usually have longer time-frames and the feedback loops are less significant at least in the short term. Awareness-raising processes therefore are much more difficult now than those appropriate for traditional environmental problems. Furthermore, environmental problems are usually strongly connected with different world-views and normative approaches. The sometimes fierce discussions about the precautionary principle bear witness to this.

Nevertheless the founding principles of steering mechanisms developed at the local and regional level might be transferable. Starting with the concept of 'spheres of authority' as developed by Rosenau, one may identify spaces of responsibility, which at least in sub-areas may regulate the interaction of ecological, social and economic dynamics, but of course have to be embedded in broader frameworks. Possible starting points, which are developed in several contributions to this book, are as follows.

Within international relations non-state actors are gaining increasing importance. This development can be traced to the negotiation processes for international environmental treaties, but also to the agenda of the World Trade Organisation (WTO), which is built on inputs and/or at least influenced by non-state actors. One main question in this regard is through which channels non-state actors influence the agenda and exert power. This question is on the one hand connected with resources and access to decision-making opportunities; on the other hand it highlights that non-governmental organisations (NGOS) may influence norms and values and discursive power. Both facets of power of NGOs might be observed within the different stages of the policy cycle, starting with agenda setting via policy formulation to implementation.

The importance of the inclusion of stakeholders in decision-making processes is increasingly recognised, as are the limits of decision processes which are, on the one side, democratically legitimised but on the other side pre-structured by experts and interest groups. Approaches as they are developed within the European Union (White Paper on Governance [EC 2001]) show the need for not treating and regulating issue areas separately, but rather integrating them in a broader view and thus identifying and implementing integrated-solution approaches.

Governance dynamics within the European Union are often exemplary for problems of multi-level governance, of course with the qualification that, at a global level, a similar supra-state organisation does not exist. One example of these multi-level approaches is the new environmental concept of an integrated product policy. This approach aims at a co-operative structure including enterprises to achieve a continuous improvement of the environmental performance of products covering the whole product cycle.

Taking the term used by Rosenau there is created a 'sphere of authority' of integrated product policy. The aim is that the responsibility for environmental protection should be taken by all actors along the product chain, producers and consumers, and an integration of economic and ecological aspects should be achieved. Under the current framework this is not a self-evident process but instead the incentive mechanisms for a dynamic process have to be developed.

Finally the enterprises become more and more a target of requests by stakeholders. The traditional discussion about corporate governance focuses mainly on the shaping of the steering structures within enterprises. This discussion usually does not include the environmental or social sphere but instead focuses on solutions concerning the principal–agent problem between capital owners and management. Recently, a broadening of firms' governance has been observed, which includes such areas as the requests for sustainability and the demand of stakeholders. A culture of accountability has developed, increasingly including aspects of sustainability in general. A broadening of the concept of corporate governance, which includes these 'external affairs', means that the responsibility on the one side towards the global commons and on the other side towards societal actors seems to be acknowledged. With this, corporations have to take into account the multiplicity of spheres of authority.

In principle many of the new governance approaches are taking into account such spheres of authority and encouraging the shared responsibility of producers, consumers and actors from civil society. Governance for sustainability therefore focuses on governance structures, which support these responsibilities and, with this, initiate the drive to improve the sustainability-oriented processes. Therewith are connected many approaches, problems and actors. The contributions to this book look at these problems and actors in order to develop processes.

Part 1. Governance and global sustainability: setting the stage

Chapter 1 discusses the aspects of governance, sustainability and globalisation, which covers both problem areas in further depth, and sets the stage for the following contributions. The first two contributions by the editors, **James Rosenau** and **Ulrich Petschow**, scan the horizon for an integrative approach, starting from two different perspectives. James Rosenau, who has substantially contributed to the governance debate, uses this background to address problems of environmental sustainability. Similar to globalisation, he characterises sustainability as a 'fragmegrative' process in which tendencies of fragmentation and integration intermingle. In an increasingly complex world without central authority this points to a dilemma, which leads him to conclude on a rather pessimistic tone. Although there are some positive signs, he sees little prospect for decentralised governance for sustainability.

Ulrich Petschow, who has a strong background in sustainability research, identifies important 'governance gaps', too, but is on balance more optimistic. In his contribution, he reviews and brings together the literatures on globalisation and its driving forces, on globalisation and the environment, as well as on governance. Pointing to a variety of governance levels and mechanisms, he emphasises the role of discourse and values for governance for sustainability. This entails chances for weaker non-state actors to contribute to the development of appropriate governance processes. Hence not only states and governmental organisations, but also decentralised market dynamics and social regulations can play an important role for reducing the governance gaps, if the spheres of authority are linked with the attribution of responsibilities . . .

The other two contributions to Part 1 take a stronger policy perspective. In his contribution, the co-editor and German Member of Parliament, **Ernst Ulrich von Weizsäcker**, emphasises the negative role of economic globalisation for environmental policy. Despite the economic potential of a significantly higher resource productivity, 'factor four' (von Weizsäcker *et al.* 1997) does not take off because global markets restrain the capacity of the nation-state to set the necessary framework conditions. Global governance as a possible substitute emerges too slowly and is difficult to establish, hence also alliances of states with civil society should be created and strengthened for enhanced environmental sustainability.

Martin Khor, leader of the non-governmental organisation Third World Network, takes an important complementary focus on governance and sustainability issues. He emphasises the development dimension of global sustainability, exemplified in the United Nations Millennium Development Goals to improve the lot of humanity in the new century. The focus of the contribution is on Goal 8, to 'develop a global partnership for development'. However, as Khor argues, the already-established global *economic* governance structures can work as impediments in this respect. He focuses on the role of the WTO and, to a lesser extent, institutions of the global financial system.

Khor claims that the dominant approach (Washington Consensus) with its focus on full, rapid and comprehensive integration of developing countries into the global economy and the corresponding main advice of international organisations to developing countries of getting domestic policies right, might be inappropriate if economic and social structures are inequitable. Therefore one main focus should be on getting international economic structures, policies and rules right. Further, he argues for a pragmatic and selective approach of developing countries to globalisation and liberalisation. Hence also the last contribution to Part 1 points to critical linkages between governance and sustainability and the need for changes in governance at both international and national levels.

Part 2. Cross-cutting issues

Part 2 addresses three types of cross-cutting issue which might strongly frame the dynamics of governance and sustainability. The first issue explored by two contributions is the dynamics of learning and innovation, which shape the conditions and prospects of governance as well as act as dynamic forces able to induce processes of change.

Starting out from a brief overview of existing approaches to conceptualising social learning processes in political science, **Bernd Siebenhüner** sketches some ideas about a more general conceptual framework on sustainability-related social learning processes. For deliberately initiating sustainability-oriented social learning processes, he points to the option of participatory procedures involving individuals from different organisations and different societal subsystems. These processes allow for the articulation and interaction between different perceptions, interpretations and argumentations by the actors involved and could, at best, result in concrete solutions, for example to sustainability-related problems. They thus have the potential to initiate both inter- and intra-organisational learning processes.

Matthias Weber emphasises first that sustainability implies giving direction to innovation processes, which involves system innovations and transition processes. For the development of an appropriate governance perspective, he further argues that it is necessary to take into account new insights about innovation processes. He proposes a dynamic conceptual framework termed 'complex innovation systems', which includes parts of governance structures as part of the system. For building on these dynamics, policies should take a forward-looking and adaptive approach, in which vision building is a key element.

The second cross-cutting issue addressed in Part 2 is co-operation and participation. **Claudia von Braunmühl** points out that gender mainstreaming might be an important instrument and institutional strategy to enrich the formal structures of democracy by making institutions and governance processes more inclusive in terms of equal opportunity and equal access for women. However, past experience with gender mainstreaming in particular in the global South indicates that, for this democratising process to happen, a debate in the public sphere is needed that encompasses a review and revision of the fundamental objectives and values of the given societal order, because neoliberal structural adjustment and corporate-driven globalisation constantly erode social development and systematically produce gender-unjust results. That kind of debate would indeed carry transformative dynamics. In Europe where an additive and institutionalised approach to gender mainstreaming prevails and works to a certain extent to keep the status quo, sustainable development could provide the necessary transformative aspect.

Angela Liberatore points out that participation is one of the main implicit pillars for institutional reform, as the Johannesburg Summit once again made clear. Environmental advocacy organisations in particular raised the question of whether the private sector was taking ownership of the sustainable development agenda. Participation has been a founding feature of discourses and practices of sustainable development, from the focus on community participation in the Brundtland Report to the experience of Local Agenda 21. Liberatore's contribution focuses on experience with governance reform in the European Union. Since governance is not an exclusive domain of governments and other public actors, the question of who participates in governance processes and institutions is a truly crucial one and the forms and impacts of involvement of non-state actors is the 'novelty' to be analysed.

While participation is increasingly presented as a key factor to address legitimacy and effectiveness problems, Liberatore points out that it provides increased legitimacy and effectiveness only under specific circumstances of accountability, balance, relevance and transparency. As to substantive democracy, it is increasingly clear that rights are not only political, but also social and economic; participatory governance can help find the balance between them when conducted within a democratic framework. The potential for extending participatory approaches that might improve policy legitimacy and effectiveness is significant; its transformation in reality will require strong commitment from all actors of European governance—from citizens to political and economic elites at various levels and in various areas of public life.

One of the central outcomes of the Johannesburg Summit was the co-operation agreements and partnerships between state and non-state actors (so called Type II initiatives). As a positive aspect of these new approaches, **Jan Martin Witte**, **Charlotte Streck** and **Thorsten Benner** recognise that they perhaps lead to some new form of environmental governance, including not only governments and international organisations but also business and NGOs. However, a serious shortcoming of the WSSD (World Summit on Sustainable Development) debate and the realised approach was its failure to clearly define the partnership concept. No comprehensive understanding was developed of what to expect from partnerships and what role various actors should play.

In order to develop an evaluation, Witte *et al.* propose that the Type II initiatives could be compared with the global public policy networks which have emerged over the past two decades. They propose the three criteria: interdependence, flexibility and learning capability, and complementarity. Furthermore they point out that different types of network have different implications for concerns about legitimacy, accountability, transparency and power asymmetries and that there is the need to develop some basic rules for the Type II initiatives in order to realise the high potential for policy implementation and policy learning.

Part 3. Actors in global governance and their changing roles

Part 3 presents a short overview of the positions of and processes within three main groups of actors in governance processes: the state, companies and civil society. One subject turns out to dominate all three groups of actors: while the possibilities of the nation-state to legislate seem to vanish, a variety of problems arise which have to do with the subsequent activities to find non-legislative means of governance. These non-legislative means of governance usually involve more actors and create multiple problems of legitimacy, power, information and agenda setting.

But concerning the role of the nation-state as the first main group of actors, **Martin Jänicke** argues that neither the fear nor the hope of a withering-away of the nation-state in times of globalisation is supported by empirical research. He sees enhanced power of states if they act in concert and he sees especially the ability of at least the advanced OECD (Organisation for Economic Co-operation and Development) countries to promote change by the adoption of a pioneering policy, the stimulation of international competition and the diffusion of best practice. Jänicke sees this potential of the highly advanced countries as a moral obligation to assume a greater responsibility for global environmental development. The advanced nations cannot hide behind the fictive monster of globalisation, seemingly legitimising any kind of inactivity. On the contrary, it is their obligation to provide the world with sustainable 'demonstration effects', with a better model of production and consumption overcoming the resource- and environment-intensive model of the past.

Taking a closer look at the example of an integrated product policy (IPP), **Frieder Rubik** demonstrates how the modern nation-state can start to influence business actors in areas where legislation is not a viable option. The focus of IPP is on business and environmental performance along the whole value chain, including upstream and downstream activities. The author presents this new approach and emphasises that, for a successful IPP, state actors have to adopt a new way of thinking, co-operating and acting in a strategic and anticipative pattern, using (product) innovation as transmission mechanism for market transformations. Hence co-operation, information and integration are key issues. The integration challenge concerning life-cycles, environmental media, actors and tools can only be dealt with by accepting a shared responsibility. In IPP, business becomes—in the best case—partner of the state in order to solve common environmental problems.

Also in many other cases voluntary initiatives of businesses are currently seen as a good opportunity to advance environmental problem-solving where legislation seems to be inappropriate or is simply impossible. In the case of transnational corporations (TNCs), voluntary initiatives might also lead to improvements in countries of operation where enforcement of local environmental legislation is weak. But these improvements might be realised only if the TNCs comply with their voluntary targets (see also the general requirements for partnerships formulated by Witte *et al.* in Part 2). **Jens Clausen**, **Kathrin Ankele** and **Ulrich Petschow** discuss in somewhat more detail the problem of compliance with voluntary initiatives. They see media and public discussion as a central means to reveal non-compliance and execute influence on non-complying TNCs by the impact this information might have on product and capital markets. Proper monitoring of and public information about target achievement of voluntary initiatives is central because the only possible mechanism of sanction lies in concerted action of public communities in markets and—indirectly—in their demand for legislative action if the success of voluntary initiatives proves to be insufficient.

From within a major TNC, **Mark Wade** from Shell International outlines the Royal Dutch/Shell Group of companies' approach to sound corporate governance. The starting point for him is a society where people are less willing than they were in the past to take the assurances of authorities such as governments, scientists and companies on trust. There is an increasing call for corporations to show what it is they are doing. And in the absence of trust—something that characterises the modern world—there is a demand for independent verification of what is being shown. Based on this view of society—which was mainly developed after the Brent Spar affair—Shell enhanced communication with stakeholder groups and redefined Shell's Business Principles. The company developed a set of instruments and organisational guidelines with which it hopes to assure compliance not only in the area of binding legislation but also concerning planned voluntary action. Not surprisingly Mark Wade strongly opts for postponing, for example, legislation in the emerging area of corporate social responsibility, which he thinks would certainly be counterproductive at this early stage and expresses general confidence in the ability of TNCs to follow voluntary codes.

In the view of **Cornelis van der Lugt** of the United Nations Environment Programme (UNEP), greater pressure from consumer-citizens moves more businesses to take moral or ethical positions and acknowledge social responsibilities. In addition to consumer pressure, questions from investors and shareholders also confirm that the business case for sustainability is becoming clear. In this situation, UN Secretary-General Kofi Annan considered it necessary to start up the UN Global Compact to advance corporate citizenship globally. By the end of 2002 a global network of over 700 companies, international trade unions, over two dozen international NGOs and supportive networks of CSR (corporate social responsibility) organisations and business schools were engaged in the effort under the Global Compact, and others co-operate in the definition of a global framework for sustainability reporting. Though van der Lugt does not explicitly mention the problem of compliance, he obviously takes it seriously. This is due to the high importance he gives to the work of the Global Reporting Initiative to foster reporting both as a means to display accountability and transparency, and as a means to improve the management systems of the reporting corporations.

Explicitly or implicitly all non-legislative approaches to governance of business rely on active consumer-citizens and their interest groups to exercise influence on corporations, either by demonstrating public opinion with influence on the companies' image, by buying or not buying goods or by investment decisions. But also national and international negotiation and legislation strives for more integration of civil society. However, both authors contributing on the role of civil society, **Nicola Bullard** and **Dieter Rucht**, see narrow limits for civil society to execute power.

From a NGO point of view, Nicola Bullard points out that, after a period of enthusiasm at the beginning of the 1990s, the Johannesburg Summit made clear that society was divided into (good) civil and (bad) uncivil society. The 'good civil society' accepts the roles of governments and business and is, for example, integrated in negotiations. The 'bad uncivil society' is kept out of the door. And, after all, the only group really achieving more power between Rio and Johannesburg is business, which has also started to use the UN to legitimise its globalisation project.

From a more scientific view Dieter Rucht arrives at similar conclusions. He also sees that TNCs start riding on the NGO ticket to gain legitimacy and organise their public relations activities accordingly. He admits that a number of NGOs use modern information and communication technology in order to exercise influence and at least obtain a lot of resonance in the media. But their real power is mostly less than it seems to be. On an international level NGOs might have some influence in the human rights negotiations, but concerning, for example, (really important) international questions of finance and development as they were negotiated in Monterrey, Mexico, their influence was low.

From the contributions of Nicola Bullard and Dieter Rucht we might conclude from Part 3 that governments and TNCs are increasingly co-operating but this is in no way a guarantee that civil society's interests are taken into account. Civil society's involvement in governance structures is still a critical point and will remain at a low level, unless the scale of problems increases and demands further integration of civil society, or the mobilising of society as a whole powerfully demands that important questions are dealt with by integrating all forces of society. Some of the thinking of TNCs as pointed out by Mark Wade strives for more integration of stakeholders but, finally, the targets of voluntary action are defined by the company alone and control of success politically or by civil society, as Clausen *et al.* remark, is scarce. And when, as Cornelis van der Lugt describes, the UN and business unite their power in the Global Compact it might make things better, but it does not finally solve problems. After all, we still need democratic nation-states, which guarantee, as far as they can, all the rights laid down in the UN human rights declaration.

Conclusion: a sustainable integration task

In a nutshell the contributions to the book make it obvious that the connection between the discussions about governance and sustainability is not a 'natural' process but instead an continuous process, characterised by conflicts, which might be enhanced by processes of learning. One main point is the solution of the integration problem, which is a consequence of fragmentation of knowledge and of the interests of actors, and this in fields that are characterised by dynamics that are increasingly fragmented. This holds true for economic and political decision-making processes. A broader view of problems is a necessary precondition for decision-making processes towards sustainability.

In economic contexts mainly regulatory approaches as well as the influences of consumers (including the actions of consumers) have shaped the way for sustainability.

With respect to the political decision-making process, it will be a matter of including the stakeholders, civil-society players and experts from the political areas concerned and other areas to put the different perspectives into competition with each other. The inclusiveness of pluralistic perspectives but at the same time sensitivity to the different contexts—for example, the structure of the environmental problem, North–South aspects and gender—is a central departing point for governance structures at least for another basis of the relationships between the different actors but also for the relationship between nature and society and with this an enabling of social–ecological transformation processes.

The contributions gathered in this book show that social–ecological transformation processes are not alone an effect of the enforcement of a more sustainable policy initiated by states but that in different areas conflicts and learning processes are needed for a change in problem awareness as well as implementation. Therefore this is not just a blueprint to follow, but a sometimes conflict-oriented and learning-oriented process.

References

EC (European Commission) (2001) *White Paper on European Governance* (COM[2001]428, 25 July 2001; Brussels: EC).

Von Weizsäcker, E., A. Lovins and H. Lovins (1997) *Factor Four: Doubling Wealth, Halving Resource Use. A Report to the Club of Rome* (London: Earthscan Publications).

Part 1
Governance and global sustainability: setting the stage

1

Globalisation and governance

SUSTAINABILITY BETWEEN FRAGMENTATION AND INTEGRATION*

James N. Rosenau

The George Washington University, USA

At first glance, the prospects for effective global governance in the realm of environmental sustainability would appear to be considerable—less because the world has advanced in its capacity for effective governance, but more because environmental issues affect everyone's desire for a more harmonious link to nature and because recent decades have witnessed a profound and discernible shift to a worldwide consciousness of the vast scope of environmental challenges. We have collectively moved from a fragmented NIMBY (not in my back yard) syndrome to a keen awareness of an integrated future symbolised by the picture of the Earth from outer space (Jasanoff 2001: 309-37).

But appearances can be deceiving. Or at least the ensuing pages argue that the prospects for effective governance leading to sustainability are, on balance, quite bleak. To be sure, the Johannesburg conclave has again drawn the world's attention to the myriad issues that constitute environmental sustainability, and doubtless that focus will continue for a long time; but there is no one-to-one correlation between extensive preoccupation and actual implementation. Enacting the commitments made at Johannesburg pose challenges to global governance that, for a variety of reasons suggested below, seem unlikely to be met in a thoroughgoing way. Accordingly, it is difficult to outline a basis for optimism.

A bleak conclusion also rests on the premise that we live in a very messy and complex world. There are far too many people who survive on or below the poverty line. There are far too many societies paralysed by division. There is too much violence within and between countries. In many places there is too little water and too many overly populated, pollution-ridden cities. And, most conspicuously, there is all too lit-

* A paper presented at the Conference on Governance and Sustainability: New Challenges for the State, Business and Civil Society, sponsored by the Friedrich-Ebert-Stiftung (Berlin, 30 September 2002). I am grateful to Ulrike Hoppner and Paul Wapner for their reactions to an earlier draft.

tle effective governance capable of ameliorating, if not resolving, these and numerous other problems that crowd high on the global agenda.

Perhaps even more troubling, our generation lacks the orientations necessary for sound assessments of how the authority of governance can be brought to bear on the challenges posed by the prevailing disarray. As will be seen, we have not adjusted our conceptual equipment to facilitate the analysis of how authority gets exercised in a decentralised world. We are still deeply ensconced in a paradigm that locates authority exclusively in states and environmental challenges exclusively in their shared problems—the so-called tragedy of the commons. In effect, we have elevated the NIMBY syndrome to the national level. Our preoccupation with global problems posed by recognising the Earth as a lonely spheroid in a vast universe has led us to minimise the extent to which environmental challenges at local levels are marked by variability. Today societies can have as much difficulty exercising authority within their own jurisdictions as they do with respect to the commons. The world, in other words, is both fragmenting and integrating, which is another way of stressing why the challenges of sustainability and global governance are so daunting.

Indeed, I contend that the world is messier today than was the case in earlier decades. Granted that every generation thinks it has more problems than its predecessors, but a case can readily be made that the present era is far messier than any other, that today's insecurities are more pervasive, its uncertainties more elusive, its ambiguities more perplexing, and its complexities more extensive. Let me briefly make that case by stressing that the central differentiation between the present epoch and previous ones involves personal, community, national and international life today being marked by rapid acceleration, even by simultaneity. Due to innovative electronic technologies, to jet aircraft that annually move millions of people around the world, and to the resulting shrinkage of time and distance, people and societies today have become substantially more interdependent than was the case in earlier eras. What is remote today is also in our back yards; what was distant is now also proximate, and the prevalence of these distant proximities underlies the messiness that sets our time apart from previous generations.[1]

One major consequence of the accelerated pace of life in our time is the breakdown of long-standing boundaries—those boundaries that differentiate the public from the private, the domestic from the foreign, the local from the global, the political from the economic, the living from the natural environment, the scientific from the experiential, to mention only a few of the distinctions that had been commonplace and that are today so obscure as to be a prime source of the widespread insecurities, uncertainties, ambiguities and complexities that prevail throughout the world. The 9/11 attacks did not initiate the insecurities, uncertainties, ambiguities and complexities; rather, the attacks simply aggravated dynamics that were already deeply rooted in the social, political and economic life of people, communities and societies.

While it goes without saying that analysts are subject to the same insecurities and uncertainties, it is also the case that some of us are, by temperament, optimistic and others are pessimistic in our approach to interpreting the prospects for sustainability. Some of us are inclined to stress the Montreal Protocol and numerous other mechanisms through which the global community has successfully addressed environmental

---

1   For an elaboration of this conception of present-day world affairs, see Rosenau 2003.

challenges, while others emphasise the flouting of commitments made at the 1992 Earth Summit in Rio and the failure of states and corporations to live up to their responsibilities. More specifically, some discern a long-term trend towards state compliance with environmental treaties (see e.g. Brown Weiss and Jacobson 1998: ch. 15) and others contend that:

> steps in the 1990s toward a more just and ecologically resilient world were too small, too slow, or too poorly rooted . . . Not surprisingly, then, global governmental problems, from climate change to species extinctions, deforestation, and water scarcity, have generally worsened since delegates met in Rio (Gardner 2002: 4).

Likewise, some regard the Global Compact framed by Kofi Annan and the UN as a huge step forward (www.unglobalcompact.org), while still others insist the Compact is 'deeply flawed' and should be 'scrapped or re-designed completely' (Bruno 2002:4). I myself am optimistic by nature, but the empiricist in me has a hard time ignoring the obstacles to progress towards effective governance that will promote environmental sustainability.

It matters, in short, how one achieves a balance between what one observes and what one wishes was the case. Wishes can prove to be self-fulfilling prophecies if they are grounded within the realm of what is realistically attainable, but all too often they ignore the empirical processes that hinder the realisation of what are seen as moral imperatives.

1.1 Between integration and fragmentation

It is in the context of the complexities that have rendered our world messier than ever that I want to examine the links between governance, sustainability and globalisation in a world that is simultaneously undergoing fragmentation and integration. First, of course, some conceptual specifications are in order. Three concepts require clarification: governance, sustainability and globalisation (which I conceive to embrace both integration and fragmentation).

1.1.1 Governance

Elsewhere I have suggested that the core of governance involves rule systems in which steering mechanisms are employed to frame and implement goals that move communities in the directions they wish to go or that enable them to maintain the institutions and policies they wish to maintain (Rosenau 1995: 13-43). Governance is not the same as government in that the rule systems of the latter are rooted in formal and legal procedures, while those of the former are also marked by informal rule systems (Rosenau 1992: ch. 1). It follows that the achievement of a modicum of governance that promotes environmental sustainability on a global scale requires the development of steering mechanisms that evoke compliant actions, not just words, on the part of the innumerable actors whose work impacts upon the myriad aspects of the natural environment that need to be sustained across generations.

Two key challenges here are especially acute. One concerns the local variability that defies an overall global solution. Some problems are global in scope, but the environmental circumstances of different communities can vary considerably, with the result that global governance must address sustainability in a host of diverse conditions. To aspire to transnational institutions that are relevant to situations everywhere is to drastically misread the governance problem and to fall back on the tragedy-of-the-commons perspective. Needs at the local level must be met without encouraging or reinforcing the NIMBY syndrome. The second involves the nature of compliance, of getting relevant actors to put aside habitual responses and, instead, to yield to authorities that act on behalf of standards that allow for the utilisation of nature's bounties without depriving future generations of the resources they will need. I shall return later to the ways in which effective governance rests on the capacity to evoke compliance with authority. For the moment it suffices to note that the sum of the world's formal and informal rule systems at all levels of community amount to what can properly be called global governance and that, for reasons elaborated below, it is a highly disaggregated and only a minimally co-ordinated system of governance.

1.1.2 Sustainability

As it has developed among activists and observers alike, environmental sustainability has both empirical and moral dimensions. On the one hand, it refers to those empirical processes whereby humankind preserves or exploits the resources of nature in such a way that present and subsequent generations do or do not have available access to comparable standards of living. Viewed in this way, sustainability is thus about meeting the needs of the future as well as the present, about the long run as well as the short term, about the capacity of people to ponder the well-being of their unborn great-grandchildren as well as the circumstances of their own generation. But efforts to promote a desirable future for both the unborn and the born are loaded with values and it is here where sustainability is pervaded with moral dimensions, with questions of right and wrong, with loaded interpretations of scientific enquiries. Empirical data—the findings of science—on whether a particular practice promotes or deters sustainable development in the future can be interpreted in diverse ways, depending on the perspectives from which they are approached.

Accordingly, it is hardly surprising that the ongoing discourse about sustainable development is marked by florid affirmations and vivid denunciations. Whatever the solidity of the empirical findings that may be uncovered about species survival, pollution, resource utilisation, and all the other foci that comprise the environmental issue-area, inevitably policies designed to achieve sustainability will be deeply ensconced in unending controversies and conflicts that make widespread compliance with the policies improbable. A major source of the controversies stems from governmental structures at local, national and international levels in which responsibility for the ecological, social and economic dimensions of sustainability is assigned to competitive agencies that must be co-ordinated for meaningful policies to be adopted. The chances of consensuses and new institutional steering mechanisms forming to overcome these bureaucratic obstacles and the environmental threats they sustain are thus dim and central to a bleak view of the prospects for the future. It is not difficult to imagine the great-grandchildren of future generations living under even more dire conditions than prevail at present.

1.1.3 Globalisation

I have found it helpful to conceive of globalisation as rooted in two basic and contrary processes. One involves all those forces that press for centralisation, integration and globalisation, and the other consists of those forces that press for decentralisation, fragmentation and localisation. In turn, these polarities can be viewed as either philosophical premises or as empirical processes. As philosophical premises, they amount to forms of either localism or globalism, both of which consist of mind-sets, of orientations, of world-views. Localism pertains to those mental sets that focus on and value the familiar and close-at-hand arrangements located within conventional community and national boundaries, while globalism involves orientations towards the distant circumstances that lie beyond national boundaries. But localism and globalism can usefully be distinguished from localisation and globalisation, which I conceive to be empirical processes rather than mind-sets, processes that are boundary-spanning in the case of globalisation and that either contract within conventional boundaries or do not span them in the case of localisation.

Whether globalism and localism are viewed as orientations towards or as processes of integration and fragmentation, they are best conceived as a singular phenomenon wherein the foregoing polarities converge. Indeed, it is the dominant phenomenon of the epoch that has emerged subsequent to the Cold War, so much so that I have coined a word designed to capture the inextricable links between the individual and societal tendencies to integrate across boundaries that are the hallmark of globalisation and the counter-tendencies towards fragmentation that are fomented by localising resistances to boundary-spanning activities. My label is that of **fragmegration**, an ungainly and contrived word that has the virtue of capturing in a single word—and thus of drawing our attention to—the extraordinarily complex phenomena that sustain the endless interactions between the forces of fragmentation and integration. I dare to suggest that, by viewing the world through fragmegrative lenses, one can discern the underlying dynamics of our epoch with a clarity that is not otherwise available.[2]

In other words, globalisation and localisation feed off each other, stimulate responses to each other, in endless interactions at every level of community. At times the interactions are co-operative, but often they are conflictual and underlie many of the issues on the global agenda. Hence, it is not far-fetched to assert that virtually every increment of globalisation gives rise to an increment of localisation, and vice versa, so thoroughly are the two contrary orientations and processes interconnected.

While fragmegrative dynamics tend to be conflictual, it is useful to reiterate that many environmental issues originate in local communities and the resolution of more than a few of them involve a measure of decentralisation founded on the perspectives of localism. In the energy field, for example, sustainable enterprises are estimated to be most efficient when they are decentralised in the private and non-profit sector

2   The concept of fragmegration is spelled out most fully in Rosenau 1997: ch. 6.

(Sachs *et al*. 2002: 29), an estimate that runs counter to practices in many countries but that is quite consistent with the underlying tendency whereby authority is undergoing a continual process of disaggregation as the fragmegrative epoch unfolds.

1.2 Sustainability as fragmegrative processes

Environmental issues and their potential for sustainability fall squarely between fragmentation and integration. They are profoundly and quintessentially fragmegrative dynamics. On the one hand, they are pervasively integrative in the sense that the value of preserving the environment and maintaining its viability is widely shared at every level of community. Rare are those who overtly argue on behalf of exploiting the resources of nature or who oppose the idea of trying to prevent their degradation. Indeed, it is precisely the integrative underpinnings of environmental issues that brought leaders of 160 national governments and representatives of thousands of non-governmental organisations (NGOs) to Rio in 1992 and comparable numbers of both types of actor to Johannesburg in 2002. And it is precisely these issues that evoked verbal affirmations of and commitments to the agreements reached in Rio throughout the subsequent decade. On the other hand, the very same issues have led to pervasive and divisive fragmentation among and within groups, communities, countries and international systems when actions designed to implement the proposed commitments proved to be highly controversial and, with some notable exceptions, largely ineffectual. It is no accident that the series of anti-globalisation protests that began with the Battle of Seattle in 1999 have in large measure focused on questions of sustainability.

Indeed, the protests have reinforced a long-term process whereby the very idea of sustainability has undergone a significant change of meaning. Now it connotes 'sustainable development', with the emphasis on sustaining economies rather than nature, a semantic shift that has enabled a vast array of diverse actors to crowd under the umbrella of sustainability and to press their goals in the context of what they regard as unquestionable sets of values (Sachs *et al*. 2002: 14). It is also a shift that has intensified controversies over whether the implementation of policies designed to achieve environmental sustainability should be undertaken by global or local jurisdictions.

1.3 Sources of fragmegration

In order to incisively probe and evaluate the challenges and tensions that seem likely to undermine the prospects for effective governance of environmental sustainability in a globalising epoch, it helps to delineate the main dynamics underlying fragmegration by way of probing what it is about the present epoch that has so markedly accelerated local–global tensions and strikingly raised their salience on the global agenda. More specifically, what is it about issues of environmental sustainability that have hastened and heightened the tensions? In short, how to devise systems of rule that enable solutions at the local and global levels to co-evolve rather than simply to co-exist and perpetuate past tensions?

I find it useful to clarify responses to these questions by identifying eight major sources of fragmegration that shape attitudes and behaviour at four levels of aggregation: the micro level of individuals, the macro level of collectivities and states, the micro–macro level at which individuals and collectivities shape and interact with each other, and the macro–macro level wherein collectivities interact and influence each other. Both the eight sources and the four levels are set forth in Table 1.1; the entries in the cells are crude hypotheses that suggest some of—though surely not all—the possible consequences that may flow at each level in response to each of the various sources.[3] At the very least Table 1.1 highlights the extraordinary complexity that marks our time.

Many more hypotheses could be listed if space permitted. None of the hypotheses has been tested. Intuitively they make sense and are consistent with much of the literature on globalisation, but I would welcome any research efforts that employ systematic data to establish or refute their validity. For present purposes, however, the ensuing analysis is confined to elaborating briefly on the eight sources and noting some of their more conspicuous consequences at the several levels as a means of facilitating assessments of the prospects for environmental sustainability and global governance.

It must be emphasised that the eight sources are interactive, that each has consequences for all the others. Indeed, so interactive are the various sources that any attempt to trace and assess their causal potency is very much an unsolvable chicken-and-egg problem that complexity theory may some day be able to solve; but all we can do here is note that all of them are relevant and suggest some of the consequences of each of them.

It should also be stressed that fragmegrative circumstances are not necessarily marked by tensions and conflict. Global orientations and actions can be supportive of local situations, and vice versa. For example, the UN's Commission on Sustainable Development created at Rio in 1992 has assisted numerous cities around the world to promote local arrangements designed to contain and reduce environmental degradation (French 2000: 161). This example is encouraging. It accords credence to the possibility of achieving widespread harmony between local circumstances and global needs as a prime goal of sustainability and global governance. However, here I want to focus on how the eight dynamics listed in Table 1.1 may serve to generate tension and conflict in the realm of environmental sustainability.

1.3.1 Microelectronic technologies

Among the consequences that may flow from the Internet, mobile phones and fax machines are an ever more effective capacity to mobilise like-minded people on behalf of shared goals. It is a capacity that serves those committed to localism as well as those inclined towards globalism. Equally important, such technologies level the playing field. Mobilisation in local communities is facilitated by word of mouth as well as communication technologies, but the latter make it possible to reach and mobilise the like-

---

3 Both the contents of Table 1.1 and parts of the ensuing discussion of the eight sources of fragmegration are adapted from Rosenau 2003: ch. 3.

Levels of aggregation → / Sources of fragmegration ↓	Micro	Macro	Micro–macro	Macro–macro
Microelectronic technologies	Enable like-minded people to be in touch with each other anywhere in the world	Render collectivities more open, connected, and vulnerable; empower them to mobilise support	Constrain governments by enabling opposition groups to mobilise more effectively	Accelerate diplomatic processes; facilitate electronic surveillance and intelligence work
Skill revolution	Expands people's horizons on a global scale; sensitises them to the relevance of distant events; facilitates a reversion to local concerns	Enlarges the capacity of governmental agencies to think 'out of the box', seize opportunities and analyse challenges	Constrains policy-making through increased capacity of individuals to know when, where and how to engage in collective action	Multiplies quantity and enhances quality of links among states; solidifies their alliances and enmities
Organisational explosion	Facilitates multiple identities, sub-groupism, and affiliation with transnational networks	Increases capacity of opposition groups to form and press for altered policies; divides publics from their elites	Contributes to the pluralism and dispersion of authority; heightens the probability of authority crises	Renders the global stage ever more transnational and dense with non-governmental actors
Bifurcation of global structures	Adds to role conflicts, divides loyalties, and foments tensions among individuals; orients people toward local spheres of authority	Facilitates formation of new spheres of authority and consolidation of existing spheres in the multi-centric world	Empowers transnational advocacy groups and special interests to pursue influence through diverse channels	Generates institutional arrangements for co-operation on major global issues such as trade, human rights, the environment, etc.
Mobility upheaval	Stimulates imaginations and provides more extensive contacts with foreign cultures; heightens salience of the outsider	Enlarges the size and relevance of subcultures, diasporas and ethnic conflicts as people seek new opportunities abroad	Increases movement across borders that lessens capacity of governments to control national boundaries	Heightens need for international co-operation to control the flow of drugs, money, immigrants and terrorists

TABLE 1.1 **Some sources of fragmegration at four levels of aggregation** (continued over)

Levels of aggregation → *Sources of* fragmegration ↓	**Micro**	**Macro**	**Micro–macro**	**Macro–macro**
Weakening of territoriality, states and sovereignty	Undermines traditions and national loyalties; increases distrust of governments and other institutions	Adds to the porosity of national boundaries and the difficulty of framing national policies	Lessens confidence in governments; renders nationwide consensuses difficult to achieve and maintain	Increases need for interstate co-operation on global issues; lessens control over cascading events
Authority crises	Redirect loyalties; encourage individuals to replace traditional criteria of legitimacy with performance criteria	Weaken ability of both governments and other organisations to frame and implement policies	Facilitate the capacity of publics to press and/or paralyse their governments, the WTO and other organisations	Enlarge the competence of some IGOs and NGOs; encourage diplomatic wariness in negotiations
Globalisation of national economies	Swells ranks of consumers; promotes uniform tastes; heightens concerns for jobs; widens gap between winners and losers	Complicates tasks of state governments *vis-à-vis* markets; promotes business alliances	Increases efforts to protect local cultures and industries; facilitates vigour of protest movements; polarises communities	Intensifies trade and investment conflicts; generates incentives for building global financial institutions

TABLE 1.1   (from previous page)

minded across national boundaries and great distances. The image of Marcos, the Zapatista commander, under a tree in the Mexican jungle with a laptop seeking support from leaders and publics around the world is but a microcosm of how microelectronic technologies can be used to generate support and give rise to fragmegrative tensions. More relevantly, the Internet has been a major factor in the surging growth of the environmental movement noted below. The involvement of so many environmental activists from so many different places in the anti-globalisation protests is testimony to the relevance of information technologies and their worldwide spread. As an organiser of the Seattle protests put it, 'The Internet has become the latest, greatest arrow in our quiver of social activism.'[4]

---

4   Mike Dolan, quoted in French 2000: 163. For a general analysis of the links between the Internet and social movements, see Deibert 2000: 255-72.

1.3.2 Skill revolution

Elsewhere I have argued at length that people everywhere—elites, activists, ordinary folk in rural areas and urban centres—have expanded their skills at dealing with the challenges and crises that mark our accelerated epoch.[5] It is no longer plausible to take publics for granted, to assume they can be led by their officials to support any course of action. Rather, equipped with a deeper understanding and more clear-cut values than, say, their great-grandparents, today they are more ready to take action in response to circumstances they find wanting. This greater readiness is perhaps especially evident with respect to environmental issues, sensitivities to which have greatly increased in recent decades as polluted air has enveloped cities and a host of other environmental crises have marred the course of events. The recurrent anti-globalisation protests are again illustrative in this regard, as many of the protestors give voice to concerns about the environment and, in so doing, intensify the clash of global and local forces. Stated in the words of one analyst, 'The local efforts of citizens have always been crucial to the environmental movement. Grassroots activism is the seedbed of more organised and enduring efforts and institutions' (Thiele 1999: 28). Furthermore, the skill revolution along with the new technologies has heightened people's sense of identity and their capacity to shoulder multiple identities. Put differently, both reflective analysis and virulent environmentalism can be traced to the greater awareness that has accompanied the skill revolution.

1.3.3 Organisational explosion

A central pattern of this accelerated epoch is the proliferation of organisations at every level of community: local, national and transnational. Spurred in good part by environmental and human rights issues but for many other reasons as well, organisations are forming and expanding at startling rates. Equally important, due largely to the Internet and the fax machine, many of them are horizontally as well as vertically structured. Networks have supplemented hierarchies as an organisational form, and many of the new organisations are conspicuously lacking in hierarchy. Combined with the processes of localisation, the organisational explosion is thus enabling people to find common cause with others in their community and to come together when the need to do so arises.[6]

The data eloquently tell this proliferation story:

> The number of NGOs working across international borders soared during the last century, climbing from just 176 in 1909 to more than 23,000 in 1998. Environmental groups have risen steadily as a share of the total, climbing from just 2 percent of all transnational social change NGOs in 1953 to 14 percent in 1993 (French 2000: 164).

---

5   For an initial discussion of the skill revolution as a micro dynamic, see Rosenau 1990: chs. 9 and 13. For an updated elaboration of the concept, see Rosenau 2003: ch. 10.
6   Furthermore, while some claim that environmental networks, unlike their organisational counterparts, are transitory and ill suited to maintaining coherence over time, they have been found to sustain local campaigns for lengthy periods in Greece, Spain and Portugal, among other countries. See, for example, Kousis 1999.

The reach of the organisational explosion is exemplified by the finding that, 'in 1984, the Citizens' Clearinghouse for Hazardous Waste worked with 600 community groups, and the figure would rise to 8,000 groups by the mid-1990s' (Thiele 1999: 18). Moreover, the reach of the organisational explosion is not a singular process. On the contrary, at least in the United States—and doubtless elsewhere—beginning in the 1980s the environmental movement underwent a 'two-pronged mainstreaming'—'from the top down through the large national organisations and from the bottom up through dispersed grassroots efforts' (Thiele 1999: 19). Nor is it the case that this growth was due only to the acceleration of email and Internet usage in the early 1990s. It has been found, for example, that 'transnational environmental organisations [grew] dramatically in absolute and relative terms, increasing from two groups in 1953 to ninety in 1993, and from 1.8 percent of total groups in 1953 to 14.3 percent in 1993' (Keck and Sikkink 1998: 10).

Since a wide variety of issues fall under the rubric of environmental concerns, it is important to note that the environmental movement is far from unified. Rather, it can be viewed as numerous environmental movements that are:

> very diverse and complex, their organisational forms ranging from the highly organised and formally institutionalised to the radically informed, the spatial scope of their activities ranging from the local to the almost global, the nature of their concerns ranging from single issues to the full panoply of global environmental concerns (Rootes 1999: 2).

Taken as a whole, the movement is thus 'defined by many different voices' which are often in conflict. 'Each cause has its own chorus of supporters and detractors', so much so that 'when advancing their own particular interests for their own political ends, environmentalists may seem less in the business of galvanising public commitment than dispersing it' (Thiele 1999: 30-31). Since some of these tensions unfold across transnational, national and local groups, it can readily be observed that the environmental movement is itself subject to fragmegrative dynamics.

1.3.4 Bifurcation of global structures

Beginning some time after the Second World War the overall structure of world politics began to undergo change, to bifurcate, with the flourishing of innumerable actors other than states clambering up on to the world stage and undertaking actions with consequences for the course of events. As a result, what I call a 'multi-centric' world evolved that consists of a great variety of collectivities and that has come to rival the long-standing, anarchical state-centric system. One can reasonably assert that overall global structures are today marked by two worlds of world politics, two worlds that sometimes co-operate, oft-times conflict, and endlessly interact. The bifurcated evolution of the global system serves to intensify fragmegrative dynamics in the sense that it contributes to a long-term process whereby authority is undergoing disaggregation. Consequently, the multi-centric world now provides avenues for local groups to articulate their needs and goals as they join with each other in persuading governments in the state-centric world to heed—or at least to hear—their claims.[7]

---

7   A conceptualisation of the bifurcated two worlds of world politics is elaborated at some length in Rosenau 1990: ch. 10.

The environmental movement has been and continues to be both a contributor to and a beneficiary of the bifurcation of global structures. It has contributed through the explosion of environmental organisations at all levels of community throughout the world. In so doing the movement has helped to institutionalise and legitimate the processes of bifurcation. At the same time it has benefited from the institutionalisation of the bifurcated structures in the sense that the movement's diverse voices now have a permanent platform from which they can express and move towards their goals. This institutionalisation of a new set of global structures can be readily demonstrated: the first in a series of moments in the last decade when the two worlds of world politics converged and interacted occurred at the 1992 environmental conference in Rio—with 160 governments represented and some 1,500 accredited NGOs at the Earth Summit and thousands more at the parallel Global Forum—and was then followed by comparable events that focused on human rights in Vienna, on population problems in Cairo, on social development in Copenhagen, on women's rights in Beijing, on cities in Istanbul, on trade, finance and other aspects of globalisation in Seattle, Washington, DC, Davos, Genoa and numerous other locales. Viewed in this way, the bifurcated setting of the Johannesburg meeting was just another instance of a global pattern that is ever more deeply rooted. It is hard to imagine any future gathering of leaders of the state-centric world that is not accompanied by a simultaneous and adjacent gathering of organisations and individuals from the multi-centric world, a reality that is profoundly and thoroughly expressive of the dynamics of fragmegration.[8]

1.3.5 Mobility upheaval

Owing in part to the advent of jet aircraft and a steady lessening of the costs of travelling in them, the accelerated epoch has witnessed a vast movement of people—everyone from the tourist to the terrorist, from the business executive to the immigrant, from illegal aliens seeking work to those fleeing persecution, from students studying abroad to artists and other professionals advancing their careers, from environmentalists attending conferences in Rio and Johannesburg to protesters converging on Seattle and Washington. To cite one quantitative example, there were 635 million international tourist arrivals in 1998, whereas the figure for 1950 was 25 million (French 2000: 29). In many ways this mobility upheaval, as I call it, has contributed to the integrative dimension of fragmentation, but in one important way it has served to intensify fragmentation. In many countries the migrant, legal as well as illegal, has fostered strong negative reactions in the host society. Immigrants and migrants represent the 'stranger' and many people in the recipient communities are uneasy about what these strangers may do to them and their ways of life. The friend and the enemy are known entities, but the stranger is not and is widely seen as a threat to long-standing traditions. Australia's handling of this problem, its refusal to let boatloads of migrants disembark on its shores, is a classic instance of this fragmegrative dynamic, but numerous other Western countries have also tried to curb this aspect of the mobility upheaval.

---

8 To be sure, the G8 have convened in remote locales that are inaccessible to protesters or groups who wish to submit policy recommendations, but such a practice cannot long withstand the bifurcated structures that facilitate demands for transparency.

1.3.6　Weakening of territoriality, states and sovereignty

As technologies shrink the world, as people become increasingly skilful, as organisations proliferate, as the multi-centric world expands, and as the mobility upheaval sustains vast movements of people, the meaning of territory becomes less compelling and states and their sovereignty become weaker. This is not to forecast the end of the state as a central political structure. Rather it is to stress that states have increasing difficulty controlling the flow of ideas, money, goods, drugs, crime, pollution and people across their borders, thus contributing substantially to the processes whereby authority is undergoing disaggregation on a worldwide scale. The fragmegrative consequences of these processes are considerable. Most notably perhaps, local communities and groups are acquiring greater autonomy and a heightened readiness to contest the integrative forces of globalisation. The recent history of the environmental movement offers numerous examples of clashes that pit local and global forces against each other.[9]

1.3.7　Authority crises

The dynamics whereby authority structures are undergoing disaggregation have contributed to a proliferation of authority crises on the part of governments, local as well as national. Such crises are most conspicuous when protesters crowd the streets and make strident demands, but an even more common form of authority crisis involves the inability of governments to frame goals and move towards them. Stalemate and paralysis, in other words, amount to authority crises, and they are pervasive. Japan's inability to confront and surmount the long-term decline of its economy and the persistence of widespread corruption and unemployment in China are illustrative of authority crises that derive their strength from stalemated political systems. Much the same can be said about other governments throughout the world. There may be increasing numbers of democratic systems, but few of these have majorities that are able to rule effectively. One need only recall how the US government closed and locked its doors twice late in 1995 to appreciate the extent to which authority crises have come to mark the prevailing global scene. Nor are these crises limited to governments. NGOs, churches, unions and a variety of other institutions are also undergoing one or another form of paralysis and upheaval. Even the Mafia has experienced an authority crisis deriving from its young members defying the dictates of its seniors. Needless to say, pervasive authority crises have important consequences for the world's capacity to maximise the governance of sustainability.

1.3.8　Globalisation of national economies

The turn towards free enterprise economic systems and a lessening of trade barriers has had a number of fragmegrative consequences. On the integrative side the emergence of a global economy has led to a greater variety of goods and services being available to more and more people, processes that have also contributed to an ever-greater interdependence among groups and societies. On the fragmenting side, the globalisation of national economies has also served to widen the gap between rich and poor both

---

9　This is a recurring theme in Litfin 1998.

within and between countries. More relevant to present concerns, the prevalence of neoliberal economic perspectives underlies the aforementioned semantic shift of the concept of sustainability to an emphasis on sustaining economies rather than nature. These perspectives have also served to move the role of transnational corporations towards the top of the global agenda, thereby generating conditions for a wide variety of fragmegrative situations, from protests against the world's economic institutions— the World Bank, the International Monetary Fund, the World Trade Organisation, the G8, the World Economic Forum—to boycotts of the goods of corporations that are considered to undermine environmental sustainability.

1.4 The governance of environmental fragmegration

The discourse that probes the problem of achieving sustainability through global governance largely bemoans the lack of progress since the 1992 convergence of the two worlds of world politics in Rio. However, when it turns to investigating how more effective global governance might be accomplished, the discourse encounters conceptual difficulties that tend to block a full appreciation of the task. Three problems are especially noteworthy. One involves the confusion noted above in which the priorities attached to sustainable and economic development get confounded. The second consists of a tendency to ignore the high degree to which authority has undergone disaggregation in recent decades and instead to focus on top-down solutions to the governance challenge. And the third amounts to a disinclination to account for local variations and, consequently, an underplaying of fragmegrative tensions and an undue stress on the universality of scientific findings.

1.4.1 Conceptual blocks: what should be developed?

Intense debate surrounds the question of whether the environment or economies should be developed. It pits environmentalists against developers, which readily becomes a debate between developed and developing countries. While some appreciate that the debate can be misleading, that the goals of each group can be compatible and need not be mutually exclusive (see e.g. Ruggie 2002), that the environment can be sustained even as economies flourish, the central tendency is for the economy and the developers to prevail over the environment and environmentalists. George W. Bush's repeated contention that the Kyoto Protocol on Climate Change would be bad for the American economy is a quintessential instance of this outcome as well as a succinct expression of how this conceptual block can prevent 'both/and' formulations from replacing 'either/or' approaches.

1.4.2 Conceptual blocks: authority

Notwithstanding the many ways in which the eight dynamics listed in Table 1.1—and especially the organisational explosion, the skill revolution, the weakening of states, and pervasive authority crises—have cumulatively fostered a global stage that is crowded with diverse actors at every level of community who take positions and pursue policies relevant to sustainability, most assessments of what has to be done start at the level of reforming international institutions and then note how the reforms have to be implemented by national and local governments. To be sure, the vulnerability of international institutions to the wishes of the member governments that created them is fully acknowledged and bottom-up solutions thereby hinted; but whether the solutions are top-down or bottom-up, they posit vertical flows of authority. The repeated calls for a World Environmental Organisation similar to the World Trade Organisation exemplify the vertical, top-down approach (see e.g. French 2000: 159; Sachs *et al.* 2002: 65).

In effect, therefore, the solutions are cast in the context of the aforementioned weakness wherein analysts still cling to traditional approaches to the nature of authority. They ignore the ways in which collectivities in both the public and private sectors sustain authority flows horizontally through networks as well as vertically through hierarchical structures. They continue to posit the state as the prime, if not the only, wielder of effective authority. Thus, still rooted in the notion that compliance involves those at the top persuading, instructing or ordering those down the chain of command to conduct themselves in specified ways, no allowance is made for requests and suggestions that evoke compliance through non-hierarchical structures. In the words of one observer,

> So dominant in contemporary consciousness is the assumption that authority must be centralised that scholars are just beginning to grapple with how decentralised authority might be understood . . . [T]he question of how to think about a world that is becoming 'domesticated' but not centralised, about a world after 'anarchy,' is one of the most important questions today facing not only students of international relations but of political theory as well (Wendt 1999: 308).

In short, it is the nature of fragmegrative processes that authority flows are not neatly structured. They go every which way, emanating from a vast array of actors whose rule systems I call 'spheres of authority' (SOAs) and who evoke compliance through a variety of means.[10] Global governance thus involves patchwork-quilt arrangements wherein authority is exercised partly by hierarchical structures, partly by horizontal networks and partly by oblique links among overlapping vertical and horizontal SOAs. Taken in its entirety, the system of global governance is comparable to a Möbius strip or web. It is a system marked by patterns that unfold when the impetus to steer a course of events derives from networked and hierarchical interactions across levels of aggregation among transnational corporations (TNCs), international non-governmental organisations (INGOs), NGOs, intergovernmental organisations (IGOs), states, elites and mass publics, interactions that are elaborate and diverse enough to constitute a hybrid structure in which the dynamics of governance are so overlapping among the several levels as to form a singular, web-like process which, like a Möbius strip, neither begins nor culminates at any level or at any point in time.[11] A Möbius web is top-down, bottom-up and side-by-side governance all at once. It is thus far more complex than the

10   For a discussion of the social contracts on which SOAs are founded, see Rosenau 2003: ch. 13.
11   A formulation that elaborates on 'Möbius-web' governance is set forth in Rosenau 2002: 81-83.

governance that flows from the principal of subsidiarity developed in the European Union.

1.4.3 Conceptual blocks: universal science and indigenous knowledge[12]

Despite widespread appreciation that many environmental problems originate in local communities, each of which has special circumstances that require responses tailored to its needs, all too many officials and their expert advisers tend to assess the local variations under the rubric of science. The impulse to posit scientific findings as having universal relevance and application has thus become so ingrained in the expertise of many environmental specialists and economists that they tend to give little credence to the idea that there are occasions when indigenous knowledge is more accurate and relevant than the knowledge generated through scientific methods. After all, experts tend to assert, the local insights are idiosyncratic and may even prove false when subjected to the rigours of scientific testing. More than that, they invite their superiors and local counterparts to consider global warming, a thinning ozone layer, species diminution, polluted air carried by high winds, and other worldwide environmental problems as indicative of the limits of indigenous knowledge, stressing that it overlooks the big picture and is therefore less compelling than universal verities uncovered through science.

This is, of course, an oversimplified characterisation. There are local experts whose knowledge is respected precisely because it stems from a familiarity with circumstances on the ground. What they offer, however, may not be scientific findings, but rather the insights of experience with local conditions. Still, for many experts the habit of positing scientific findings as more reliable than any other form of knowledge is a habitual perspective not easily abandoned. For many experts forsaking the habit is viewed as a capitulation to local pressures. Expertise, in short, can be a basis for perpetuating rather than ameliorating fragmegrative tensions.

1.5 Conclusions

It is the patchwork-quilt nature of global governance, along with the failure to conceptually allow for it, that underlies my bleak assessment of the prospects for achieving worldwide sustainability. For the agreements reached in Johannesburg to be translated into effective authority that inches the world towards sustainability, a wide variety of numerous actors, both individuals and collectivities, have to be co-ordinated and their differences at least minimally subordinated to the interests of their great-grandchildren. More than that, given the boundary-spanning nature of environmental dynamics, all concerned have to recognise that people everywhere have an interest in your grandchildren as well as their own.

---

12   A penetrating discussion of the distinction between science and indigenous knowledge can be found in Jasanoff and Martello 2004.

The chances of such Möbius webs being fashioned as effective rule systems seem very slim indeed. Too many actors can introduce ruptures into the webs. Whether they are corporate executives who sacrifice the well-being of future generations for the sake of immediate profits, states that pursue economic goals at the expense of sustainable development, sovereignty-protective officials who are oblivious to the great-grandchildren of publics other than their own, NGOs that put their narrow interests ahead of collective ecological policies, the United States that withdraws from treaties, individuals whose corrupt practices undermine efforts to preserve endangered species, or bureaucrats and analysts mired in conceptual confusion who do not fully appreciate the numerous local foundations of global structures—to mention only a few of the ways in which the diverse actors on the global stage can divert movement away from a sustainable world—the co-ordination needed to implement the goals articulated in Johannesburg seems unlikely to surmount the disaggregated authority structures on which global governance rests. Stated less pessimistically, 'reversing ecological decline in the early decades of the new century will require innovative partnerships between many different actors, including NGOs, businesses, governments, and international organisations' (French 2000: 164). Cast in even more general terms, 'Contemporary dynamics of globalisation have not yet resulted in the homogenisation of environmental governance' (Sonnenfeld and Mol 2002: 1,457).

This is not to suggest that the prevailing global governance accords all actors a veto over the pace of reform and progress. Rather, it is to highlight the extraordinary complexity and barriers that confront efforts to move a world marked by highly disaggregated SOAs in meaningful and desired directions.

Nor is it to suggest that no progress towards meaningful sustainability lies ahead. Already there has been a proliferation of environmental regimes: 'fourteen different global environmental agreements [were] concluded in the rather short period between 1985 and 1997' (Anderson 2001: 117) (though, to be sure, the record of compliance with these treaties has been, at best, chequered). Equally relevant, there is no lack of good, knowledgeable leaders and activists who expend a lot of energy on behalf of decent goals. Nor is there a shortage of research centres and other organisations of civil society that can make constructive inputs into governance processes. Pockets of progress will thus doubtless occur as some countries, corporations and NGOs sign on to constructive rule systems designed to advance sustainability as the skill and organisational revolutions lead to public pressures on recalcitrant collectivities. One observer expresses the difficulty of coming to a conclusion on whether progress or decline lie ahead by asking an upbeat question and then offering a downbeat answer:

> Is the world witnessing the beginning of such a phase shift [toward rapid change] in the antiglobalisation protests, in the unprecedented initiatives undertaken by both private corporations and local communities, in the growth of NGOs and their innovations, in scientists speaking up and speaking out, and in the outpouring of environmental initiatives by the religious community? We must certainly hope so. The alarms sounded 20 years ago have not been heeded, and soon it will be too late to prevent an appalling deterioration of the natural world (Speth 2002: 76).

My own view is that, on balance, the dynamics that underlie the disaggregated character of global governance seem likely to thwart movement towards a viable and worldwide sustainability. It was neither an accident nor pervasive malevolence that prevented the earlier alarms from being heeded and the commitments made at the 1992 Rio meeting from being implemented. The pervasive inaction appears, rather, to be inherent in the structural constraints and conceptual blocks that currently prevail in the global system.

References

Anderson, W.T. (2001) *All Connected Now: Life in the First Global Civilization* (Boulder, CO: Westview Press).

Brown Weiss, E., and H.K. Jacobson (eds.) (1998) *Engaging Countries: Strengthening Compliance with International Environmental Accords* (Cambridge, MA: MIT Press).

Bruno, K. (2002) 'The UN's Global Compact, Corporate Accountability and the Johannesburg Earth Summit', www.corpwatch.org/campaigns/PCD.jsp?articleid=1348, 24 January 2002.

Deibert, R.J. (2000) 'International Plug 'n Play? Citizen Activism, the Internet, and Global Public Policy', *International Studies Perspectives* 1: 255-72.

French, H. (2000) *Vanishing Borders: Protecting the Planet in the Age of Globalization* (New York: W.W. Norton).

Gardner, G. (2002) 'The Challenge of Johannesburg: Creating a More Secure World', in L. Starke (ed.), *State of the World 2002: A Worldwatch Institute Report on Progress Toward a Sustainable Society* (New York: W.W. Norton).

Jasanoff, S. (2001) 'Image and Imagination: The Formation of Global Environmental Consciousness', in P. Edwards and C.A. Miller (eds.), *Changing the Atmosphere: Science and the Politics of Global Warming* (Cambridge, MA: MIT Press).

—— and M.L. Martello (eds.) (2004) *Earthly Politics: Local and Global in Environmental Politics* (Cambridge, MA: MIT Press:): Introduction.

Keck, M.E., and K. Sikkink (1998) *Activists beyond Borders: Advocacy Networks in International Politics* (Ithaca, NY: Cornell University Press).

Kousis, M. (1999) 'Environmental Movements, Ecological Modernization and Political Opportunity Structures', in C.A. Rootes (ed.), *Environmental Movements: Local, National, and Global* (London: Frank Cass).

Litfin, K.T. (ed.) (1998) *The Greening of Sovereignty in World Politics* (Cambridge, MA: MIT Press).

Rootes, C.A. (1999) 'Environmental Movements from the Local to the Global', in C.A. Rootes (ed.), *Environmental Movements: Local, National, and Global* (London: Frank Cass).

Rosenau, J.N. (1990) *Turbulence in World Politics: A Theory of Change and Continuity* (Princeton, NJ: Princeton University Press).

—— (1992) 'Governance, Order, and Change in World Politics', in J.N. Rosenau and E.O. Czempiel (eds.), *Governance without Government: Order and Change in World Politics* (Cambridge, UK: Cambridge University Press).

—— (1995) 'Governance in the 21st Century', *Global Governance* 1: 13-43.

—— (1997) *Along the Domestic–Foreign Frontier: Exploring Governance in a Turbulent World* (Cambridge, UK: Cambridge University Press).

—— (2002) 'Governance in a New Global Order', in D. Held and A. McGrew (eds.), *Governing Globalization: Power, Authority and Global Governance* (Cambridge, UK: Polity Press): 70-86.

—— (2003) *Distant Proximities: Dynamics beyond Globalization* (Princeton, NJ: Princeton University Press).

Ruggie, J.G. (2002) 'Taking Embedded Liberalism Global: The Corporate Connection', *Canadian Congress of the Social Sciences and Humanities*, Toronto, 29 May 2002.

Sachs, W. (ed.) (2002) *The Jo'burg Memo: Fairness in a Fragile World* (Berlin: Heinrich Böll Foundation).

Sonnenfeld, D.A., and A.P.J. Mol (2002) 'Ecological Modernization, Governance, and Globalization', in D.A. Sonnenfeld and A.P.J. Mol (eds.), *Globalization, Governance, and the Environment* (Thousand Oaks, CA: Sage Publications).

Speth, J.G. (2002) 'Recycling Environmentalism', *Foreign Policy* 131 (July/August 2002): 74-76.

Thiele, L.P. (1999) *Environmentalism for a New Millennium: The Challenge of Coevolution* (New York: Oxford University Press).

Wendt, A. (1999) *Social Theory of International Politics* (Cambridge, UK: Cambridge University Press).

2
Governance and sustainability in a dynamic world

Ulrich Petschow

Institute for Ecological Economic Research (IÖW), Germany

Sustainability issues at a global level are mentioned and discussed in various documents drawn up by international organisations. Central issues refer to aspects of the fight against hunger and poverty and eventually also to aspects of the environment. Sustainability problems are caused by 'governance gaps'; that is, control structures of different regions and sectors result in sustainability problems on a global platform.

These issues are clearly ranked differently on the international agenda. Goals such as poverty control rank very highly and partially include operative goals and implementation dates such as the Millennium Development Goals (cf. Khor, Chapter 4, this volume). Environmental protection or the conservation of life-support systems play a rather weak role in this context. Agreements far less often include goals and deadlines, and control mechanisms are mostly rather poor.[1]

This is partially based on the fact that, by reason of differences in valuation, there is no real understanding of the goals.

To a great degree, the Brundtland Report of 1987 as well as the Rio Conference in 1992 and its follow-up process have determined the discussion on sustainable development. Moreover, it has been determined by the tension between growth and environmental conservation as well as the different interests of industrialised and developing countries. Thus, sustainability has turned out to be a global area of conflict. At the same time, it is a complex problem; solution of this problem by purely governmental control attempts is possible only in a limited way.

Sustainability problems have fundamentally resulted from industrialisation-oriented development paths and the alignment of governance structures with this development model. In this connection, environmental interests such as the preservation of the common good (e.g. the life-support function of nature) have been ignored.[2] The

---

1   It is, all the same, a fact that the strategies conceived to solve poverty and development problems also have major implementation weaknesses.
2   This does not mean, however, that the market as a control mechanism has caused these crucial sustainability problems. Especially against the background of development in the former socialist countries, it seems to be the basic development model of industrialisation and centralisation that has been a major determinant in this respect.

limits of this development model, manifested among other things in the climate issue, create new requirements for governance structures. Thus, one may demand a 'governance for sustainability'.

Besides the necessity to move towards sustainability, however, there is a second governance challenge connected with globalisation. Globalisation trends are accompanied by a diffusion of authority, limiting the scope for manoeuvre on the part of governmental actors. The variety of new actors and their concurrence change the possibilities of traditional forms of control.[3] As a result, control structures, which are often still nationally oriented, are confronted with a major requirement to adjust to modified structures and distributions of power.

This chapter, as a priority, questions the consequences of globalisation trends for control structures in general and environmental problems in particular. It also seeks to address which governance approaches could contribute to sustainable development against this background. An analysis of globalisation processes (Section 2.1) is followed by a glance at the interconnection between globalisation and environmental impacts. The latter both illuminates the sustainability debate and identifies governance gaps. Section 2.3 analyses resulting changes in control structures, paying particular attention to the multiplicity of forms and levels of regulation, including the level of norms and values. Section 2.4 considers changes in control structures in terms of regulation possibilities and subsequently attempts to analyse possible approaches to governance for sustainability. It is argued that co-operation is becoming increasingly complex and that some sort of market regulation is becoming increasingly significant. The conclusions outline how proposals for action could be constructed. Against this complex background, simple solutions are inconceivable. Sustainability cannot be prescribed. It must be realised within the process.

2.1 Changes within the framework of the global economy

The globalisation discourse takes place on the basis of different premises and assessments and is therefore characterised by different spectra. Some proclaim an unrestricted economy (Ohmae 1994). Some hold that, in the final analysis, the degree of globalisation does not differ from the situation before the First World War (Baldwin and Martin 1999). In others, the approach is more pragmatic and identifies a globalisation process, which, however, has not yet brought about a global economy (Hübner and Petschow 2001).

These different interpretations of the globalisation process concurrently involve statements regarding the capacity to act on the part of different actors, often focusing on governmental and economic actors.

---

3   This does not mean, however, that the traditional and, often, state-centred types of regulation are better suited to solving sustainability problems. One finds, rather, that a multitude of global environmental problems have come into existence in spite of the supposedly better control capacity of governmental actors. This also means that it is necessary to enquire about control possibilities in complex societies in favour of sustainability in general.

In this context, one proceeds on the assumption that globalisation should be understood to be a process that is nowhere near completed and may not be invulnerable to setbacks.[4] Nevertheless, it leaves marks in the traditional institutional fabric and consequently highlights the necessity to act against the background of the goals of sustainability and fairness.

Moreover, globalisation is not only discussed in economic terms. References are also made in particular to technological and cultural influence factors. Within the framework of the economic discussion, the increasing economic entwining of trade, direct investments, and capital markets in particular is emphasised, as well as technological changes.

In a nutshell, at least five substantially undisputed factors influencing globalisation can be set forth:

1. The (politically deliberate) **liberalisation** of markets since the end of the Second World War, which the triumphant advance of the neoclassical paradigm of the welfare-increasing effect of 1980s trade liberalisation has intensified. This can be deduced particularly from the transition of the GATT system, by lifting trade barriers, to the World Trade Organisation (WTO), from the development of a corresponding institutional fabric and from the almost complete departure from the model of import substitution in developing countries. These countries now also count on opening their markets to the world and attracting foreign capital.

2. The increasing privatisation of government activities. This is very often closely connected with the first factor. Greater efficiency is attributed to the co-ordination effect of the market in comparison with other types of co-ordination. In conformity with the management literature of the 1990s, one focuses on the 'withdrawal of the state to its core competences' and the 'outsourcing of state activities'.

3. Expanded means of communication and thus a faster flow of information. This leads to a considerable improvement in the possibilities for international co-ordination of economic activities: for instance, by multinational companies.

4. Change in production structures from the Fordist to the post-Fordist method of production, which in turn exerts major effects on corporate structures, increasingly seen as co-ordination networks.

5. Simultaneously with these rather economic globalisation trends, however, one must pay attention to social and cultural globalisation trends, which in turn can eventually integrate an economy. This also suggests that scope for

---

4   James (2001) depicts three political developments that have entailed such setbacks. Among other things, nation-states were meant to: (i) offer social welfare state protection; (ii) provide for protectionism; and (iii) provide the international financial capital throwing the national economies off balance from outside. These are still relevant discussion topics as shown by the increasingly unilateral actions taken by the US, for example, in connection with international environmental agreements and the International Criminal Court of Justice.

manoeuvre exists at nation-state level and that the change in economic structures does not necessarily lead to a convergence of the nation-states' forms of
action.

These change processes should not automatically be rated as negative. Economic
globalisation may, however, become problematic, particularly when the reduction or
removal of national frontiers for economic transactions (liberalisation) is accompanied
by a political deregulation within nation-states. This decreases the capacity to intervene on the part of national political actors. There is no 're-regulation' effected simultaneously at a higher level. Under these framework conditions, globalisation displays
asymmetric effects. For a certain category of actors, exit options are expanded enor-
mously. For another category of actors, options are restricted. This may produce a new
balance, where a few actors reappear in a structurally better position, while the majority are in a structurally more defenceless position than before. In contrast to the economic mainstream, it is therefore impossible to assume that the net effects of the globalisation process, particularly also from a social and ecological point of view, will turn
out to be positive.

Thus, the compromise of **embedded liberalism** (Ruggie 1982) effected in the postwar period, where a balance between the efficiency of markets and the protection of
the community was created by means of social security systems, is increasingly questioned. The opening of markets, which is identical to increased volatility of economic
activities and thus a reduction of security, was accompanied by governmental provision
of social protection to cushion adjustment processes. In this context, states also had
control facilities pertaining to foreign trade by means of monetary policy, customs
levies and taxes, etc. Thus, the opening of markets went together with increased state
activities (cf. Hübner and Petschow 2001). It rendered the possibilities of trade liberalisation socially acceptable to all. Those countries that advanced the opening of markets
most were the countries whose social security systems were most developed.[5]

The increasing liberalisation of world economies by means of flexible exchange rates
and the lifting of capital transaction barriers, whereby the nation-states increasingly
relinquished their scope for manoeuvre, as well as the switch to neoliberal political
approaches from the 1980s in the USA and UK, however, put an end to this compromise.
Embedded liberalism was eventually substituted by the so-called Washington Consensus, which wagered on extensive liberalisation and privatisation, and, in the final
analysis, on the primacy of the market. Thereby, the facilities of social negotiation
processes at a national level are questioned or qualified. Against this background, the
embedding issue must be reformulated. This also requires new forms and levels of regulation; that is, these can no longer be oriented to the nation-state alone.

This control problem is aggravated by the fact that, within the framework of economic integration processes, negative integration is at the fore. Market-creating international institutions are successfully being developed but positive integration, i.e. market-correcting intervention at an international level, has not been possible (cf. Scharpf
1998 using the example of Europe). However, international environmental regimes and

---

5   It must be emphasised, however, that this did not inevitably place environmental protection or
    even issues regarding the development of the so-called third world in the fore; very often the com-
    promise and the strong co-ordination within states prevented development in this direction.

other solutions to common-good problems require market-correcting intervention. At the EU level and also at a global level, possible solutions to the dilemmas connected with the common good, which ideally existed at nation-state level, are non-existent, or continue to exist only in a limited way. This means that, in a situation where hierarchical forms of control do not exist, new forms of problem definition, decision-making as well as institutional and instrumental solutions must be identified and translated.

This bias may be clarified by means of the development of international rules and regulations during recent decades. The rules and regulations of international trade (GATT) with their transition to the WTO (in 1995) have experienced considerable strengthening: for instance, by their dispute settlement machinery and its better enforceability. At the same time, however, this latter aspect extensively restricts the scope for manoeuvre in trade issues on the part of nation-states. On the other hand, rules and regulations have been massively extended by including a multitude of fields that were previously not covered: for instance, intellectual property within the framework of the TRIPS (Trade-Related Aspects of Intellectual Property Rights) agreement. Thus, the trade regime severely challenges regulation at nation-state level because national regulation systems must be adjusted and new regulations must be WTO-compatible.[6]

As a consequence of these changes, most contributions to the discussion proceed on the assumption that a state's scope for manoeuvre decreases, whereas that of companies increases (Hübner and Petschow 2001).[7] This is mainly explained by the fact that the mobile factors (capital, companies, etc.) ultimately already confer different negotiating power by threat of the exit option. States competing to attract firms and public revenue as well as immobile factors (workers) must accept a weakening of their negotiating position and make concessions. It is often suspected that a 'race to the bottom', both in the ecological and social fields, could be a result of this development.

From a state-centred perspective, these changed structures connected with the processes of Europeanisation and globalisation are often defined by the notion of a policy at several levels (Scharpf 1998). Supra- and transnational regulation systems, which increasingly influence regulation systems at nation-state level and restrict their capacity to act, must, however, develop capacities to regulate and solve problems beyond the nation-state hierarchy. However, this is usually only possible in so far as nation-states co-operate.

Relations between states are more and more regulated by international agreements. In the final analysis, this means that the states make commitments and the capacity to act in regulated areas is thus restricted at least in principle. Nevertheless, authority and means of control are not only transferred, as described, bottom-up but sometimes also top-down (devolution). An example of this is the strengthening of regions in the UK and Spain.

---

6   In individual cases, however, this may also have positive environmental effects. For example, the EU is compelled by WTO regulations to reform its agricultural policy. Thereby, an environmentally profoundly harmful policy has been put under pressure and at least the beginnings of a policy observing environmental issues to a greater extent could be implemented.

7   However, this view is not universal. Some contributions proceed on the assumption that the states will still be able to maintain their freedom of action, although in a modified form, by way of co-operation.

2.2 Globalisation and environmental effects

Sustainability issues are not an outcome of the globalisation process alone. A globalisation of environmental issues had already occurred before international exchange intensified. As early as in the 1960s, the global consequences of industrialisation became clear. Thus, Carson's book *Silent Spring* (1962) demonstrated the global impacts of pesticide use; related problems were already discussed at the Stockholm Conference in 1970. In simple terms: at that time, the powerful national scope for manoeuvre did not result in a more comprehensive means of tackling particularly cross-border environmental issues. On the contrary, in the first international environmental agreements, this capacity for manoeuvre was used only in a very limited way.

To this extent, governance gaps relating to environmental issues were already visible when the internal political capacity to act was stronger than today. The reactions of the local population varied in strength from country to country. In the USA and some other countries, environmental movements formed, tackling at least their national problems and leading to political reactions. Subsequently, a multitude of environmental and production areas have been regulated. Environmental issues have, however, not decreased; new problems have arisen and old problems have sometimes been shifted rather than resolved.

In particular, environmental problems on a global scale have increased. In this context, two aspects of the globalisation of environmental issues must be distinguished:

- On the one hand, environmental issues with impacts only at a global level with no regional impact (CO_2 or CFCs; as a continental issue: acid rain). To overcome these, global strategies are required. However, the strategies must be appropriate to be pursued vertically down to the regional level in order to, for instance, approach the goal of climate stabilisation.

- On the other hand, environmental issues manifesting themselves regionally, but at the same time in many places on Earth (fresh water availability, soil erosion, etc.). A typical example of local or regional problems is soil erosion, whose global impacts are triggered by the more or less global adoption of production practices in agriculture (taking into account different capacities to solve problems).

For classification purposes, the following reasons for the globalisation of environmental issues can be identified:

1. Beyond economic globalisation, national development paths may entail environmental problems on a global scale (emissions to the air [CO_2] or into the sea).

2. Indirect impacts through open markets and trade relations: due to an adjustment to competition conditions, there may be considerable pressure to adjust to non-sustainable production patterns.

3. Diffusion of techniques and practices from other countries without any import of goods or adjustment by reason of the opening of markets having necessarily taken place.

Thus, it must be emphasised that some environmental issues have arisen more or less bottom-up as a result of national industrial competition dynamics and associated development expectations. It is not only the processes of economic globalisation that are significant in terms of global environmental issues, but also the general dynamics of the industrial development paradigm and its worldwide implementation.

Assessments of globalisation effects on the environment vary markedly. On the one hand, economic globalisation is held responsible for increasing environmental problems on a global scale (Sachs 2000). On the other hand, it is emphasised that economic development processes enable environmental protection and ensure that the latter achieves at least some importance in developing states. The associated discussion on environmental Kuznets curves (e.g. de Bruyn *et al.* 1998), first and predominantly carried on in terms of an automatism between economic development and growing environmental awareness, has recently changed to increasingly include the issue of political control. For these developments do not occur autonomously, but crucially also depend on the articulation skills of the actors concerned.

The problematic aspect of these rather optimistic assessments consists in the fact that references to these correlations are usually made by means of traditional pollutants such as SO_2 emissions, which can be decreased relatively easily by technical solutions. However, for environmental issues associated with structural factors such as the loss of biodiversity, not even appropriate indicator systems for possible control purposes have been developed (CEC 2001). An important influencing factor here consists in the embedding of traditional life forms and the far-reaching interventions associated with this into the structures of the interaction between humans and nature, where sustainable socio-ecological contexts are dissolved and concurrently only insufficient re-regulation measures are taken. In addition, the success of classic environmental politics often involves regional and also media-related problem shifts within the environmental field.

As a whole, an increase in environmental burdens and a growing threat to the functions of nature, in spite of international environmental agreements and manifold environmental measures at a national level, are acknowledged.

The emergence of the term 'sustainability' as well as its openness and interpretability elucidate the outlined problem. The term was created in an international political discussion (WCED 1987) and is ultimately another element of the globalisation process. With all its ambiguities, it provides a stage for discussions on development paths and is generally appropriate for global application both in the overall context and for very different contexts.

From a governance perspective, however, at least two further aspects arise through the opening of markets and an increasing world market integration, which may impede steps to overcome global environmental problems and strengthen governance gaps. On the one hand, negative integration via the WTO results in a situation where different general approaches clash and conflicts arise. A typical example is the conflict between industrial states over the import of hormone-enhanced meat. The EU refers to the precautionary principle, whereas the US approach is rather in line with the principle 'do and see'.[8] Furthermore, the developing industrial states often perceive the EU's envi-

---

8   Cf. Commission of the European Communities (2000) communication on the precautionary principle, but also the manifold critical reactions to this.

ronmental approach as a barrier to trade and thus to their own development. The WTO currently modulates these different models and views of the world in principle at an international level by means of a risk assessment approach, which is based on supposedly objective analyses and evaluations. On the other hand, national environmental politics, by reason of the global reach of commodity chains associated with increasing international trade flows, always also touch trade aspects and, therefore, against the background of WTO regulation, have only limited reach left.

2.3 Governance

Subsequent to the liberalisation trends and the, at least in principle, decreasing capacities to act on the part of nation-states, new arrangements have developed that can no longer be grasped by the classical term 'governing', which works on the principle of a decision monopoly. Instead, the term 'governance' has been increasingly used.

2.3.1 Attempt at a conceptual approach

Hewson and Sinclair (1999) identify several sources of the term 'global governance': for instance, the discussions on globalisation and 'global change' in general as well as the literature on transnational relations, international regimes and international organisations. Furthermore, this concept is closely connected with the reform of public sectors (public policy) in the 1980s and 1990s, which, to a different degree, was accompanied by a redefinition of the authority of states, of the international governmental organisations (IGOs) and of private actors. Therefore, the notion is also closely connected with trends in terms of individualisation, deregulation and privatisation. All things considered, the term 'governance' thus refers to the transformation of the state or governmental nature. Subsequently, one finds that 'global public policy-making has become much more complex and fragmented, and has covered ever more levels, issues, arenas and agents' (Arts 2003). At the same time, the governance approach is not at all limited to global governance, but is used at different levels and in different sectors. For the trends mentioned above are also connected with modified control structures of companies, regions, etc.

At the international level, there is a multitude of international institutions, which, in terms of their territorial reach, are oriented to both the regional and the global levels. Regime theory has developed a number of systematisations. Koenig-Archibugi (2003), for instance, distinguishes between four categories: embedded arrangements, nested regimes, clustered regimes and overlapping regimes.

These regimes were developed on very different occasions and with different aims. A central WTO goal, for example, is the overcoming of trade barriers and thus the advancement of international competition. The side-effects of this removal of trade barriers are hardly acknowledged as a problem within this regime. Non-intended side-effects of corresponding regimes are subsequently tackled in a problem–solution-oriented manner by setting up other regimes in order to enable the embedding of the side-effects of unimpeded trade flows. Meanwhile, a multitude of conflict potentials between environmental issues and the exchange of goods becomes apparent. These conflicts have often not yet been decided so that the question comes up in how far the embedding regimes can prevail against the trade regime, which is increasingly defined in a broader sense.

The total of these often-conflicting regulations makes up global governance (Zürn 1998: 175). Zürn distinguishes between three basic forms of governance in terms of the role a superior organisation plays as a regulating agency:

1. Governance by government

2. Governance with government

3. Governance without government

The first form of governance corresponds to the classical hierarchical control exerted by states. The second form, however, can be instead defined as 'co-operative governing', where the latter refers to a self-organisation of actors, who succeed in developing rules of behaviour, which are observed without any resort to a superior central agency.

Nevertheless, the term 'governance' is used in very different ways. On the one hand, the European Union and international organisations, for example, perceive it more or less as classic governing; the key phrase here is 'good governance' (Adam 2000; EU Commission 2001). On the other hand, only those forms of regulation that differ from classical governing are grouped under governance (Zürn 1998; van Kersbergen and van Warden 2001)—thus including only new forms of public co-ordination (governance without government). Finally, there is also a comprehensive definition covering both the classic form of governing and any 'mode of public co-ordinating individual actions to provide for the common good', no matter whether it arises from public, private or mixed groups (Knill and Lehmkuhl 2002).

A similarly open, mainly analytically determined definition is also used by the Commission on Global Governance (CGG): 'Governance is the sum of the many ways in which individuals and institutions, both private and public, manage their common affairs' (CGG 1995: 2). This definition does not include an objective. Thus, the question is not what is meant to be, but how the control structures used to regulate common matters are organised.

Normative issues become important when it comes to rating the outcome of regulation attempts and querying how far requirements for a change of control mechanisms can flow from the latter. Particularly against the background of the normative goal of sustainable development, requirements for a corresponding adjustment of control structures may arise.

In those international relations where the governance discussion including its normative level is most advanced, the focus is on 'governance without government' or 'rule without a ruler' (Rosenau and Czempiel 1992) exclusively because in this case there is no central authority.

2.3.2 Global governance and spheres of authority

The ideas developed so far fit Rosenau's considerations on global governance. Similarly to the CGG, Rosenau (1999) basically proceeds on the assumption that global governance is first and foremost an analytical concept. This, however, does not stand for integration and good order. Instead, Rosenau conceives global governance as a catch-all term for profoundly complex and often disparate activities, whose outcome remains open. In principle, global governance stands for the total of all activities of very different actors (including nation-states), who pursue their goals within most different contexts, networks and structures. By reason of such complexity of processes, central control will not be possible. Therefore, states are only a source of authority and global governance is simultaneously characterised by trends towards fragmentation and integration (cf. Chapter 1 in this volume).

For this purpose, Rosenau has developed the concept of spheres of authority, saying that authority is very often no longer connected with formal characteristics but is rather the outcome of processes. What is important is that these spheres of authority are automatically tied to neither territories nor legal relations. They can easily be linked with the recent discussion on the role of **epistemic communities** and other non-governmental actors in tackling environmental issues within the globalisation process (cf. Section 2.3.4).

Not least by reason of the globalisation and privatisation trends, these aspects of differentiation of governance structures hint at the significance of non-governmental control activities. Companies and business associations, for instance, increasingly aim at developing rules for areas that have not yet been covered by international law. As a consequence, and in a similar way to the historical emergence of trade rules, a sort of new lex mercatoria is developing as a global legal framework. This will, in some cases, become the model for national or international regulations. On the one hand, this refers to the settlement of legal disputes and on the other hand to the development of standards enabling an exchange between companies in different legal systems.

At present, the relevant rules are primarily intended to decrease transaction costs. With regard to environmental or social standards, such development does not take place, or, only in a limited way. Corresponding approaches, for instance, exist in terms of standards generated for suppliers such as the ISO standards. At the moment, the efforts made by companies and the developing approaches to self-regulation are mainly driven by disputes with, and pressure by, social actors to whom certain forms of behaviour are not acceptable and who question the reputation of companies. In order to protect their reputation, companies develop their own voluntary standards (cf. e.g. Olins 1999).

2.3.3 Levels of governance structures

Social (self-)regulation processes take place at different levels and time scales. Within the framework of institutional economic considerations, Williamson (2000) has distinguished at least four levels which are significant for social (self-)regulation processes and have proved to be modifiable in different periods of time.[9]

- Level 1: embeddedness. Informal institutions, customs, traditions, norms, religions

9   Differentiations similar to those described here are also used in other scientific disciplines—however, with different notions of governance and institutions (e.g. North 1990; Göhler 1997; von Prittwitz 2000).

- Level 2: institutional environment. Formal rules of the game—especially property (polity, judiciary, bureaucracy)

- Level 3: governance. Conduct of the game, especially contracts

- Level 4: resource allocation; incentive alignment

This systemisation proceeds on the assumption that the different levels are closely intertwined and influence each other. In a concise and schematic representation, level 1 results in values and models that are manifested in formal institutions and determine the rules at level 3. Level 4 is oriented towards the efficient use of resources. These intertwinings and structures may in turn refer to different geographical and functional levels (issue areas) and their links.

By reason of the globalisation processes, these intertwinings at different levels can no longer be conceived of in terms of one country. The processes of opening markets rather result in a situation where the informal and formal regulations increasingly enter into competition—a situation that brings about a continuous need for change and adjustment, but also for reorganisation. This coexistence, overlapping and coincidence of different traditions, values, formal rules, systems of incentives, etc. often leads to processes of adjustment to hegemonic systems and is thus prestructured by power factors. For, along with modified control structures, distribution positions are also affected.

Sustainability governance, however, is not only a question of power. For sustainability proves to be an approach that is, in principle, oriented towards all four dimensions. It does not touch the level of currently visible control mechanisms alone, but above all also contains those basic beliefs and values that are ultimately required to attain sustainability (SRU 1996). This level therefore must be included when control structures are sought that may advance steps towards sustainability.

An example of the significance of different norms and conflicts arising therefrom by reason of globalisation trends is the debate about the TRIPS agreement. The Western form of property rights as individual property and the rules concerning the handling of traditional knowledge, which are often oriented towards common property with indigenous peoples, are often diametrically opposed. This means that institutional forms are ultimately shaped by norms and values and have significant influence on formal control levels.

2.3.4 Governance and sustainability: the significance of norms and values as a control level

The significance of individual and social norms and value systems for issues of social organisation has already been pointed out by North (1990). The development of international environmental agreements and individual cases of success in environmental politics in general suggest that these are closely connected with perceptions and learning processes. Norms and beliefs are very important and learning processes to change these are central requisites for the development of sustainable strategies.

According to Jänicke *et al.* (1999: 92), knowledge and awareness or the informatory and cognitive conditions of action prove to be the 'essential resources of environmental politics'. This is a question of dominating interpretation patterns, of if and how environmental issues are perceived. Social science calls it 'cognitive structuring' of action or the structure of 'knowledge reserves and thought processes'. The studies Jänicke conducted on environmental success stories reveal that in almost all cases the background condition of public awareness was significant. In half of the cases, success came through direct public pressure. This pressure, however, must be exerted by journalistic means.

Zürn (1998: 188) has also pointed out that the development of a common understanding of problems is of central importance in order to achieve positive integration processes: for instance, on the occasion of international environmental agreements.[10] Positive solutions may therefore be possible when the normative and cognitive dispositions of the actors are also taken into consideration so that blockade situations are overcome (Messner 1995). In this connection, the establishment of so-called **border institutions** may be of particular importance. These can enable and advance border crossings.

The significance of normative and cognitive approaches is increasingly reflected on by political science by referring to the so-called 'argumentative turn' or 'cognitive turn' (Arts 2003). These turns were promoted by the emergence of poststructuralism, postmodernism and social constructivism in social science. The classical political variables, such as interests, power and bargaining, were increased to include new variables such as arguments, norms and persuasion. This is a reflection of processes that enable materially weak actors to also exert influence on development processes.[11] Environmentally relevant examples are analyses of the influence exerted by so-called epistemic communities. These problem-oriented communities of scientists play a central role in naming problems. They have often contributed to moving problems to the political agenda and thus prepared the ground for environmental agreements at a regional or global level.

Part of the literature deals with the role of non-government actors in knowledge construction and the setting-up of norms, as well as in discourse formulation within international politics. The central hypothesis is that these actors, by shaping and disseminating politically relevant values, norms, theories and stories, also determine the behaviour of states and other participants in the global arena and thereby exercise discursive power. Examples of this 'capacity to (re-)frame discourse' are climate change and biodiversity. Moral authority, access to mass media and the legitimacy of the dominant discourse challenged are named as three essential factors for the relative success of discursive power strategies (Risse 2001).

Departing from an informal control level that is focused on values, this opens up the possibility for non-governmental actors to exercise regulatory power. Risse refers to differentiation as is usual in regime theories and clarifies that regulatory power refers to principles (moral and causal belief), norms (rights and duties), regulation (pre- or proscription for action) and procedures (decision-making rules).

10   As further central factors Zürn (1998) specifies environmental trend-setters (or trend-setter countries), the generation of capacities as well as verification and reporting obligations.

11   The analysis of these processes is effected in different studies: for instance, with respect to the science–politics interface (Andresen *et al.* 2000; Boehmer-Christiansen 1995; Litfin 1995), the norm 'creation' and norm-driven behaviour in the international system (Kratochwil and Ruggie 1986; Risse 2001), and within the framework of discourse analyses at a global level (Hajer 1995).

The significance of norms set up by non-governmental actors in regulation processes, however, is controversial. On the one hand, it is emphasised that norms, particularly by reason of the activities of non-governmental organisations (NGOs) at an international level, play a role. On the other hand, the underlying conditions of this are not clear because implementation fundamentally depends on the context at the time. Norms can only play a role when certain conditions such as the openness of the situation are given. Epistemic communities, for example, depend on corresponding possibility structures so that their ideas can become effective.

All in all, governance is a concept trying to grasp the change processes and increasingly complex regulation structures mentioned above in an analytical way. In addition, there is a socio-ecological extension to include those norms and values into the governance concept that ultimately form the basis of regulation structures. Socio-ecological transformation towards sustainability depends on change processes at the level of norms and values which ultimately determine how common affairs are managed.

2.4 Approaches to sustainable change processes to reduce governance gaps

As already demonstrated in Section 2.2, one may first of all note as a starting point that governance gaps exist on a considerable scale. This is, to a large extent, undisputed in literature, at least regarding the supply of global collective goods. In this respect, the global system must be described as distorted global governance.[12]

The identification of these gaps and disturbances of global governance immediately entails the question of whether these regulatory structures should be modified in the sense of sustainable governance and thus raises the issue of a corresponding transition. Subsequently, it is crucial to determine which sustainability gaps exist, which governance structures have contributed to this situation and what sort of transformation can be effected (cf. e.g. Kates and Parris 2003; Parris and Kates 2003).

2.4.1 Possible approaches to overcoming governance gaps

In principle, this is a question of (environmental) over-exploitation and corresponding institutional adjustments at different levels. Theoretically, it is important to bring the regulation and the problem levels together in order to avoid 'externalities'. On the one hand, however, this is barely possible on a global scale by reason of an extensive lack of effective control agencies or environmental agreements. On the other hand, the realisation of such a harmonisation is, also at other levels, confronted with the problem that the enforceability of environmental regulation is limited because of, one suspects, disadvantages in global competition.

12   The evaluation of global governance, however, turns out differently. Cable (2000), for instance, proceeds on the assumption that the international fabric of institutions in principle exists and on the whole also functions, but that conflicts over values increasingly emerge: for instance, over women's rights.

All the same, regulatory approaches beyond the nation-state are developing, namely:

- Above the nation-state (international agreements and treaties in co-operation between nation-states)

- Beside (between companies and social actors)

- Below the nation-state (e.g. regional governance, integrated product policy)

Success conditions for the avoidance of governance gaps have been examined by Ostrom (1990): for example, with respect to regional and local common pool resources. On the one hand, it could be demonstrated that, even over long periods, the over-exploitation of natural resources could be avoided by means of institutional adjustments, carried out at several levels and even in different ways. On the other hand, it became clear that this could also occur on the basis of self-organisation without any resort to central authorities. This is subject, however, to a number of success conditions of the issue in question. In this connection, Ostrom (2000) names:

- **Feasible improvement**. Resource conditions are not at a point of deterioration such that it is useless to organise or so under-utilised that little advantage results from organising.

- **Indicators**. Reliable and valid indicators of the condition of the resource system are frequently available at relatively low cost.

- **Predictability**. The flow of resource units is relatively predictable.

- **Spatial event**. The resource system is sufficiently small, given the transport and communication technology in use, that appropriators can develop accurate knowledge of external boundaries, and internal microenvironments.

According to Ostrom (2000), some further success conditions refer to the composition of the actors concerned:

- **Salience**. Appropriators are dependent on the resource system for a major portion of their livelihood.

- **Common understanding**. Appropriators have a shared image of how the resource system operates and how their actions affect each other and the resource system.

- **Low discount rate**. Appropriators use a sufficiently low discount rate in relation to future benefits to be achieved from the resource.

In cases of global problems which are not, or not sufficiently, regulated by international agreements and thus represent governance gaps, this approach, heuristically, may therefore also serve as a means to identify and develop potentials for problem solutions—and without the necessity for a central decision-making authority. The different spheres of authority of global governance may be regarded as spheres of responsibility, each of which must make its contribution to sustainable development. On a global scale, it is clearly much more difficult to achieve such institutional solution approaches not least by reason of the multitude of the actors concerned, the multitude of different environmental situations and the problems of a policy at several levels that should ultimately implement global solution approaches also at a local level. All the same, there are approaches to self-organisation, i.e. beyond or below a peripheral involvement of states, even at a global level, partially only as basic approaches, but partially also in terms of developed structures: for instance, within the framework of ISO standards.

The following is not meant to rank certain types of and possibilities for regulation, or to say that governmental environmental policies no longer play a role. It is rather meant to demonstrate different forms of governance, how they work together, and to illuminate the role of non-governmental actors in particular. Particularly in international relations, there are actors who increasingly become established beside states. These at least address governance gaps and the need for control and are possibly also in a position to offer solutions for these issues. This does not, however, always occur without the integration of states or their supranational organisations, but often in co-operation with states or at least with individual interested states.

In this context, different approaches to change, which are specified below, can be differentiated:

- Market-oriented approaches

- (Inter-)governmental approaches

- Non-governmental social regulations and eventually as a combination of these approaches

- Co-operation between companies, NGOs and states

An example of this multifariousness is the development and dissemination of environmental standards. In global competition, states, for instance, adopt environmental standards that have been developed in other countries (e.g. vehicle emission standards). Other standards are developed at governmental level by international organisations (e.g. OECD code for multinational companies), others by private international standardisation bodies (e.g. ISO environmental management standards), international corporate organisations (Responsible Care associated with the chemical industry) or through co-operation between NGOs and companies (e.g. FSC label for sustainable forestry).

2.4.2 Market-oriented governance approaches

Market-oriented approaches cover processes that are ultimately driven or confirmed by the market. It must be emphasised, however, that markets are social institutions, which are always shaped by norms and values and other institutions. Therefore, markets are inconceivable without regulation and thus without aspects of the other governance approaches.

Market-oriented approaches start with the observance that, in spite of globalisation, the suspected environmental race to the bottom in many sectors has not come about. The latter is usually employed as a rule by the environmental movement and refers to the **exit option** of companies, which can avoid the environmental regulation of a state by means of relocation. Hence, states can easily be compelled to adjust whereby any further development of environmental standards is prevented. It is often emphasised that such relocations particularly occur in developing countries. Empirical studies, however, predominantly show that such developments have not been proved. Only a few studies have yielded adverse results.[13]

This is contrasted particularly by Vogel's idea of a **race to the top** (Vogel and Kagan 2002). The basic idea of this refers to the empirical finding that solutions to problems in one region are adopted by other regions and states and subsequently become apparent as an active market demand. An example is Californian environmental standards for car emissions, which, not least by reason of the natural space situation in California, are among the strictest standards worldwide. These standards serve as models worldwide and have also been adopted by companies.

Conditions for success are related to the global dissemination mechanisms of market-driven (environmental) innovations, also beyond pure regulation, and to political dissemination mechanisms (policy learning). New coalitions, particularly between companies and NGOs, also play an important role. These include process standards and are as significant as dynamics.

Politically, this effect may be used, for instance, within the framework of ecological lead market strategies. Here, one starts from precise regional or national environmental problems, and investigates how technical and/or social solutions can be generated that could be used in other countries with similar problems and could therefore contribute to the export of sustainable technologies.

Similar approaches are pursued within the context of the so-called 'strategic niche management' (e.g. Hoogma *et al.* 2002). By means of experiments, the latter aims to identify sustainable solution approaches and implement these in niches, involving the idea that a market-driven transition from the niche would become possible subsequently.

These examples of market-driven change processes towards sustainability refer to the partially complex mechanisms by which markets can contribute to sustainability. All cases require, however, a corresponding simultaneous development of general social conditions and values and subsequently of the market demand.

One should note critically that the discussion about market-oriented governance approaches predominantly refers to technical product and already less to production standards and leaves structural factors more or less outside. Thus, the focus is on the reduction of emissions; with respect to other environmental issues such as the preservation of biodiversity and alluvial landscapes or water pollution control, however, positive international competition for standards cannot be established.

So far, market-oriented influence factors significantly contribute to the dynamic forces necessary to overcome governance gaps. This contribution is, however, only effective in partial sectors. Therefore, more measures are necessary: also governmental measures. These will be considered below.

2.4.3 (Inter-)governmental approaches

In the sense of the harmonisation approach of problem and regulation as outlined above, global environmental issues and solutions to those environmental issues that

---

13   For an overview of different empirical studies see Petschow *et al.* 1998. For a discussion of theoretical arguments see, for example, Nill 1999.

supposedly have a local or regional origin but become effective on a global scale, in principle require the setting-up of global institutions. Corresponding strategies, however, pose a co-operation problem between the different groups concerned and the problem of distributing profits and losses. The multitude of existing international environmental agreements (WTO 2001), their clearly diverging success stories and the different problem situations regulated by these agreements clarify that there is no 'one size fits all'. It is rather the institutional design and the individual relation of forces that play fundamental roles.

It is true that studies on the development of environmental agreements exist. However, most of these refer only to individual environmental agreements and regimes. It was only recently that a long-term comparative study was submitted. On the one hand, it emphasises individual peculiarities; on the other hand, also things in common, particularly with respect to the actors concerned (Social Learning Group 2001). Important success factors turned out to be the co-operation between scientists, for instance, who put the subject on the agenda, and the integration of states that adopt the issue in question and also try to incorporate others. Basically, it takes political entrepreneurs, epistemic communities and standard entrepreneurs to put the subjects on the agenda and eventually enable their implementation. The assertiveness of corresponding subjects in turn depends on a multitude of further conditions.

In assessments of the current status, it is often held that entering into corresponding international agreements is already crucial. For it simultaneously generates capacities and possibly triggers developmental dynamics which eventually reach far beyond initial goals. On the other hand, it can be established that, while international agreements on environmental protection, particularly on the protection of global commons, have clearly increased in number, their assertiveness relative to existing trade rules, however, has quite definitely been less developed. In this conflict between environmental and trade rules, the latter, apart from a few individual cases such as the Montreal Protocol on the protection of the ozone layer and the Basel Convention on hazardous wastes, clearly take precedence. Ultimately, environmental protection instruments must be WTO-compatible, and may in principle be challenged at any time before the WTO arbitral tribunal.

Thus, market-creating inter-governmental agreements have by far more impact than market-correcting regulations. The latter can usually only be asserted at a minimal consensus level between almost all states. Consequently, considerable regulation gaps remain in both the social and the environmental realms, but also in a number of further sectors that are especially important for companies.

In a global dimension, it therefore seems to be difficult to find a solution to sustainability problems by means of inter-governmental co-operation. It is true that, in some sectors, corresponding institutions such as the Food and Agriculture Organisation (FAO) or the World Health Organisation (WHO) exist. Against the background of dynamic globalisation processes, however, these cannot or can only in a limited way enable positive regulation processes. This suggests that a, hitherto non-existent and in the discussion often demanded, global environmental agency and similar institutional solutions would also have only limited effectiveness (see, for example, Biermann 2002). This will be true, at least until market-creating institutional settings such as the WTO are organised in this sense.

2.4.4 Non-governmental social regulations

Moreover, one can increasingly observe the development of private regulative standards caused not least by reason of governance gaps. These private regulative standards primarily gain assertiveness in sectors that are connected with transnational corporate activities and where they contribute to the reduction of transaction cost. An important sector here is the formulation of standards, predominantly in the technical sector, where governmental actors normally only have limited expertise, but also in the sense of behavioural standards where private actors set normative standards: for example, with respect to 'right' sustainable behaviour (Braithwaite and Drahos 2000). Those private regulative standards aimed at the common good, however, have clearly less assertiveness.

The normative governance debate about such private standards on the one hand points out the increasing inefficiency and the legitimacy deficits of traditional governmental regulations in view of globalisation trends, the increasing scientific lack of confidence and the existing multitude of regulations. On the other hand, private regulations are also considered to be complementary to governmental action; participation and self-regulation could contribute to an improved legitimacy of both political procedures and results. How far this is actually the case can only be analysed within a specific context.

Ruggie (2003) has observed the development of a global public sphere, where NGOs and companies co-operate and companies are therefore interested in paving the way for global governance. Schneider and Ronit (2001) clarified that business associations, which basically focus on their own interests in order to protect their own reputation, all the same produce club goods which at least provide contributions to the supply of public goods.

To this extent, spheres of authority definitely exist to which responsibility for overcoming severe sustainability problems can be assigned, and which subsequently can contribute to a provision of public goods. Political control has had only partial access to these sustainability problems. This means the aim consists in establishing an 'interest and responsibility group' of actors who basically act in markets, but who are united by reason of their interest in a common product. Thus, governance structures are created that are, to a certain extent, similar to those in connection with the social regulation of local and regional common goods.

An example of this is the global protection of forests. The breakdown of the forest convention at an international level resulted in the·formation of a coalition of companies and NGOs that have developed, within the framework of the Forest Stewardship Council (FSC), a label to limit governance gaps. This coalition was rather successful in advancing sustainable timber industry and forest exploitation. The marketing of the FSC seal benefits from the readiness to pay for goods produced in a sustainable way and thus aims at a value level at which sustainability can exist. For the success of corresponding initiatives, it is crucial that market dynamics enable such approaches.

Another example is the development of criteria for sustainable financial services and their marketing through private organisations. Such private standards moreover turn out to be a fundamental aspect with regard to accountability and thus the liability to account towards third parties.

The increasingly differentiated governance structures going along with globalisation trends represented here result in the fact that, also with respect to sustainability, other actors become established beside the world of states, that at least address these regulation needs and are possibly also able to offer solutions. This does not always occur without the integration of states or their supranational organisations, but often even in co-operation with states or at least with individual interested states.

2.5 Conclusions

Globalisation and its impacts have reduced governmental control facilities and simultaneously resulted in the development of new forms of governance. The sustainability discussion points out governance gaps concerning public goods that are not territorially bound and, in connection with these, changed regulation needs. It seems to be appropriate that strategies to overcome these governance gaps should therefore proceed from existing new forms of governance and partial structures and their dynamics. While doing so, the essential control elements at these levels must be clarified and possibly extended by way of an opening into society.

The predominant goal consists of shaping processes that could generate more sustainability. This process shaping has to proceed from many different levels. In this connection, it must be emphasised that such processes are both fragmented and integrated and that they involve the participation of very different actors and networks. Thus, it appears to be doubtful how far sufficient change could be achieved through a central institution such as a global environmental organisation. Sustainability governance occurs rather at all levels and in a multitude of issue areas. One cannot expect a reversal on a global scale even where some indications can be found. It is crucial, however, that at the other levels, including the micro level, fundamental impulses occur, which by way of being disseminated contribute to the assertiveness of more sustainable modes of behaviour. In this connection, central aspects are that:

- On the one hand, states are not at all the only central initiators, although they can eventually be implementers or are involved in other ways.

- On the other hand, non-governmental actors can play an important role as trailblazers or standard entrepreneurs with their own approaches to overcoming regulation deficits.

On a global scale, aside from governmental agreements, market- and competition-oriented approaches such as the establishment of ecological lead markets and the influence exerted by private actors such as scientists, companies, NGOs and other social movements may be effective. In this context, it is crucial that opportunities for social action in favour of a contribution of self-regulation to sustainable development are provided.

New regional and sectional environmental approaches may serve here as an important orientation. Examples of this are river basin management initiatives within the framework of the implementation of the General European Water Directive. The basic idea of these activities, which often also have a cross-border character, is to combine the problem and the management levels of natural areas and manage ecological and socioeconomic areas in an integrated way in order to avoid externalities. The idea of a central ecosystem control is rejected. Instead, the power to act is returned to the partial regions in question and efforts are being made to strengthen social relations between actors by incorporating participative aspects. At a global level, such ecosystem approaches of place-based management are outlined within the framework of the Biodiversity Convention, but not yet precisely supported. Another, rather sector-based, example is the development of integrated product policy by way of co-operation between the actors along the net value added chains, which has also been pushed by the EU.

In principle, such approaches correspond with the finding of Ostrom (1990) that common pool resources can be protected even without the existence of a central regulatory authority. Applied to the global level, this would mean that it is ultimately also important to create corresponding spheres of authority by establishing a connection between those who cause problems and those who solve them within that framework. In accordance with Ostrom it would then be necessary to examine how far these spheres of authority, which are vested at least with informal power, can be developed in order to combine this power with responsibility and thus develop some sort of accountability. Particular difficulties on a global scale can be found in the fact that relevant background control is less developed, the perception of activities of different actors is rather limited and there is hardly any or sometimes no experience with such approaches.

A precise starting point when it comes to getting a grip on these problems could be voluntary and controllable self-commitments at a global level. For example, business associations usually understand the behaviour of their members, but also that of non-members. Moreover, the relevant world congresses on different techniques also convey a global overview of the behaviour of companies and corporate actors. Similarly to the trade-related lex mercatoria, where regulative standards relating to corporate behaviour were developed, which later on often became state laws, a lex mercatoria with respect to 'corporate behaviour' would be a central aspect in advancing dynamics towards sustainability. In this connection, central aspects against the background of globalisation are the creation of publicity, the creation of transparency and the accountability of the actors concerned.

In this light, the results yielded by the world sustainability summit in Johannesburg, where it was not possible to generate momentum as had been achieved at the Rio summit, must be interpreted. At the same time, Johannesburg revealed that there is a multitude of initiatives and movements that do not automatically require any world conference. In this context, initiatives have been founded that even contribute to putting new subjects on the agenda. All this proves that public discussion and the moral authority of civil-society actors, but also of scientific actors, may contribute to the achievement of sustainable goals. Corresponding approaches have become visible within the framework of the Type II agreements of the Johannesburg summit. They also clarify, however, that an evaluation of results has not been effected in these cases, i.e. that an external control in this sense does not work.

Maybe these aspects are of greater importance than inter-governmental agreements. For non-governmental initiatives are more flexible, negotiation- and power-oriented than the nation-states themselves, which are ultimately determined by different interest groups within the nation-state in question. New forms of co-operation between companies, civil-society actors and individual states may eventually also entail modified forms of control. This represents only a limited solution, however, to overlapping governance regimes: for example, between trade and environment. The latter is particularly emphasised by globalisation critics holding that the continuous dynamics of globalisation and liberalisation at the same time challenge the existing, relatively more sustainable, structures. As a consequence, processes to achieve more sustainable structures must be developed in turn. The sustainability model with its various possibilities for interpretation may, however, be an element to move from fragmentation towards integrated regulation approaches.

References

Adam, M. (2000) 'Die Entstehung des Governance-Konzepts bei Weltbank und UN: Die EZ wird politischer', *E+Z: Entwicklung und Zusammenarbeit* 10.00: 272-74.

Andresen, S., T. Skodwin, A. Underdal and J. Wettestad (eds.) (2000) *Science and Politics in International Environmental Regimes* (Manchester, UK: Manchester University Press).

Arts, B. (2003) *Non-state Actors in Global Governance: Three Faces of Power* (Bonn: Preprints aus der Max-Planck-Projektgruppe Recht der Gemeinschaftsgüter).

Baldwin, R.E., and P. Martin (1999) *Two Waves of Globalization: Superficial Similarities, Fundamental Differences* (NBER Working Paper 6904; Tübingen, Netherlands: J.C.B. Mohr for Kiel Institute of World Economics).

Biermann, F. (2002) 'Green Global Governance: The Case for a World Environment Organisation', *New Economy* 9.2: 82-86.

Boehmer-Christiansen, S. (1995) 'Reflections on the Politics Linking Science, Environment and Innovation', *Innovation* 8.03/95: 275-87.

Braithwaite, J., and P. Drahos (2000) *Global Business Regulation* (Cambridge UK: Cambridge University Press).

Cable, V. (2000) *Globalization and Global Governance* (House Papers; London: The Royal Institute of International Affairs).

Carson, R. (1962) *Silent Spring* (Boston, MA: Houghton Mifflin).

CEC (Commission for Environmental Cooperation) (2001) *Changing Biodiversity, Changing Markets: Links between Agricultural Trade, Markets and Biodiversity* (Montreal: CEC).

CGG (Commission on Global Governance) (1995) *Our Global Neighbourhood* (Oxford UK: Oxford University Press).

Commission of the European Communities (2000) *Communication from the Commission on the Precautionary Principle* (Brussels: Commission of the European Communities).

De Bruyn, S.M., J. van den Bergh and J.B. Opschoor (1998) 'Economic Growth and Emissions: Reconsidering the Empirical Basis of Environmental Kuznets Curves', *Ecological Economics* 25: 161-75.

European Commission (2001) *Europäisches Regieren: Ein Weißbuch* (Brussels: European Commission).

Göhler, G. (1997) *Institution–Macht–Repräsentation* (Baden-Baden, Germany: Nomos Verlag).

Hajer, M.A. (1995) *The Politics of Environmental Discourse* (Oxford, UK: Oxford University Press).

Hewson, M., and T.J. Sinclair (1999) *Approaches to Global Governance Theory* (Albany, NY: State University of New York Press).

Hoogma, R., *et al.* (2002) *Experimenting for Sustainable Transport: The Approach of Strategic Niche Management* (London: Spon).

Hübner, K., and U. Petschow (2001) *Spiel mit Grenzen: Ökonomische Globalisierung und Soziale Kohäsion* (Berlin: Edition Sigma).

James, H. (2001) *The End of Globalization: Lessons from the Great Depression* (Cambridge, MA: Harvard University Press).

Jänicke, M., P. Kunig and M. Stitzel (1999) *Lern- und Arbeitsbuch Umweltpolitik* (Bonn: Verlag Dietz).

Kates, R.W., and T.M. Parris (2003) 'Long-term Trends and a Sustainable Transition', *PNAS* 100.14: 8,062-67.

Knill, C., and D. Lehmkuhl (2002) 'Private Actors and the State: Internationalisation and Changing Patterns of Governance', *Governance* 15.1/02: 41-63.

Koenig-Archibugi, M., and D. Held (2003) Taming Globalisation: Frontiers of Governance (Cambridge, UK: Polity Press).

Kratochwil, F., and J.G. Ruggie (1986) 'International Organization: A State of the Art on the State', *International Organization* 40.4 (Autumn 1986): 762-75.

Litfin, K. (1995) 'Framing Science: Precautionary Discourse and the Ozone Treaties', *Millennium* 24.2: 251-77.

Messner, D. (1995) *Die Netzwerkgesellschaft: Wirtschaftliche Entwicklungsfähigkeit und internationale Wettbewerbsfähigkeit als Probleme gesellschaftlicher Steuerung* (Cologne: Weltforum-Verlag).

Nill, J. (1999) 'Zwischen Öko-Dumping und First-Mover-Vorteilen: Die Perspektive der Neuen Außenwirtschaftstheorie auf Umweltpolitik und eine explorative Anwendung auf die Osterweiterung der Europäischen Union', *IÖW-Schriftenreihe* (Berlin) 139.99.

North, D.C. (1990) *Institutions, Institutional Change and Economic Performance* (Cambridge, UK: Cambridge University Press).

Ohmae, K. (1994) *Die neue Logik der Weltwirtschaft: Zukunftsstrategien der internationalen Konzerne* (Frankfurt am Main: Fischer-Taschenbuch-Verlag).

Olins, W. (1999) *Trading Identities: Why Countries and Companies are Taking Each Others' Role* (London: Foreign Policy Centre).

Ostrom, E. (1990) *Governing the Commons: The Evolution of Institutions for Collective Action* (Cambridge, UK: Cambridge University Press).

—— (2000) 'Reformulating the Commons', *Swiss Political Science Review* 6.1: 29-52.

Parris, T.M., and R.W. Kates (2003) 'Characterizing a Sustainable Transition: Goals Targets, Trends, and Driving Forces', *PNAS* 100.14: 8,068-73.

Petschow, U., K. Hübner and S. Dröge (1998) *Nachhaltigkeit und Globalisierung: Herausforderungen und Handlungsansätze* (Berlin: Springer Verlag).

Risse, T. (2001) 'Transnational Actors, Networks, and Global Governance', in W. Carlsnaes, T. Risse and B. Simmons (eds.), *Handbook of International Relations* (London: Sage).

Rosenau, J.N. (1999) 'Towards an Ontology for Global Governance', in M. Hewson and T.J. Sinclair (eds.), *Approaches to Global Governance Theory* (New York: State University of New York Press).

—— and E.-O. Czempiel (1992) *Governance without Government: Order and Change in World Politics* (Cambridge, UK: Cambridge University Press).

Ruggie, J.G. (1982) 'International Regimes, Transactions and Change: Embedded Liberalism in the Postwar Economic Order', *International Organization* 36 (Spring 1982): 379-415.

—— (2003) *Taking Embedded Liberalism Global: The Corporate Connection* (Working Paper IILJ 02/03; New York: Institute for International Law and Justice New York University School of Law).

—— (2000) 'Wie zukunftsfähig ist Globalisierung?', *Wuppertal Papers* 99.01/00: 3-7.

Scharpf, W.F. (1998) 'Die Problemlösungsfähigkeit der Mehrebenenpolitik in Europa', in B. Kohler-Koch (ed.), *Regieren in entgrenzten Räumen* (PVS Sonderheft 29.98; Opladen, Germany: Westdeutscher Verlag): 121-44.

Schneider, V., and C. Ronit (2001) 'Übersehener Beitrag: Internationale Unternehmerorganisationen und die Produktion globaler öffentlicher Güter', *Ökologisches Wirtschaften* 3-4.01: 18-20.

Social Learning Group (2001) *Learning to Manage Global Environmental Risks* (Cambridge, MA: MIT Press).

SRU (Der Rat von Sachverständigen für Umweltfragen) (1996) *Umweltgutachten 1996: Zur Umsetzung einer dauerhaft umweltgerechten Entwicklung* (Stuttgart, Germany: SRU).

Van Kersbergen, K., and F. van Waarden (2001) *Shifts in Governance: Problems of Legitimacy and Accountability* (Background Report NWO 2002–2005; Dutch Organisation for Scientific Research [NWO]): 77.

Vogel, D., and R.A. Kagan (2002) 'National Regulations in a Global Economy', in D. Vogel and R.A. Kagan (eds.), *Dynamics of Regulatory Change: How Globalization Affects National Regulatory Policies* (Berkeley, CA: University of California Press).

Von Prittwitz, V. (2000) *Institutionelle Arrangements in der Umweltpolitik: Zukunftsfähigkeit durch innovative Verfahrenskombinationen?* (Opladen, Germany: Leske & Budrich).

Williamson, O.E. (2000) 'The New Institutional Economics: Taking Stock, Looking Ahead', *Journal of Economic Literature* 38.3: 595-613.

WTO Committee on Trade and Environment (2001) *Matrix on Trade Measures Pursuant to Selected MEAs* (WT/CTE/W/160/Rev.1, 14 June 2001; docsonline.wto.org:80/DDFDocuments/t/WT/CTE/W160R1.doc).

Zürn, M. (1998) *Regieren jenseits des Nationalstaates* (Frankfurt am Main: Suhrkamp).

3
Globalisation means new challenges for sustainability

Ernst Ulrich von Weizsäcker
Bundestag Environment Committee, Germany

3.1 Pollution control versus sustainable development

Sustainable development emerged as a powerful new concept from the Brundtland Report in 1987. Concerning the focus of the environmental debate, it pulled attention away from the classical pollution control paradigm and shifted it towards global equity, the needs of developing countries and global environmental challenges.

The pollution control agenda has, in a sense, been very convenient. You could argue that you first have to become rich in order later to afford expensive pollution control. It allowed industry and economists both in the South and the North to quote Indira Gandhi, who said in Stockholm in 1972 that 'poverty is the biggest polluter'. And industrialised countries proved well that a near-complete decoupling is available between pollution and economic wealth.

Troubles pop up when you start analysing the ecological meaning of pollution-free wealth. You soon see that countries that have reached that stage are among the biggest culprits when it comes to climate change, the over-use of natural resources and of land (direct and indirect) and associated biodiversity losses. Pollution control is not automatically 'sustainable'. One may go as far as inverting Indira Gandhi's statement by saying that *economic wealth involves the greatest (per capita) environmental problems*.

Globalisation tends to be helpful for pollution control. International companies have a tendency to keep the same level of pollution control in their factories around the world. It simply does not pay for them to go for lower levels of protection in less developed countries: it would impede staff mobility, it involves extra administrative costs and it can be hazardous for the firm's public image.

Sustainable development, on the other hand, seems rather more difficult under the conditions of globalisation. It has to be assumed that all countries and all companies try to maximise their economic wealth. Under conditions of intensified competition, companies try to cut costs per unit of output, meaning that they go for economies of scale. Scale benefits are a lot more important in most cases than are resource costs. In fact, international competition among commodity suppliers has led to a systematic trend since the early 1980s of falling commodity prices. This all means that globalisation and the increase of resource consumption go hand in hand.

Market theory suggests that resource prices will go upwards as scarcity signals set in. However, climate change may be more worrying than the depletion of fossil energy resources and does not by itself send scarcity signals into the global commodity markets. Also biodiversity losses caused by excessive land use or by excessive material turnover don't create any scarcity signals by themselves.

Anyway, it remains an open question whether market signals can help at all to create a situation of 'sustainable prosperity'. If resource productivity were something like a technological constant, the outlook would be very dim for reconciling prosperity with climate protection and biodiversity conservation (to name but the two most prominent ecological challenges).

Fortunately, resource productivity is not a constant at all. It has, in fact risen by roughly 1% per annum throughout the world during the last 50 years, and that under the conditions of mostly falling resource prices! During the late 1970s, when energy prices skyrocketed, the world saw a much more rapid increase in energy productivity.

At least a factor of four appears still to be available in the increase of energy and material resource productivity. Fifty examples have been collected of quadrupling resource productivity using existing or proven technologies from all conceivable sectors of the economy (von Weizsäcker *et al.* 1997). And there are prospects of achieving a factor of ten or more in the long run.

Multiplying resource productivity, however, is tantamount to launching a new industrial revolution, reaching *much* deeper than pollution control which, after all, can be done 'at the end of the pipe' without interfering with the manufacturing process.

3.2 Markets beat public interest

Alas, the 'factor four' revolution has not taken off the ground. The main reason, as mentioned above, seems to be that market signals tend to reward resource use, not efficiency.

In the old days when the state could intervene and change market signals, the conclusion would have been to raise public awareness about the calamity and induce politicians to design an appropriate intervention. But again, globalisation does not allow that.

Globalisation can be seen as the trend of giving markets ever more steering powers on technology and societal developments.

Until the 1970s, nation-states were able to autonomously set the frame conditions for business. But then, after the turbulence of the oil crisis and in its wake the novel arrogance of Islamic fundamentalism, first culminating in the Iran hostage crisis, the USA underwent profound changes. Ronald Reagan, enjoying a landslide victory in 1980, strategically reduced welfare benefits and in foreign policy steered the country into harsh confrontation against what he called the 'evil empire'. He promised to reduce taxes for the achievers and invited private business to take their profits home. The state was in retreat.

Similar developments could be observed in the UK, Germany and several other countries. At the time, I believe, it was good for these countries that the private sector assumed additional responsibilities and introduced efficiencies unknown to some state-owned agencies. But in some cases, such as the privatisation of British Rail, it all went wrong.

When the Soviet bloc collapsed, around 1990, many nation-states in the West and in the developing world all of a sudden lost much of their bargaining position towards international capital markets. This bargaining position had been rooted to a large extent in the very existence of the communist threat. It seems to have forced capital owners to accept progressive income taxes, co-determination, generous social security benefits and environmental regulation. The result was the socially inclusive market economy which capital owners found still preferable to any inclination of a country to go communist.

Now, after 1990, that comfortable bargaining position of the nation-state had gone. What now happened was called *globalisation* and was characterised by the dominance over the nation-states of international capital markets. It is striking that the term 'globalisation' was not in use in any major language. In German, it first appeared in 1993 (Deutscher Bundestag 2002).

Globalisation is characteristic of our situation today. In the early days after 1990, the world (and not only business) was celebrating the new freedom. The spectre of a Third World War had disappeared. Hundreds of millions of people were liberated from dull, authoritarian and inefficient regimes. Huge peace dividends were expected to arrive. The stock markets soared. Francis Fukuyama in America called it the end of history: that is, the end of ideological quarrels. Markets were believed to give guidance towards ever-increasing prosperity.

Nobody dared to raise doubts about the legitimacy of the dominance of the private sector because the dominance of the state had conspicuously lost *its* legitimacy.

However, the euphoria didn't last very long. Soon people began to realise that the gap between the rich and the poor was steadily widening. The income gap between the richest and the poorest 20% of the world population rose to a shocking factor of 75 during the 1990s, after having stayed essentially stable at a factor of 30 during the 1960s and reaching 45 during the 1980s.

Environmental policy became a nightmarish task because everybody's immediate concern was now to survive in the unforgiving struggles of globalisation.

Even on their home turf, financial markets performed a lot more poorly than expected. In rapid succession, currencies from Eastern Europe, Western Europe, Mexico, the Asian emerging markets, Turkey and Argentina were subject to extremely damaging turbulence. Worst of all, the 'new economy bubble' eventually imploded and with it the entire euphoria of the global stock markets.

The states, guardians of the public goods, suffered from stagnating revenues, in part self-inflicted through a rat-race for ever-decreasing corporate taxation. Corporate tax rates in the OECD (Organisation for Economic Co-operation and Development) countries were at 36.6% in 1996 and plummeted to 31.4% by 2002.

Ordinary people became increasingly worried and angry about the arrogance of the dominant market ideology. In Seattle, Gothenburg and Genoa you could see them marching and protesting. Protesters mostly represented the losers of globalisation. They also represented in a great variety of ways *public goods* such as the environment, human rights, social equity, farmers' rights, cultural diversity, or the rights of indigenous people.

3.3 Global governance and civil society

Let us take stock for a moment. The victory of what we all considered the superior system, namely the democracy-based market economy, appears to be in the doldrums. People worldwide are seeking a new sense of direction and of recovering the powers for the defence of public goods. However, there is no way back to the autonomous nation-state.

What else can beat the powers of the blind market that is governed by short-term profit considerations?

One suggestion is global governance. States can join with other states to form regional entities such as the European Union (EU). The EU has become a major player in the creation of European and even global rules. This helps to prevent financial markets from blackmailing nation-states. Wider steps are global rules concerning human rights, anti-dumping clauses and the environment. Strengthening the UN is perhaps the most important feature of global governance.

There are three weaknesses of global governance: it's a very slow process; the US doesn't like it and tends to block it; and, for ordinary people, the mechanisms of global governance are very remote and don't invite for participation.

Hence, a *second* path should be followed in addition: the creation of alliances between states, or parliaments, and *civil society*. Both parts have a mission of defending public goods. States still own the privilege of setting binding rules (national laws and internationally binding agreements). Civil society, on the other hand, is highly international and can help create public opinion in favour of social and ecological goals. Civil society is accessible to the ordinary citizen.

Building up public goods alliances fortified by global governance structures is a slow and long-term process. It may take decades. But, then, the creation of national democracies after absolutist kingdoms also took about half a century.

3.4 A final remark on Japan

There is one country in the world that appears to be well advanced as regards sustainable development under the conditions of globalisation: namely Japan. What is usually called the Japanese disease may actually be a special state of health.

Japan is an economic giant. It can be proud of its history, or most of it. It has the highest life expectancy in the world. There is no destitution, very little crime and violence and hardly any hatred towards foreign countries or religions. Japanese firms operate successfully on highly competitive world markets. The basis for this is an excellent education system and a high-technology industry. The service sector is more sophisticated than in essentially all other countries. Infrastructure is well functioning, trains are punctual, and the country is clean.

What is missing is economic growth. But then let us reflect for a moment. What is the meaning of zero growth in a situation of a stable population and of high prosperity? It still means a huge turnover; it can mean an increasing *stock* of wealth. It only means that the *flow*, covering both increase and maintenance of wealth, is not bigger than it was in the preceding year. As a matter of fact, private financial assets are nearly four times as high as the notorious state deficit, and increasing, meaning that the country as a whole is not at all indebted. Japan seems to live close to what can be called sustainable prosperity.

There are only three worrying facts associated with the Japanese zero-growth model: one is that certain competitors, notably China, may eventually outgrow Japan. The second is that technological advances produce higher labour productivity, which means an increase of unemployment, a phenomenon unknown to Japan for many happy decades. And the third is that Japan has *exported* quite a few of its environmental liabilities: Japanese fishermen are among the worst in depleting fish stock all around the world; energy-intensive and highly polluting industries were shifted to other, mostly tropical countries; and the per capita energy consumption (to a large extent from nuclear power) is still too high to be sustainable.

I am not suggesting that Japan cannot be improved, both in ecological and economic terms. But I submit that it does a lot better than all other prosperous countries in both regards.

References

Deutscher Bundestag (2002) *Schlußbericht der Enquetekommission Globalisierung der Weltwirtschaft* (Opladen, Germany: Leske & Budrich; English, French and Spanish summaries are available from the Bundestag): 49.

Von Weizsäcker, E., A. Lovins and H. Lovins (1997) *Factor Four: Doubling Wealth, Halving Resource Use. A Report to the Club of Rome* (London: Earthscan Publications).

4

Developing a global partnership for development
CRITICAL ISSUES AND PROPOSALS FOR TRADE AND FINANCE

Martin Khor
Director, Third World Network

From the developing countries' perspective, ensuring successful development is key for sustainability. The Millennium Development Goals (MDGs) of the United Nations (UN) translate this claim into a set of time-bound and measurable goals and targets. The origins of the Millennium Development Goals lie in the United Nations Millennium Declaration, which was adopted by all 189 UN Member States (147 of them represented by their head of state or government) on 8 September 2000. The Declaration embodies many commitments for improving the lot of humanity in the new century (United Nations 2001). Subsequently the UN Secretariat drew up a list of eight MDGs, each of them accompanied by specific targets and indicators.

The extent, however, to which a developing country is able to make progress on many of the MDGs (especially Goal 1 to eradicate poverty and hunger, but also Goals 4, 5 and 6 relating to health, and Goal 7 on environmental sustainability) depends not only on domestic policy choices. International factors have become proportionately more important in recent years as a result of the globalisation process. Developing countries have generally become more integrated in the world economy and thus their development prospects and performance are more dependent on global economic structures and trends. More importantly, many policies that used to be made solely or primarily at the national level are now very significantly influenced or shaped at international forums and by international institutions. This applies especially to those developing countries that are dependent on the international financial institutions for loans and debt restructuring and have to abide by loan conditionalities. However, it also applies to most developing countries, who are members of the World Trade Organisation (WTO), as they are obliged to align or realign national laws and policies to be in line with the WTO's legally binding agreements.

Thus, the economic policies determined or influenced by international agencies such as the International Monetary Fund (IMF), the World Bank, the WTO, the UN, and developed-country groupings such as the Group of Eight, the Organisation for Economic Co-operation and Development (OECD) and bilateral aid agencies do impact tremendously on a typical developing country. For example, many developing countries have suffered declines in or threats to their industrial jobs and farmers' livelihoods as a result of inappropriate import liberalisation policies, partly or mainly due to external policy influences resulting from loan conditionalities or multilateral trade rules. Moreover, cutbacks in social-sector expenditure, as well as the introduction of the 'user should pay' principle, as a result of structural-adjustment policies in the past on behalf of the IMF have been identified as a significant factor in the deterioration of social well-being of vulnerable and poor groups in several developing countries.

The only goal of the MDGs that generally and specifically covers international relations is Goal 8, namely to 'develop a global partnership for development'. Hence this goal is extremely critical in the overall scheme of the MDGs. This chapter provides a view on Goal 8. There are seven targets listed under Goal 8, as well as 17 indicators. The selection of indicators is subject to further refinement.

Owing to the wide range of issues covered by Goal 8, the chapter will focus on only some aspects of the governance structure of the global economic system, their effects on development, and what needs to be done to contribute to realising Goal 8. The main focus will be on international trade and multilateral rules under the WTO. The global financial system will also be discussed, but in outline form and not in the same level of detail. In the discussion, some of the specific targets will be commented on. Suggestions will also be made on clarifying or adding to the targets or indicators.

Another general point is that in the effort to meet the MDG targets, 'getting policies right' is of crucial importance. If economic and social structures are inequitable and if policies (either for preserving the status quo or for reform) are inappropriate, then the mere expansion of funds and programmes in a country would not be enough, and may indeed increase the problems. This applies to structures and policies at both national and international levels. Efforts to attain Goal 8 for developing a global partnership for development should therefore, as a priority, focus on getting international economic structures, policies and rules right. The rest of this chapter will further discuss this governance aspect.

4.1 Need for an appropriate approach to the integration of developing countries in the world economy

Perhaps the most important, and most difficult, set of development policies that a developing country has to decide on is in the interface between domestic policies and the world economy. Whether, how, when, to what extent, in which sectors, and in which sequence, to integrate the domestic economy and society with the international economy and society are simple but large questions and issues that face developing countries. In the international discussion on these issues, there is no consensus and instead there is much debate and many controversies on the definition, nature and consequences of globalisation.

The dominant approach of the past two decades, favoured by the 'Washington Consensus', of the major developed countries and the agencies under their influence, is that full, rapid and comprehensive integration of developing countries into the global economy is both beneficial and essential for their development. The dominance of this paradigm is now rapidly eroding as a result of the empirical record of developing countries that have followed (or attempted to follow) the policies of rapid liberalisation. The East Asian financial crisis of 1997–99 and other subsequent crises (including in Argentina and Uruguay) have undermined the policy prescription that developing countries should rapidly liberalise their financial systems. It is now more widely recognised that financial liberalisation is qualitatively different from trade liberalisation, and that developing countries should be cautious about how to (or even whether to) open their capital account.

In the area of trade liberalisation, there is also empirical evidence that excessive import liberalisation has caused dislocation to local industries and farms in several developing countries, and at the same time there has not been an increase in export opportunities or performance to offset these adverse developments. There is now an emerging trade-policy paradigm that stresses the importance of addressing other factors (such as the need to tailor the rate of import liberalisation to the increase in competitiveness of local firms, and the need to increase the supply-side capacity of local firms in order to realise the country's export potential). Failure to address these can lead to serious problems of domestic economic dislocation and worsening trade imbalances, should a country liberalise its imports (TWN 2001).

In the area of foreign direct investment, host developing countries are now being cautioned to take an even-handed approach and to have policies that seek to maximise the benefits (for example, through equity-sharing and profit-sharing and technology-transfer arrangements) and to take account of and minimise the risks (especially of potentially large drains on foreign exchange through high import content and large profit repatriation).

The emerging paradigm calls for developing countries to take a pragmatic approach to globalisation and liberalisation, and to be selective and deliberate in choosing how and when, and in which sectors and to what extent, to integrate their domestic economy with the global economy, in the areas of finance, trade and investment. This approach recognises that interaction with the global economy can benefit (potentially significantly) a developing country. However, the terms of interaction are crucial if the potential benefits are to be realised, and if costs and damage is to be avoided. Too rapid a rate of integration, or integration in the wrong areas and in the wrong way, can be harmful rather than helpful. For example, too great a dependence on commodity exports, and an increase in export volume when there is a global over-supply of a particular commodity, can be detrimental. Excessive financial liberalisation (for example, in allowing local institutions to freely borrow from abroad in foreign currency) can lead to a debt repayment crisis if the right regulations and conditions are not in place. The approach of selective integration, done carefully and appropriately, suited to the needs and particular conditions of a country, is therefore of the utmost importance. It should replace the still-dominant approach of 'big-bang' rapid liberalisation, done inappropriately in a one-size-fits-all manner.

This change in paradigm and approach should first be considered at the national level, when governments choose their development strategy. However, it must be recognised that most developing countries do not have the 'luxury' or space to choose their approach to economic integration, because of the determining influence of loan and aid conditionalities, or because of the rules they had agreed to in the WTO. Thus, Millennium Development Goal 8 assumes central importance. In developing a global partnership for development, there is an underlying need for an understanding that developing countries should have the right to take an appropriate and pragmatic approach towards selectively integrating their domestic economy with the world economy. This understanding should be the basis for the systems of international trade, finance, investment, aid and intellectual property rights. The policies, rules and conditionalities arising from these systems should reflect these realities facing developing countries, and their needs. Without this change in attitude and approach at international level, it would be difficult or even impossible to attain Goal 8 of a global partnership for development; and it would also be difficult for developing countries to attain the other MDGs.

4.2 Trade, development and reform of the multilateral trading system

4.2.1 Need for a reform of the governance of the international trading system

Trade is an important component of development. Ideally, trade and trade policy should serve the needs of development within a country's overall policy framework. There is thus the need to 'mainstream development concerns in trade and trade policy'. In practice, development needs are often compromised when a developing country participates in an inappropriate way in international trade (for example, by being too dependent on export commodities whose prices are on a trend of decline) or when domestic policies and laws are amended in line with the country's obligations to meet the rules of the WTO or to meet loan conditionalities (and where aspects of the rules or policy conditionalities are unfavourable to the country's development interests). 'Mainstreaming trade in development', which is a recent slogan in international agencies, can inadvertently have adverse effects, if the policies underlying trade (or if the international trade rules) are inappropriate and damaging to development needs. In considering the policy approach for Goal 8, this distinction (between 'mainstreaming development in trade' and 'mainstreaming trade in development') should be carefully kept in mind.

The international trading system has brought benefits in various ways to several countries, especially the developed countries and some developing countries that have managed to take advantage of it. However, the system is also imbalanced in ways that disadvantage many developing countries. One example is the decline in commodity prices.

It should be recognised that the decline in commodity prices constitutes the most important factor that hinders many developing countries from benefiting from trade, and also suppresses the incomes of millions of commodity producers, thus making it difficult for Millennium Development Goal 1 (eradicating poverty and hunger) to be realised. It is imperative that such huge income losses incurred by poor countries be

stemmed and if possible reversed. Between the 1960s and the 1980s, attempts to stabilise commodity prices at reasonable levels were perhaps the most concrete manifestation of a 'global partnership for development'. This partnership took the form of several producer–consumer commodity agreements, under the UNCTAD umbrella, and the
establishment of a Common Fund for Commodities. Many agreements succeeded in
price stabilisation. However most of the agreements closed or became ineffective after
the withdrawal of interest and commitment by the consumer countries.

There should thus be a target under Goal 8 to 'address the problem of commodity-
exporting developing countries through international measures to ensure commodity
prices are stabilised at levels enabling adequate incomes for the countries and producers'. The need for action on commodities was also recognised in the Implementation
Plan of the World Summit on Sustainable Development. One possibility is for countries
to initiate a new round of producer–consumer commodity agreements aimed at ratio-
nalising the supply of raw materials (to take into account the need to reduce depletion
of non-renewable natural resources) while ensuring fair and sufficiently high prices (to
reflect ecological and social values of the resources).

Also the rules of the WTO themselves are an important aspect of the imbalance of the
global trading system.

4.2.2 Problems facing the developing countries in the WTO system

There is at present considerable rethinking on the nature of the multilateral trading
system as embodied in the WTO. This rethinking is being carried out by developing-
country members of the WTO, many of which have become disillusioned by various
aspects of the system. Meanwhile there is also a high and growing level of criticism
from public-interest groups worldwide. The collapse of the WTO Ministerial Conference
in Cancún, Mexico, in September 2003 is an important signal of the problems.

There is now widespread acceptance that the rules and processes at the WTO are
imbalanced and that much needs to be done to improve the situation (Das 1998, 1999).
Perhaps the most important decision to be taken in the next few years is whether the
WTO members do their best to rectify the problems and imbalances in the existing rules
and system, or whether the developed countries still succeed in their proposals to add
more new issues (such as investment, competition and government procurement) to
the WTO ambit despite rejection of these in Cancún. The addition of these non-trade
issues is likely to distort the trading system and add to the existing imbalances.

Some of the concerns of the developing countries are outlined below.

4.2.2.1 Non-realisation of the expected benefits of the Uruguay Round for
them

The developing countries' main expectation of benefit from the Uruguay Round was
that the developed countries would open their agriculture and textiles markets to their
products. However, there has been little progress. In agriculture, tariffs of many agriculture items of interest to developing countries are prohibitively high (some are over
200–300%). Domestic subsidies in the industrialised countries of the OECD rose from
US$275 billion (annual average for base period 1986–88) to US$326 billion in 1999
(according to OECD data; see OECD 2000) instead of declining as expected, because the

increase in permitted subsidies more than offset the decrease in subsidy categories that are under discipline in the WTO Agriculture Agreement. The recent decisions of the US administration to increase subsidies under the US Farm Bill and of the European Union leaders to continue its level of subsidies under the Common Agricultural Policy have dashed expectations of a serious reduction in domestic support by the US and EU.

In textiles and clothing, the developed countries agreed to progressively phase out their quotas over ten years to January 2005, but they in fact retained most of their quotas even near the end of the implementation period. Genuine liberalisation was avoided by the device of choosing in the first phases to 'liberalise' mainly products that were not actually restrained in the past, thus leaving quotas on the bulk of significant products, which would be eliminated only at the end of the ten-year transition period. This, together with the absence of structural adjustment in the North to prepare for the ending of the quotas, has raised doubts as to whether other trade measures (such as anti-dumping and safeguard measures) will be taken, besides high tariffs, to continue the protection of this sector.

There is thus an important asymmetry here: the developed countries have not lived up to their liberalisation commitments, yet there is an assumption pressed on the developing countries that it is unquestionably beneficial for them (the developing countries) to liberalise their imports and investments as fast as possible. Developing countries are asked to bear for a little while the pain of rapid adjustment which will surely be good for them after a few years, whereas the developed countries that advocate this policy themselves ask for more time to adjust in agriculture and textiles which have been protected for so many decades.

Developed countries also have tariff peaks and tariff escalation in other products that are of export interest to developing countries. Developing countries have also been concerned at the non-tariff barriers in the developed countries that have hampered their exports. These include the use of anti-dumping measures and countervailing duties on the products of developing countries.

The tariff and non-tariff barriers in the North are costly to the developing countries in terms of the potential exports forgone. According to an UNCTAD report:

> Developing countries have been striving hard, often at considerable cost, to integrate more closely into the world economy. But protectionism in the developed countries has prevented them from fully exploiting their existing or potential competitive advantage. In low-technology industries alone, developing countries are missing out on an additional $700 billion in annual export earnings as a result of trade barriers. This represents at least four times the average annual private foreign capital inflows in the 1990s (including FDI) (UNCTAD 1999).

4.2.2.2 Problems faced by developing countries in implementing their WTO obligations

Implementing their obligations under the WTO agreements has brought many problems for developing countries. The prohibition of investment measures (such as local-content policy) and many types of subsidy (under the trade-related investment measures agreement and the subsidies agreement) has made it harder for developing countries to adopt measures to encourage domestic industry.

The Agriculture Agreement enables the developed countries to maintain high protection while also continuing with large subsidies. This enables them to export agriculture products at artificially cheap prices. However, many developing countries have low tariffs (in many cases they were reduced under structural adjustment programmes) and low or no domestic subsidies, and are not allowed to increase the tariffs (beyond a certain rate) or increase their subsidies. There is thus a basic imbalance in the Agriculture Agreement. Many developing countries are facing problems from having liberalised their agricultural imports, as cheaper imports are threatening the viability and livelihoods of small farmers. An FAO study of the experience of 16 developing countries in implementing the Agriculture Agreement concluded that:

> A common reported concern was with a general trend towards the concentration of farms. In the virtual absence of safety nets, the process also marginalised small producers and added to unemployment and poverty. Similarly, most studies pointed to continued problems of adjustment. As an example, the rice and sugar sectors in Senegal were facing difficulties in coping with import competition despite the substantive devaluation in 1994 (FAO 2000, 2001).

An ideal regime of intellectual property rights (IPRs) would strike an appropriate balance between the interests of owners and users of technology, and between the IPR holder and the consumer. However, the WTO Agreement on Trade-Related Aspects of Intellectual Property Rights (TRIPS) has heavily tilted the balance in favour of the IPR holder, causing difficulties for technology users and consumers. The effects of a high-standard IPR regime in developing countries have included: high and often exorbitant prices for medicines, reducing access of the consumer to affordable medicines; high pricing (due to monopolies created by IPRs) of other consumer items, including computer software; the patenting by Northern corporations of biological materials originating in the South (often referred to as 'biopiracy'); and higher cost for and lower access by developing countries to industrial technology (Khor 2001).

The services agreement has many imbalances. Service enterprises in developed countries have far greater capacity to export and to invest abroad, while developing countries' services firms lack the capacity to operate in developed countries, and thus there will be an unequal outcome in benefits. The right of capital to move across frontiers (which is favourable to developed countries which are the main providers of capital) is given far more weight than the movement of persons (where developing countries have an advantage). The agreement also puts pressure on developing countries to liberalise various services sectors, which could lead to the smaller local services enterprises in developing countries losing their market share or even becoming unviable. At the same time, developing countries' service providers are generally unable to penetrate the markets of developed countries (TWN 2001).

These problems raise the serious issue of whether developing countries can presently or in future pursue development strategies or meet development needs (including industrialisation, technology upgrading, development of local industries, food security and maintenance of local farms and agriculture, survival of local service providers, and fulfilment of health and medicinal needs). These problems arise from the structural imbalances and weaknesses of the WTO agreements. There is now an urgent need to redress the imbalances and problems. Surely the WTO was not created with the intention to hurt the majority of its members or deprive them of development.

The developing countries have put forward their problems of implementation and their proposals for redressing these problems in the WTO. These requests have been taken up under the rubric of 'implementation issues' in the past several years (see WTO 2001a, b, c). They have been discussed on numerous occasions in the WTO General Council special sessions on implementation and in various committees and councils. Unfortunately the developed countries have so far not responded positively. Their attitude seems to be that the developing countries entered into legally binding commitments and must abide by them however painful; any changes require new concessions on their part. Such an attitude does not augur well for the WTO, for it implies that the state of imbalance will have to remain and, if developing countries 'pay twice' or 'pay three or four times', the imbalances will become worse and the burden more heavy.

4.2.2.3 Proposals by developed countries to expand the WTO's mandate to 'new issues'

The biggest immediate problem facing the developing countries in the WTO is the immense pressure on them to accept the proposals by developed countries to expand the WTO's mandate to non-trade issues including establishing new agreements on investment, competition and transparency in government procurement. Developing countries are being asked to accept these new obligations as an exchange for developed countries opening their agriculture markets or for favourably considering the 'implementation issues'. However, the agreements and obligations in these new areas would be detrimental to the developing countries' development prospects, and at the same time (given the past poor record of the developed countries) it is uncertain that the developed countries will really provide more meaningful market access to the developing countries or resolve their implementation problems.

The three proposed new agreements have a common theme: increasing the rights of the foreign firms to have much greater access to the markets of developing countries. The investment agreement aims to expand the right of foreign firms to enter, invest and operate in developing countries with minimum regulation (as performance requirements would be prohibited) and to be given 'national treatment' (treated at least as well as locals). The competition agreement is meant to oblige developing countries to adopt competition laws and policies, which would result in 'effective equality of opportunity' for foreign firms *vis-à-vis* local firms. In effect this would mean that governments would not be able to assist local firms. The proposed agreement on transparency in government procurement is planned as the first stage of an eventual agreement that would grant foreign firms the same right as local firms to bid for the business of government supplies, contracts and projects. These agreements would seriously tie the hands of government, preventing it from regulating foreign firms and also from providing assistance or preferences to local firms and other productive units. It would severely restrict the ability of developing countries to build the capacity of their domestic sectors, enterprises and farms (Khor 2002).

4.2.3 Conclusions and proposals on WTO

In the context of the MDGs, there is a clear rationale for improving and reforming the WTO system of multilateral rules and decision-making process. The developed countries need to provide greater opportunities for developing countries so that the latter's export opportunities can expand. If this is done properly, it can lead to increased export earnings, foreign exchange and income, thus helping provide the extra resources for financing measures to meet the MDGs. However it must be recognised that many developing countries will be unable to take up the opportunity because of supply-side constraints. On the other hand, the problems caused to developing countries by the existing agreements must be rectified. Failure to do so can adversely affect the realisation of several of the Goals. It would hinder Goal 8's striving for a global partnership for development, as the WTO rules are today recognised as representing an unequal partnership between North and South. The agreement on agriculture, by allowing artificially cheap subsidised imports to threaten small farmers' livelihoods in developing countries, threatens the realisation of Goal 1 (eradicate poverty and hunger). Unless there is a satisfactory clarification or amendment of the TRIPS agreement, access to healthcare and other services will be adversely affected, thus threatening Goal 6 on combating HIV/AIDS and other diseases. The pressures for liberalising services under the GATS (General Agreement on Trade in Services) could adversely affect the access of the public, especially the poor, to essential services such as education (thus affecting Goal 2), healthcare (thus affecting Goals 4, 5 and 6) and water supply (thus affecting Goal 7 on environment).

The following measures are thus proposed in order to further the goal of developing a global partnership for development:

1. The developed countries should commit to meaningfully opening their markets to developing countries in sectors, products and services in which the latter are able to benefit. These include textiles, agriculture and products processed from raw materials, as well as labour services. A meaningful expansion of market access for developing countries will be able to provide large opportunities for earning more revenues that could be the basis for significant extra financing for meeting the MDGs.

2. The process in the WTO of reviewing the implementation problems arising from the existing agreements should result in appropriate changes to the rules or authoritative interpretations of the rules that help resolve the imbalances and the problems facing developing countries. For example, the following are among the changes that should be considered:

    – Developing countries should be given adequate flexibility in implementing their obligations in the Agriculture Agreement on the grounds of the need for food security, defence of rural livelihoods and poverty alleviation. In developing countries, food produced for domestic consumption and the products of small farmers should be exempted from the Agriculture Agreement's disciplines on import liberalisation and domestic subsidies.

    – In the Agreement on Trade-Related Investment Measures (TRIMs), 'investment measures' such as the local-content requirement (obliging firms to use at least a specified minimal amount of local inputs) and foreign exchange balancing (limiting the import of inputs by firms to a certain percentage of their exports) have been prohibited. Such measures had been introduced to protect the country's balance of payments, promote local firms and enable more linkages to the local economy. Prohibiting them causes developing countries to lose some important policy options to pursue their industrialisation. The TRIMs Agreement should be amended to provide developing countries with the flexibility to continue using such investment measures to meet their development goals.

- The TRIPS Agreement should be amended to take into account development, social and environmental concerns. For example, full clarification or amendments are still required to ensure that members can effectively take measures to provide medicines at affordable prices. Members should also be allowed to prohibit the patenting of life forms, and to protect the traditional knowledge and practices of farmers, indigenous people and local communities. Other amendments are also needed to re-balance the agreement towards the interests of consumers and technology users in developing countries. The issue of whether IPRs should be covered at all under the WTO should also be reviewed.

- It should be clarified that essential services required by the public, and especially by the poor, such as water supply, healthcare and education, should or can be exempted from the general rules and the specific sectoral schedules of the GATS.

3. There should be a reorientation in the operational principles and rules of the WTO so that the development principle is accorded the highest priority. The preamble to the Marrakesh Agreement recognises the objective of sustainable development and also the need for positive efforts to ensure the developing countries secure a share in international trade growth commensurate with the needs of their economic development. The objective of development should become the overriding principle guiding the work of the WTO, and its rules and operations should be designed to produce development as the outcome. Since the developing countries form the majority of the WTO membership, the development of these countries should be the first and foremost concern of the WTO. The test of a rule, proposal or policy being considered in the WTO should not be whether that is 'trade-distorting' but whether it is 'development-distorting'. Since development is the ultimate objective, while reduction of trade barriers is only a means, the need to avoid development distortions should have primacy over the avoidance of trade distortion. So-called 'trade distortions' could in some circumstances constitute a necessary condition for meeting development objectives. From this perspective, the prevention of development-distorting rules, measures, policies and approaches should be the overriding concern of the WTO (TWN 2001).

The reorientation of the WTO towards this perspective and approach is essential if there is to be progress towards a fair and balanced multilateral trading system with more benefits rather than costs for developing countries. Such a reorientation would make the rules and judgement of future proposals more in line with empirical reality and practical necessities. Taking this approach, the goal for developing countries would be to attain 'appropriate liberalisation' rather than to come under the pressure of attaining 'maximum liberalisation'. The rules of the WTO should be reviewed to screen out those that are 'development-distorting', and a decision could be made that, at the least, developing countries be exempted from being obliged to follow rules or measures that prevent them from meeting their development objectives. These exemptions can be on the basis of special and differential treatment.

4. Cancún was an important signal that, instead of opening 'new issues', the next phase of the WTO's activities should focus on the above three areas, in order that the review of existing rules, the realising of opportunities in the developed countries' markets, and the reorientation of the WTO to developing countries' needs and interests, can be carried out. These processes would in themselves be a massive task, requiring the commitment, energy and resources of WTO members. However this is needed to build a mutually beneficial multilateral trading system.

5. The process of decision-making in the WTO must be democratised, made more transparent and enable the full participation of developing countries. At present, the system of participation is flawed. The so-called consensus system enables the developed countries to pressurise developing countries to accept what has been agreed among the developed countries. Moreover, non-inclusive and non-transparent processes are used, especially surrounding the Ministerial Conferences during which the key decisions are taken. For example, at the Singapore Ministerial Conference in 1996, only 30 countries were invited to the 'informal' meeting where the major decisions were taken, and the remaining countries were asked to accept the decisions on the last night. At the Doha Conference in 2001, the proposals of a majority of developing countries on key subjects were not included in the drafts of the Declaration, despite their objections. This put them at a great disadvantage. The decision-making processes should therefore be reformed, and the absence of such reform would make it difficult or impossible for the other improvements being suggested to be realised. At the least:

    - All members must be allowed to be present and participate in meetings.
    - The views of all members must be adequately reflected in negotiating texts.
    - Pressure should not be applied on members to accept views of other members.
    - Adequate time must be given to all members to consider proposals being put forward.
    - The practice of late-night exclusive meetings at Ministerial Conferences should be discontinued.

6. There should also be a rethinking on the scope of the WTO's mandate over issues and the role of other agencies. It is misleading to equate the WTO with the 'multilateral trading system', as is often done in many discussions. In fact the WTO is less than and more than the global trade system. There are key issues regarding world trade that the WTO is not seriously concerned with, including low commodity prices. On the other hand, the WTO has become deeply involved in domestic policy issues such as intellectual property laws, domestic investment and subsidy policies. There are also proposals to bring in

other non-trade issues including labour and environment standards as well as investment and competition. The WTO and its predecessor the GATT have evolved trade principles (such as non-discrimination, MFN [most favoured nation] and national treatment) that were derived in the context of trade in goods. It is by no means assured or agreed that the application of the same principles to areas outside of trade would lead to positive outcomes. Indeed, the incorporation of non-trade issues into the WTO system could distort the work of the WTO itself and the multilateral trading system. Therefore, a fundamental rethinking of the mandate and scope of the WTO is required. First, issues that are not trade issues should not be introduced in the WTO as subjects for rules. Second, a review should be made of the issues that are currently in the WTO to determine whether the WTO is the appropriate venue for them (the obvious issue to consider here is IPRs).

4.2.4 Conclusion

The processes of reviews, reforms and changes to the WTO suggested above are important elements of contributing towards Goal 8 of 'developing a global partnership for development'. In fact the above measures could be included as new targets, with accompanying indicators. Within its traditional ambit of trade in goods, the WTO should reorient its primary operational objectives and principles towards development, as elaborated in the sections above. The imbalances in the agreements relating to goods should be ironed out, with the 're-balancing' designed to meet the development needs of developing countries and to be more in line with the realities of the liberalisation and development processes. With these changes, the WTO could better play its role in the design and maintenance of fair rules for trade, and thus contribute towards a balanced, predictable international trading system which is designed to produce and promote development. The WTO, reformed along the lines above, should then be seen as a key component of the international trading system, co-existing, complementing and co-operating with other organisations, and together the WTO and these other organisations would operate within the framework of the trading system, in a 'global partnership for development'.

4.3 Developing reforms to the global financial system

4.3.1 The need for global financial reform

In working towards Goal 8 for a global development partnership, a major element to develop is the reform of the global financial architecture. This reform is embedded within the first target accompanying Goal 8: 'Develop further an open, rule-based, predictable, non-discriminatory trading and financial system'. A note under the target says that this 'includes a commitment to good governance, development and poverty reduction, both nationally and internationally'.

It can be argued that the present global financial system is not open (in that many financial transactions, including those involving speculative activities, highly leveraged institutions such as hedge funds, and derivatives are non-transparent and non-account-able), it is not adequately rule-based (as there is absence of or inadequate regulation over many kinds of activity by the financial institutions, and over the massive international flows of funds), and it is also not predictable (witnessed by the volatility, fluctuations and unpredictability of exchange rates, and inflows and outflows of funds that countries are subjected to).

The lack of regulation and predictability of the global financial system has been a source of financial and economic destabilisation for many developing countries. In recent years there has been a continual series of devastating financial and economic crises, including those that hit Mexico, Thailand, Indonesia, South Korea, Malaysia, Russia, Turkey, Argentina, Uruguay and Brazil. There have been conflicting reasons given for these crises. One of the dominant explanations is that the affected countries suffered from bad political and economic governance. This is quite remarkable, as most of the affected countries had been lavishly praised just prior to their crises as shining examples of good economic management.

A more accurate and credible explanation is that these crises were caused by the financial liberalisation and deregulation that has swept the world since the early 1970s (when the Bretton Woods system of fixed exchange rates collapsed). As a result, there has been an explosive increase in financial speculation as investment funds and speculators move rapidly across borders in search of profits. In recent years, many developing countries were also advised to deregulate and liberalise their financial systems. The controls over the inflow and outflow of funds, which these countries previously had, were relaxed very significantly. This led to excessive short-term borrowing by local firms and banks, as well as the entrance of international funds and players that invested, speculated and manipulated currencies and stock markets in the countries.

The prevailing mainstream view that liberalisation was beneficial and posed little danger to developing countries had been promoted by the international financial institutions and the major developed countries. The latter were eager to obtain more market access for their financial institutions to the emerging markets. It is now widely recognised that when the crisis struck in the East Asian countries in 1997, the IMF made it worse by misdiagnosing the cause and promoting even further financial liberalisation as part of its loan conditionality, as well as a policy package (which included high interest rates, tight monetary and fiscal policies and closure of local financial institutions) that converted a financial-debt problem into a structural economic recession. A report of the IMF also denied that hedge funds and other highly leveraged institutions had played a destabilising role in the Asian crisis, and it took the near-collapse of Long-Term Capital Management (LTCM) to expose the extremely high leverage and market power of these speculative funds.

In order that a global financial system can be developed as part of a 'global partnership for development', two categories of measures are required at international level in the interests of developing countries.

4.3.2 Measures to avoid new institutional pressures for financial liberalisation

The first set of proposals involves the need to avoid new policies or agreements that would 'lock in', oblige or pressurise the developing countries to adopt policies that further financial liberalisation. Each developing country should be enabled to decide on its own, without pressure, the degree, rate and type of financial liberalisation it should undertake. Moreover, the country should have the degree of flexibility to 'backtrack' and reintroduce regulations, should it decide that this is in its interests, following a change in circumstances or judgement. The following are proposed:

1. The IMF should no longer pursue the goal of amending its Articles of Agreement to give it jurisdiction over capital account convertibility, with the aim of disciplining developing countries to open up their capital account and markets. The IMF had been pursuing the amendment, until the series of financial crises beginning in 1997 slowed down the process.

2. The OECD countries should stop altogether any attempt to revive their proposed Multilateral Agreement on Investment, which would have given unfettered freedom of mobility to all types of capital flow. The negotiations stalled in 1998 following discontent by civil-society organisations and the withdrawal from negotiations by France.

3. The proposal for a multilateral investment agreement under the aegis of the WTO should also not proceed, as such an agreement would put intense pressures on developing countries to deregulate the flows of investments and financial flows into and out of their countries. This will make them more susceptible to the instability of financial flows.

4. There should be a review of the financial services agreement in the WTO to take into account the understanding gained and lessons learned from the negative effects of financial liberalisation resulting from the latest round of financial crisis. Developing countries should not be pressurised in the present or future rounds of services negotiations in the WTO to further liberalise their financial sectors. The decision to liberalise should be left to the developing countries to make, without pressure placed on them. Developing countries should be cautious about liberalisation commitments.

4.3.3 Proposals for global financial reform

The second set of proposals relates to international policies and measures that are required in order to develop a stable and development-oriented global financial system.

1. The development of measures and guidelines to assist developing countries to prevent or avoid future debt and financial crises. These should include measures that regulate and control the type and extent of foreign loans that the public and private sectors are allowed to obtain; and regulations to prevent speculation and manipulation in the stock market and the currency markets.

2. If, nevertheless, a financial crisis breaks out, in which a country is unable to service its external debt, international measures and mechanisms are required to enable the affected country to manage the crisis effectively and in which the debtors and creditors share the burden equitably. At present there is no systemic treatment for debt workout, rescheduling and relief, and usually the debtor developing countries are left carrying an unfairly large share of the burden, and the outstanding debt in many cases remains or even grows. The measures required include an arrangement in which a country in financial trouble can opt for a debt standstill arrangement, and have recourse to an independent international debt arbitration court or panel, which would then arrange for a debt workout that fairly shares the cost and burden between creditors and debtors, and also facilitate the provision of fresh credit to aid the affected country's recovery. This proposal for an 'international bankruptcy mechanism' had been notably put forward in detail by UNCTAD in its Trade and Development Reports 1998 and 2001, and the IMF Secretariat has in the past year also been actively promoting the concept. It would be a major breakthrough towards a new financial architecture if this concept were to be appropriately developed and implemented.

3. A framework that allows and freely permits developing countries, without fear of attracting penalties, to establish systems of regulation and control over the inflow and outflow of funds, especially of the speculative variety.

4. Governments of countries that are the sources of internationally mobile funds should be obliged to discipline and regulate their financial institutions and players to prevent them from unhealthy speculative activities abroad and from causing volatile capital flows.

5. Systems of international regulation need to be developed to control the activities of hedge funds, investment banks and other highly leveraged institutions, offshore centres, the currency markets and the derivatives trade.

6. An international monetary system that enables the stability of currency exchange rates is also urgently required.

7. A reform of the decision-making system in international financial institutions (IFIs), especially the IMF and the World Bank, is required, so that developing countries can have a fairer and more effective role in the policies and processes of these institutions that have so much influence and power over their economic and social policies. The distribution of quotas in the equity of the IFIs should be reviewed and reformed, so that developing countries are enabled to have a greater proportion of the total shares (for example, half or more than half).

8. A review of and appropriate changes to the set of conditionalities that accompany IMF–World Bank loans is urgently required as it has become increasingly obvious that in many cases the sets of policy prescriptions have had adverse rather than positive effects, specifically as well as overall. Recent UN reports have pointed out criticisms, including by finance ministers of heavily indebted poor countries (HIPCs), that some elements of macroeconomic conditionality

have focused on reducing inflation at the expense of growth and employment. Although the previously termed 'structural adjustment policies' have now been renamed, the newly established 'poverty reduction strategy papers' (PRSPs) that are meant to be oriented towards poverty reduction, also contain policy elements that are very similar to the macroeconomic and structural adjustment programmes implemented in many poor countries over the past two decades (United Nations 2002; UNCTAD 2002). The scope of conditionality should be streamlined and reduced to appropriate topics, and the appropriateness of the policy assumptions and the policies themselves should be openly debated and the needed corrections made, so that the economic frameworks are growth- and development-oriented rather than having contractionary effects. Recipient countries should be enabled to 'own' the process of establishing the priorities and assumptions of the policy frameworks and the policies themselves. Civil society should also be adequately consulted. The recipient countries should have options to choose among appropriate financial, monetary, fiscal, macroeconomic, trade, ownership and other economic and social policies, instead of being obliged to merely follow the IMF and World Bank prescriptions.

9. As recognised by target 15 under Goal 8 of the MDGs, there is a need to 'deal comprehensively with the debt problems of developing countries through national and international measures in order to make debt sustainable in the long run'. The comprehensive treatment needs to cover all types of debt (private, public, bilateral and multilateral) and for low- as well as middle-income developing countries facing debt servicing problems, and other developing countries that are on the verge of debt repayment crisis. The HIPC initiative has had only limited effects, and its coverage, framework, procedures and content of conditionality should be reformed to give much deeper relief to many more HIPC countries. A more serious and systemic approach to debt relief and fair creditor–debtor burden sharing should be made for middle-income developing countries. The mechanism for debt arbitration or an international insolvency court could be an important part of the resolution of the debt crisis.

10. To prevent future debt problems and financial crises, the possible sources of these problems and crises should be identified, including outside of the financial arena. For example, there should also be a review of the appropriateness of trade policies. The decline in commodity prices, the lack of export opportunities and inappropriate import liberalisation (and especially the combination of all these three factors) can cause, contribute to or worsen a financial crisis. For example, when a country liberalises its imports when its local sectors are not yet prepared to compete while at the same time it is unable to earn more export revenue, the country's trade and balance-of-payments deficits may worsen significantly, adding to debt pressures, and possibly triggering a full-scale external financial crisis.

4.3.4 Conclusion

This section on the global financial system has outlined only some of the critical areas where reform is required, and the discussion and proposals have not been as detailed as the section on the trading system and the WTO because of the limited scope of the chapter.

However, it is clear that reforms are urgently required, as a great number of developing countries are still heavily indebted even after a decade or two in that situation, while increasing numbers of other developing countries (including the more developed among them) have also become heavily indebted. The financial system as a whole, which is increasingly characterised by liberalised cross-border flows of funds, by the absence of regulations, transparency or a fair rules-based way of resolving the burden between debtor and creditor countries, requires an overhaul. In the reforms, the interests of developing countries should be placed at the highest priority.

In the context of the MDGs, Goal 8 does not have a detailed enough target to capture the manifold objectives and actions that are needed in the area of global finance, including the problem of debt, capital flows and a healthy system of financing for development. Therefore, more detailed targets in this field should be developed, as well as more and better indicators. Most important, however, is the need to flesh out in more detail and greater accuracy the various measures, policies and frameworks required to make the financial system a key component to a 'global partnership for development' rather than the problem it now is.

References

Das, Bhagirath Lal (1998) *The WTO Agreements: Deficiencies, Imbalances and Required Changes* (Penang, Malaysia: Third World Network).

—— (1999) *Some Suggestions for Improvements in the WTO Agreements* (Penang, Malaysia: Third World Network).

FAO (Food and Agriculture Organisation) (2000) *Agriculture, Trade and Food Security* (vol. I; Rome: FAO).

—— (2001) *Agriculture, Trade and Food Security* (vol. II; Rome: FAO).

Khor, M. (2001) *Rethinking IPRs and the TRIPS Agreement* (paper; Penang, Malaysia: Third World Network).

—— (2002) *The WTO, the Post-Doha Agenda and the Future of the Trade System: A Development Perspective* (Penang, Malaysia: Third World Network).

OECD (Organisation for Economic Development and Co-operation) (2000) *Agricultural Policies in OECD Countries: Monitoring and Evaluation 2000* (Paris: OECD Secretariat).

TWN (Third World Network) (2001) *The Multilateral Trading System: A Development Perspective* (report prepared for UNDP; New York: UNDP [United Nations Development Programme]).

UNCTAD (1999) 'Industrial countries must work harder for development if globalisation is to deliver on its promises', press release UNCTAD/INF/2816, 1 September 1999.

—— (2002) *Economic Development in Africa. From Adjustment to Poverty Reduction: What is New?* (Geneva: United Nations).

United Nations (2001) *Road Map towards the Implementation of the United Nations Millennium Declaration: Report of the Secretary General* (General Assembly document A/56/326; United Nations).

—— (2002) *External Debt Crisis and Development: Report of the Secretary General* (General Assembly document A/57/253; United Nations).

WTO (World Trade Organisation) (2001a) *Implementation-Related Issues and Concerns* (decision of 14 November; Geneva: WTO).

—— (2001b) *Compilation of Outstanding Implementation Issues Raised by Members* (General Council document JOB[01]152/Rev.1, dated 27 October 2001; Geneva: WTO).

—— (2001c) *Implementation-Related Issues and Concerns* (General Council document JOB[01]/14 dated 20 February 2001; Geneva: WTO).

Part 2
Cross-cutting issues

5

The role of social learning on the road to sustainability*

Bernd Siebenhüner[†]

Carl von Ossietzky University Oldenburg, Germany

Many social and ecological problems addressed under the umbrella of sustainability prove to be rather resistant to regulatory policy measures, in particular when it comes to diffuse sources of pollution, long-term consequences and changes in consumption patterns and individual behaviour. In these fields, directive approaches are limited in their ability to achieve social change with measurable outcomes in terms of alleviated ecological stresses and social improvements. Since individual and group behaviours are to a large extent governed by value structures, cultural norms as well as individual and collective perceptions, changing these underlying causes requires policy approaches that leave room for self-organisation and learning by individuals and collective social actors based on their own decision-making (see, for example, Minsch *et al.* 1998). To achieve measurable results on a macro scale, changes and learning will have to be fostered on a societal level beyond mere individual approaches which might be neutralised through contrasting behaviours by other members of society.

This is not to say that regulatory policy measures are futile. But, given the complex, long-term and uncertain character of the interactive social and ecological problems, they exhibit significant limitations with regard to their flexibility, comprehensiveness and motivational strength which must be acknowledged when sustainable development strategies are to be implemented (Council 1999). Nonetheless, we have to question how these kinds of social processes come about, how they are triggered, which driving factors play key roles in them, in which situations and environments they take place, what outcomes can be expected, how they might be directed towards sustainable development and how social learning might interrelate with the governance systems of collective decision-making.

* A version of this chapter first appeared in *The International Journal of Ecological Economics and Statistics* (IJEES), Volume 3, Number S05 (2005), pp. 42-61.

† The author is grateful for highly valuable comments and suggestions by Thomas Beschorner and Jens Clausen. Research for this paper has been carried out as part of GELENA project on Social Learning and Sustainability hosted by Carl von Ossietzky University Oldenburg and IÖW Berlin (see www.gelena.net). Funding by BMBF (German Federal Ministry of Education and Research) is gratefully acknowledged.

The general insight into the pivotal role of societal change through social learning is somehow negatively mirrored by the situation in the social sciences where attention has been focused on regulatory and economic instruments in environmental policy based on a focus on economic interests and political power as key drivers of social change. In political science, for instance, most scholars viewed social change as triggered by strong social forces such as economic interests or military power (Nordlinger 1981). It has only been in recent years that a growing number of researchers have increasingly focused on other social drivers and illustrated the role that knowledge, ideas and values play in public policy-making in particular and in social change in general. These concepts and research findings have, however, scarcely been applied to problems of sustainable development: 'Generally lacking are theories of social dynamics that can complement the emerging theories of ecosystem dynamics to produce real understanding of the long-term, large-scale interactions of environment and development' (Parson and Clark 1995: 428-29).

This chapter draws on some existing approaches from political science, sociology, management studies and social psychology in order to outline a conceptual framework for the analysis of social learning processes towards sustainability. The line of argumentation is structured as follows. The subsequent section will highlight the need for social learning in the context of sustainability and it will lead to a related definition of social learning. Section 5.2 discusses concepts of social and political learning that have been developed in political science. These concepts particularly focus on learning processes within the governance system. In Section 5.3, I will sketch out a conceptual framework that focuses on societal actors as change agents in social learning processes towards sustainability. Finally, some conclusions will be drawn concerning possible triggers for social learning processes towards sustainability and in relation to the questions of social learning and its role within the governance system under the perspective of sustainable development.

5.1 Social learning and sustainability

Social learning has many different connotations and meanings in a number of contexts and disciplinary perspectives. It is the objective of this chapter to specify the meaning of social learning that is relevant for a transition towards sustainable development. Therefore, we first have to clarify the meaning of social learning before we can discuss the relationship between social learning and sustainability.

In social psychology, learning phenomena on the individual level have been examined for a long time. A broad definition was developed by Swenson (1980: 3), who framed learning as 'the most important process (or processes) by which we manage to change, adapt, and become (hopefully) more competent'. Therefore, he focused on the outcomes of the learning process resulting in changes in behaviour. However, this definition does not contain any indication about the processes behind the changes in behaviour and individual capabilities. By contrast, Schunk (1996: 2) attempted to capture this phenomenon in his definition when he states that 'learning is an enduring change in behaviour, or in the capacity to behave in a given fashion, which results from practice or other forms of experience'. Both definitions encompass changes in behaviour and changes in the capabilities to behave in a certain manner, whereas the latter particularly highlights the need for training or experience from which people learn.

In the field of political science, a number of theories emerged that contribute to the topic of social learning. Definitions of learning in this area partly draw on the general notion of learning in social psychology. For example, Heclo (1974: 306) formulates that 'learning can be taken to mean a relatively enduring alteration in behaviour that results from experience; usually this alteration is conceptualised as a change in response made in reaction to some perceived stimulus'. In a shorter form, Ernst Haas (1991: 63) has a similar idea of the topic: 'I define learning as any change in behaviour due to a change in perception about how to solve a problem.' Thereby, Haas gives a clear direction for the learning process similar to the definition of social learning given above. However, the changes that are viewed as learning are behavioural changes that are based on cognitive development within the learning agent. This notion is challenged by Sabatier's definition of policy-oriented learning. He states that learning processes are 'relatively enduring alterations of thought or behavioural intentions that result from experience and that are concerned with the attainment or revision of the precepts of one's belief system' (Sabatier 1987: 673). His reference to the belief system incorporates more than mere cognitive processes but it comprises values and emotions that lay behind the actual cognition. Thus, a wider understanding of knowledge behind behavioural changes seems necessary.

Building on these bodies of literature, it can be concluded that learning is a process of long-lasting change in the behaviour or the general ability to behave in a certain way that is founded on changes in knowledge.[1] Thereby, knowledge is understood in a broad sense incorporating cognitive, normative and affective elements but it still has to be specified in which respect learning distinguishes itself from other kinds of behavioural change. Moreover, these definitions solely refer to individuals and not to collective actors such as groups, networks or organisations, and they do not specify the direction of what should be learned and why.

Most theories of social learning as opposed to individual learning adopt the concept of individual learning in one form or another and apply it to collective entities such as groups, organisations, networks, political systems or society as a whole. Some authors also conceive of social learning as those processes where individuals learn within groups of other people, i.e. social environments (e.g. Bandura 1977; Goldstein 1981; Gale 1996). In this chapter, I refer to social learning as processes of learning that take place on a collective level constituting changes that are more than the mere sum of individual contributions to it. However, this understanding comprises collective learning processes on a spectrum of different levels of aggregation ranging from local community groups, to commercial or non-profit organisations, to societal subsystems such as the economy, the scientific community or the governmental system up to the entire society. This wide scope of subjects of social learning will require further conceptual efforts in the remainder of the chapter in order to acquire a better understanding of the links between social learning and governance processes.

1   By referring to changes, most of these definitions oppose the idea of a simple increase in knowledge because there always have to be losses of knowledge at the same time that allow for the acceptance and memorisation of new knowledge. Hence, learning is more a change than a steady growth of the knowledge of the learning system.

Since individuals and groups can learn virtually anything—from co-operating with others to torturing them—a more focused definition of learning is required for this context. The concept of social learning employed here builds on the normative perspective of sustainable development as a guideline for the progress made in the learning process. It focuses on those learning processes that can be expected to lead to sustainable solutions to actual problems. Therefore, sustainability-oriented social learning has to be judged to which extent it might help to bring about sustainable solutions. Other learning processes might also count as social learning under different perspectives but they have to remain outside the particular focus of this chapter.

Despite being a concept that is somewhat open to new interpretations and developments, sustainability provides some landmarks about the direction of these learning processes. Elements of social learning under this perspective have been identified by a number of authors (Parson and Clark 1995; Board on Sustainable Development of the National Research Council 1999; Social Learning Group 2001; Kopfmüller *et al.* 2001; Stagl 2001):

- Improvements of cognitive knowledge about human impacts on social and natural systems and possible solutions (sustainability knowledge)

- Integration of different bodies of knowledge from different academic disciplines and from different social actors (inter- and transdisciplinarity)

- Better understanding of long-term consequences of human action and finding better ways to deal with uncertainties (long-term perspectives)

- Moral development of social groups and societies to integrate norms of social justice, equity and ecological preservation into the existing system of social norms (moral and ethical growth)

- Advancements in societal conflict resolution and discursive capabilities

- Enhancement of a society's capacity to solve environmental and social problems: for example, through intelligent institution building and the implementation of learning mechanisms

In conclusion, it is the underlying conviction of this chapter that social learning is a *process of change on the level of collective actors or even in a society that is based on newly acquired knowledge, a change in predominant value structures, or of social norms which results in sizeable practical outcomes*. It is the particular focus of this chapter to concentrate on those practical outcomes that foster sustainable development. Social learning thus transcends both individual learning and mere changes in the cognitive abilities of certain individuals. However, it is the problem of nearly all concepts of social learning to find a clear dividing line between processes of individual, group and social learning since all of them are closely interconnected and one depends on the other. The following discussion of existing concepts in the realm of political science will exhibit this problem and will demonstrate ways to capture the essence of social learning in some clarity.

5.2 Social learning in political science

Scholars from political science have discovered the field of social learning rather late. There is not yet a consistent set of concepts and empirical case studies of social learning, and theories of social learning with respect to sustainability issues are extremely scant. The following paragraphs will give an account of existing approaches that have been developed and applied to different social and political spheres. In a preliminary systematisation the following foci can be distinguished:[2]

5.2.1 Local arena

Crucial arenas for actual progress in the direction of sustainable development are communities, neighbourhoods and initiatives on the local level. Promoting sustainable lifestyles, implementing Local Agenda 21 initiatives, launching community projects, bringing together local actors and reaching out to other communities and regions are challenges and learning tasks for local communities in this respect. In most cases, social learning has been organised in public participation processes. Webler *et al.* (1995) report on a deliberative process conducted in Switzerland to decide about a waste disposal site. They found significant cognitive and moral developments taking place on the side of the participants in these processes which led to better-informed and consensual decisions. In the Sustainable Community Projects discussed by Smith *et al.* (1999), it has mostly been certain individuals who triggered learning processes within social groups and the individual participants. They were needed as 'catalysts' to new solutions and projects. The action-oriented research effort undertaken by Johnson and Wilson (2000) detected 'learning points' in participatory development projects in the different perspectives of the participating actors. Building on a study of the Columbia River Basin water management, Lee (1993: 110) emphasises the role of trust and confidence in participatory approaches and their sustained solutions: 'Learning is a gradual ascent towards confidence punctuated by the slippery panic of disappointments.'

5.2.2 Domestic politics

This class of approaches addresses questions such as: How do political systems and particularly political decision-makers learn? Where does the knowledge come from that is applied and diffused in the learning process? What has been learned? How could the resulting changes be measured? The different concepts in this field vary in their focus on the learning agents. Some focus exclusively on governments, such as Etheredge (1981), while others such as Heclo (1974) and Sabatier (1987, 1988) additionally examine societal actors such as elites, networks and other social groups as learning agents. The latter approaches stress the role of norms and belief systems in learning processes within a network structure, called 'advocacy coalition' by Sabatier. Studies with a focus on sustainability are particularly rare.

---

2   A meta-analysis of pre-existing approaches on policy learning is included in Bennett and Howlett 1992.

5.2.3 International relations and comparative studies of different countries

Another group of studies in policy learning addresses the international arena and investigates whether and how states learn from each other and whether and how international communities are able to learn. Rose (1991, 1994) addresses issues of 'lesson-drawing' where one state benefits from the experiences gained by other states. The concept of epistemic communities as developed by Peter Haas (1992) and Adler (1992) draws the attention to mostly internationally organised networks that are united by their shared beliefs and convictions about particular political problems and the favourable solutions to them. These networks usually consist of scientists, lobbyists, political decision-makers and advocacy groups. With their particular interest in US–Soviet relations during the Cold War, Breslauer and Tetlock (1991) apply learning concepts to individuals as well as to political structures and cultures and demonstrate how, over time, both sides developed patterns of interaction and conflict resolution to deal with the nuclear threat. Some insights on issues of sustainability in the field of learning between countries can be found in diffusion studies that analyse the spreading of (environmental) policy innovations across countries (Jänicke and Jörgens 2000; Tews *et al.* 2003). These studies identified national pressure groups, public administration and its traditions, and public opinion channelled through the media as key drivers for the acceptance of certain policy innovations.

5.2.4 Global society as a whole

Many environmental problems such as climate change, ozone depletion and biodiversity loss, and health problems such as the life-threatening diseases malaria, tuberculosis, HIV/AIDS and others are global phenomena threatening all of human society. Humankind has combated a number of these problems successfully through some form of collective learning processes. Therefore, a number of authors attempt to develop a conceptual framework for this kind of global learning mostly building on empirical case studies of particular learning areas such as combating plague, cholera and smallpox (Cooper 1989), implementing Keynesian economic policy (Hall 1989) or managing global environmental change (Social Learning Group 2001). Key factors for social learning identified in these studies have been innovative ideas mostly brought about by scientific research and engaged individuals who promoted these ideas—be they findings about new kinds of problems or new solutions to old problems.

In the face of this variety of ways to conceptualise social learning in the political realm one should bear in mind that all of them address phenomena where groups or social actors change their behaviour on the basis of new knowledge or an alteration of the norms and values underlying their behavioural patterns. Therefore, they—in one way or another—provide blueprints for projected social changes towards sustainable development. They identified the key role of certain individuals, collective actors or networks as promoters of change of social discourse and scientific information for social learning, which can guide pathways for the design of social learning processes for sustainable development.

5.3 Conceptualising social learning in an actor-centred approach

Modern societies are highly differentiated and compartmentalised into various functional subsystems and a large variety of societal actors. Obtaining a clearer picture of the processes of social learning and their interaction with governance processes in modern societies necessitates a closer conceptual look into these levels and the actors which might generate some fruitful insights.

In a systems theory perspective, sociologists distinguish between different functional social subsystems such as the economy, politics, science, the media and others. According to Luhmann (1998), each of these is dominated by a specific communication code which limits the possibilities for communication between the different systems. For instance, the political system is structured along the discourse about power whereas the science system largely focuses its communication around the issue of truth and the economic system is centred on monetary interaction. In this perspective, societal change is based on subsystem-specific forms of functional differentiation. Social subsystems tend to reaffirm their boundaries and to foster internal communication at the expense of communication with external systems. These systems inherently produce problems with the integration of external rationalities and other communicative structures. They are increasingly unable to find solutions to societal problems that cross their boundaries, such as environmental problems (Luhmann 1986).

Therefore, the political system is put in charge to mitigate the most extreme dysfunctionalities of the interaction between the subsystems. However, the political system can build only on the informational and conceptual inputs and contributions from the other systems in the governance process. It requires common cognitions and reflection on certain problems across the different subsystems for the integration of societal forces, which are extremely limited according to Luhmann's view. This process can, however, be understood as social learning that crosses the borders of single social systems and leads to society-wide solutions to problems that affect or threaten more than one societal subsystem.

In this process of integration, framing and development of common notions and solutions to societal problems, sociologists focus on organisations as particular forms of social structures that could claim actor status (Schimank 2001). This focus can prove helpful in the attempt to capture the dynamics of social learning on a societal level given the contributions of diverse social actors in their respective frames of reference and rationalities. Moreover, it can heal a significant shortcoming of the sociological systems-theory approach, which to a large extent abstracts from actors given its focus on systems dynamics. Thereby the specific possible contributions and capacities of social actors move out of sight. By contrast, organisations can be understood as any form of collective actor that builds on decisions by individuals to participate in the organisations and to acknowledge the specific norms and rules governing this particular organisation. They include business corporations as well as public authorities, non-profit associations, advocacy networks and political parties.

The perspective on organisations as collective actors in processes of social learning allows us to apply categories of collective knowledge and practices that might even be located far beyond the specific code of a subsystem. These types of organisation usually act within different social subsystems and might develop specific cognitions that contradict or transcend the general communication code of one system. However, these cognitions might turn out to be highly influential for the solution of specific problems such as sustainability-related problems.

In this perspective, processes of social learning have to be analysed from two angles. First there will be internal organisational learning processes, which refer to changes in the internal cognitions, norms and rules of an organisation building on reflections by the individual members of an organisation. These processes have been studied in management science under the label of organisational learning. Second, larger social learning processes will emerge from the interaction of different organisations. The latter can be described as inter-organisational social learning whereas the former would be intra-organisational social learning. Both have their specific dynamics and forms.

5.3.1 Intra-organisational learning in collective actors

The analysis of intra-organisational learning processes can largely draw on the literature on organisational learning as it has evolved in management studies over the past 20 years. Concepts of organisational learning—also described as 'the learning organisation'—have been developed in management studies to describe processes of organisational change that take place at a collective level.[3] In this body of literature the distinction between individual and collective action is crucial—in particular for the choice of the appropriate theoretical and analytical approach. It is commonly assumed that organisations exist on the basis of collective action. According to Argyris and Schön (1996: 8), it is the precondition of collective action that the individual member 'must (1) devise agreed-upon procedures for making decisions in the name of the collectivity, (2) delegate to individuals the authority to act for the collectivity, and (3) set boundaries between the collectivity and the rest of the world'. These requirements can be found fulfilled in most organisations with some kind of formal membership.

Studies of intra-organisational learning processes have to pay special attention to the relationship between individuals and the collective level and to the relation between their learning processes. Although the notion of collective learning implies that it is more than the mere sum of individual learning by its members, it is dependent on individuals, their learning and their behavioural changes. In this line of thought, collective learning can be seen as the change of procedures, structures, shared beliefs and knowledge that are assembled from individual contributions. For instance, the knowledge of how to produce cars, telephones or computers is inherent in the relevant organisation but individuals usually oversee only a small part of the whole production process. In general, one can conclude that the necessary division of labour and responsibilities in an organisation allow for the possibility of collective learning.

Another argument comes from systems theory in management, which regards organisations as emergent systems that are more than the sum of their individuals. In this view, organisational learning is mostly studied on the basis of analogies to individual learning. Probst and Büchel (1997: 15) define organisational learning as 'the process by

3 For related studies see Fiol and Lyles 1985; Argyris 1990; Senge 1990; Dodgson 1993; Probst and Büchel 1997; Denton 1998; Schreyögg and Eberl 1998; Argote 1999; Wilkesmann 1999; Gilley and Maycunich 2000; Schreyögg 2000; Schwandt and Marquard 2000; Pawlowsky 2001.

which the organisation's knowledge and value base changes, leading to improved prob-lem-solving ability and capacity for action'. Similarly, Marquardt (1996: 22) points out that:

> organisational learning represents the enhanced intellectual and productive capability gained through corporate-wide commitment and opportunity for continuous improvement. [It] occurs through the shared insights, knowl-edge, and mental models of members of the organisation [and it] builds on past knowledge and experience—that is on organisational memory which depends on institutional mechanisms (e.g. policies, strategies, and explicit models) used to retain knowledge.

In sum, it is the general assumption underlying most of the studies in organisational learning that numerous forms of organisation can be analysed under a perspective of collective learning and that this form of intra-organisational learning cannot be reduced to the sum of the individual learning processes although it is based on indi-vidual contributions and on individuals as 'change agents'. This assumption does not imply a complete analogy between all forms of organisations ranging from commercial corporations to charity associations or public authorities. It merely states that learning of and in organisations can be more than mere individual learning because of the exis-tence of division of labour and an existing structural framework of internal relation-ships between the members of the organisation.

In the various models of learning, different kinds of learning process have been dis-tinguished. With regard to the definition of learning employed in this chapter, further specification seems appropriate. Therefore, I adopt a typology based on Argyris and Schön (1996). The fundamental criterion for this classification is how far the underly-ing objectives, norms and beliefs of the organisation have changed during the learning process. The authors focus particularly on changes in the underlying 'theory in use': that is, the often tacitly used set of values and causal beliefs that the members of an organisation share. Individual members of the collectivity are seen as the carriers and developers of the theory-in-use, which might be changed through learning. Argyris and Schön distinguish the following types of learning:

- **Single-loop learning**. The simplest form of learning is the adaptation of new knowledge to existing frameworks of objectives and causal beliefs. Based on a simple feedback loop between given expectations and the real outcomes of a process, this instrumental type of learning allows for error correction and leads to adjustment of results that differ from the pre-existing expectations. For example, a product manager may detect unexpectedly high emission rates from one production process and a search for the causes might lead him or her to a technical flaw that has to be corrected. In this case no change in the the-ory-in-use would be required.

- **Double-loop learning**. The advanced form of learning is framed as 'double-loop learning', which includes the underlying objectives, values, norms and belief structures into the learning process. Thus, there will be two feedback loops, an instrumental one of error correction and a more fundamental one that connects the former to changes in the general framework of beliefs, norms and objectives. For example, new results in ecological research might require a company to overturn existing orientations on a certain product type, e.g. CFCs (chlorofluorocarbons), and call for a reorientation on substitution technologies with far-reaching consequences for the whole organisational set-up.

- **Deutero learning**. If learning takes place on a meta level of how to learn, Argyris and Schön speak of deutero learning. This is a form of learning of the ability to learn itself. For example, an organisation might gather experiences with certain approaches to learning and attempt to improve its internal learning system consisting of—among others—communication channels, information systems, training procedures and routines.

In their studies of business corporations, Argyris and Schön could hardly find forms of deutero learning. Most learning processes usually remain in the scope of the first two categories of learning. In general, single-loop learning is largely sufficient when limited errors or deviations from goals have to be corrected, but it is no longer sufficient when the underlying norms and belief systems of an organisation conflict with new internal or external developments or requirements.

What can be gained from an organisational-learning perspective in the analysis of social learning towards sustainable development? First, the literature on organisational learning provides a rich body of knowledge mostly from the management of private corporations but increasingly also from other forms of organisations that offer fruitful insights even for processes of relevance for sustainability (see e.g. LaPalombara 2001; Siebenhüner 2002). The interaction of different forms of knowledge and the role of explicit and tacit belief systems, norms and cognitions are equally relevant for sustainability-related learning processes, even if they are in part substantially different from business-related issues (Lam 2000). Second, it can be concluded that different forms of social learning process towards sustainable development can be distinguished. There are rather simple adaptive forms of learning as opposed to more comprehensive reflection processes reversing the underlying value and belief systems towards a recognition of sustainability problems. Even processes of deutero learning that take place on a meta level can prove highly influential for changes towards sustainability since they enable individuals and groups to learn more effectively in general. Third, the numerous studies of organisational learning processes identified a large set of factors influencing these processes. They range from internal driving forces such as internal communication, organisational slack, the regular exchange of individuals across the divisions of the organisation to hampering factors such as the existence of certain taboos which cannot be addressed explicitly and external factors. As yet, organisational learning studies have hardly addressed inter-organisational learning processes, which seem to be crucial for sustainable development as a society-wide endeavour.

5.3.2 Inter-organisational learning between collective actors

Intra-organisational learning takes place in a societal environment and is dependent on impulses and support from this background. In particular, different discourses with specific forms of commonly accepted knowledge govern the interaction between individuals and different collective actors. For instance, views of the connectedness of

humans with the larger globe as claimed by deep ecologists have little bearing for market-related transactions between companies in the car industry, for example, where a
strong belief in the merits of modern technology is the underlying consensus (Levy and
Rothenberg 1999). Processes of sustainability-related inter-organisational learning will
look largely different in these different spheres. The analysis of these discourses can
profit from the insights from studies of epistemic communities (Adler 1992; Haas 1992),
which focus on specific belief systems and problem-oriented forms of knowledge. They
show how different social actors form coalitions on the basis of commonly shared
knowledge and how new knowledge is being processed across the different individual
and collective actors of the community.

In a similar direction, DiMaggio and Powell (1983) developed the notion of the
organisational field in which network structures govern the interaction between different organisations. The organisational field is characterised by close interactions
between the organisations, a higher density of information transferred and the emergence of commonly shared belief systems. These fields can cut across different economic sectors or even different social subsystems.

Starting out from a slightly different angle, the Social Learning Group (2001) analysed social learning processes between different social actors and between particular
individuals or organisations as agents within the framework of social actors. This analysis of the role of specific actors conveys the pivotal contribution of scientists to initiate
and support social learning processes through the provision of relevant information
and its communication to the public and to decision-makers. Most cases demonstrate
that independent media and environmental NGOs play key roles in raising public awareness and in pushing environmental issues into the agenda of political decision-making
processes. In contrast, industry is more ambivalent an actor since industries often oppose
proactive regulatory measures to combat global environmental risks, most prominently
in the case of climate change, but business actors also serve as innovators and supporters of certain response strategies. Inter-organisational learning processes thus do
not always lead to changes in the whole field or economic sector but they could spread
to a certain extent across different organisations. In most cases of social learning, the
group found networks of actors to be of crucial importance. In these networks, scientists, public administrators and some pioneering companies worked together for the
advancement of a certain form of regulation or solution to an environmental problem.

5.4 Conclusions

Starting out from a brief overview of existing approaches to conceptualise social learning processes in political science, this chapter has sketched out some ideas about a
more general conceptual framework on sustainability-related social learning processes. It has distinguished between intra- and inter-organisational learning and suggested ways to analyse these two domains. To evaluate the merits of such an endeavour one has to ask for new insights for the practically relevant question: how can social
learning towards sustainability on an intra- and an inter-organisational level be initi-

ated? Given the multitude of processes and influencing factors that are involved in social learning processes, a general answer to this question seems difficult. There have been several quite different starting points for social learning processes in the direction of sustainability in the past. It could be new scientific findings, immediate catastrophes, media attention, or advocacy-group activities that triggered these processes (see the Social Learning Group 2001). Therefore, only a rather pragmatic answer can be given to the initial question.

One interesting option to initiate sustainability-oriented social learning processes can be seen in participatory procedures involving individuals from different organisations and different societal subsystems. According to their proponents, participatory processes offer a potential for mutual learning between different actors and groups, to launch socio-ecological innovations, to trigger organisational change and to facilitate decision-making processes in conflict-stricken areas. They allow for the articulation and interaction between different perceptions, interpretations and argumentations by the actors involved and can, at best, result in concrete solutions: for example, to sustainability-related problems. They thus have the potential to initiate both inter- and intra-organisational learning processes (Webler and Renn 1995).

On the other hand, it can be expected that participatory processes might result in internal organisational changes and learning processes of the organisations themselves. Once having opened up to new knowledge from external groups and organisations such as critical consumer groups, environmental groups or critical scientists, organisations such as companies are likely to continue on the path of organisational development. Therefore, an integration of both research fields on social learning and participatory procedures might deliver fruitful insights into ways to spark off social learning processes that have the potential to address problems of sustainability. It has to be linked to theories of social and institutional change in order to address the question of how single participatory procedures can trigger ongoing processes of society-wide and inter-organisational learning.

References

Adler, E. (1992) 'The Emergence of Cooperation: National Epistemic Communities and the International Revolution of the Idea of Nuclear Arms Control', *International Organization* 46.1: 101-45.

Argote, L. (1999) *Organizational Learning: Creating, Retaining, and Transferring Knowledge* (Boston, MA: Kluwer).

Argyris, C. (1990) *Overcoming Organizational Defenses: Facilitating Organizational Learning* (Englewood Cliffs, NJ: Prentice Hall).

—— and D.A. Schön (1996) *Organizational Learning. II. Theory, Method, and Practice* (Reading, MA: Addison-Wesley).

Bandura, A. (1977) *Social Learning Theory* (Englewood Cliffs, NJ: Prentice Hall).

Bennett, C.J., and M. Howlett (1992) 'The Lessons of Learning: Reconciling Theories of Policy Learning and Policy Change', *Policy Sciences* 25: 275-94.

Board on Sustainable Development of the National Research Council (1999) *Our Common Journey: A Transition toward Sustainability* (Washington, DC: National Academy Press).

Breslauer, G.W., and P.E. Tetlock (1991) *Learning in US and Soviet Foreign Policy* (Boulder, CO: Westview Press).

Cooper, R.N. (1989) 'International Cooperation in Public Health as a Prologue to Macroeconomic Cooperation: Can Nations Agree?', in R.N. Cooper, B. Eichengreen, C.R. Henning, G. Holtham and R.D.
Putnam (eds.), *Issues in International Economic Cooperation* (Washington, DC: The Brookings Institution): 178-254.

DiMaggio, P., and W.W. Powell (1983) 'The Iron Cage Revisited: Institutional Isomorphism and Collective Rationality in Organizational Fields', *American Sociological Review* 48: 147-60.

Denton, J. (1998) *Organisational Learning and Effectiveness* (London: Routledge).

Dodgson, M. (1993) 'Organizational Learning: A Review of Some Literatures', *Organization Studies* 14.3:
375-94.

Etheredge, L. (1981) 'Government Learning: An Overview', in S.L. Long (ed.), *The Handbook of Political
Behavior 2* (New York: Pergamon).

Fiol, C.M., and M.A. Lyles (1985) 'Organizational Learning', *Academy of Management Review* 10.4: 803-
13.

Gale, D. (1996) 'What Have We Learned from Social Learning?', *European Economic Review* 40: 617-28.

Gilley, J.W., and A. Maycunich (2000) *Organizational Learning, Performance, and Change: An Introduction to Strategic Human Resource Development* (Cambridge, UK: Perseus Publishing).

Goldstein, H. (1981) *Social Learning and Change: A Cognitive Approach to Human Services* (Columbia, SC:
University of South Carolina Press).

Haas, E.B. (1991) 'Collective Learning: Some Theoretical Speculations', in G.W. Breslauer and P.E. Tetlock (eds.), *Learning in US and Soviet Foreign Policy* (Boulder, CO: Westview Press).

Haas, P.M. (1992) 'Introduction: Epistemic Communities and International Policy Coordination', *International Organization* 46.1: 1-35.

Hall, P. (1989) *The Political Power of Economic Ideas: Keynesianism across Nations* (Princeton, NJ: Princeton University Press).

Heclo, H. (1974) *Modern Social Politics in Britain and Sweden: From Relief to Income Maintenance* (New
Haven, CT: Yale University Press).

Jänicke, M., and H. Jörgens (2000) 'Strategic Environmental Planning and Uncertainty: A Cross-
national Comparison of Green Plans in Industrialized Countries', *Policy Studies Journal* 28.3: 612-
32.

Johnson, H., and G. Wilson (2000) 'Biting the Bullet: Civil Society, Social Learning and the Transformation of Local Governance', *World Development* 28.11: 1,891-906.

Kopfmüller, J., V. Brandl, H.J. Jörissen, M. Paetau, G. Banse, R. Coenen and A. Grunwald (2001) *Nach-
haltige Entwicklung integrativ betrachtet: Konstitutive Elemente, Regeln, Indikatoren* (Berlin: Edition
Sigma).

Lam, A. (2000) 'Tacit Knowledge, Organizational Learning and Societal Institutions: An Integrated
Framework', *Organization Studies* 21.3: 487-513.

LaPalombara, J. (2001) 'The Underestimated Contributions of Political Science to Organizational
Learning', in H.M. Dierkes, A. Berthoin Antal, J. Child and I. Nonaka (eds.), *Handbook of Organizational Learning and Knowledge* (London: Oxford University Press): 137-61.

Lee, K.N. (1993) *Compass and Gyroscope: Integrating Science and Politics for the Environment* (Washington, DC: Island Press).

Levy, D.L., and S. Rothenberg (1999) *Corporate Strategy and Climate Change: Heterogeneity and Change
in the Global Automobile Industry* (Cambridge, MA: Kennedy School of Government, Harvard University).

Luhmann, N. (1986) *Ökologische Kommunikation: Kann die moderne Gesellschaft sich auf ökologische
Gefährdungen einstellen?* (Opladen, Germany: Westdeutscher Verlag).

—— (1998) *Die Gesellschaft der Gesellschaft* (Frankfurt am Main: Suhrkamp Verlag).

Marquardt, M.J. (1996) *Building the Learning Organization* (New York: McGraw-Hill).

Minsch, J., P.-H. Feindt, H.-P. Meister, U. Schneidewind and T. Schulz (1998) *Institutionelle Reformen
für eine Politik der Nachhaltigkeit* (Berlin: Springer).

Nordlinger, E. (1981) *On the Autonomy of the Democratic State* (Cambridge, MA: Harvard University
Press).

Parson, E., and W.C. Clark (1995) 'Sustainable Development as Social Learning: Theoretical Perspectives and Practical Challenges for the Design of a Research Program', in L.H. Gunderson, C.S. Holling and S.S. Light (eds.), *Barriers and Bridges to the Renewal of Ecosystems and Institutions* (New York: Columbia University Press).

Pawlowsky, P. (2001) 'The Treatment of Organizational Learning in Management Science', in H.M. Dierkes, A. Berthoin Antal, J. Child and I. Nonaka (eds.), *Handbook of Organizational Learning and Knowledge* (London: Oxford University Press): 61-88.

Probst, G., and B. Büchel (1997) *Organizational Learning: The Competitive Advantage of the Future* (London/New York: Prentice Hall).

Rose, R. (1991) 'What is Lesson-Drawing?', *Journal of Public Policy* 11.1: 3-30.

—— (1994) *Lesson-Drawing in Public Policy: A Guide to Learning across Time and Space* (Chatham, NJ: Chatham House Publishers).

Sabatier, P. (1987) 'Knowledge, Policy-Oriented Learning, and Policy Change', *Knowledge: Creation, Diffusion, Utilization* 8: 649-92.

—— (1988) 'An Advocacy Coalition Framework of Policy Change and the Role of Policy-Oriented Learning Therein', *Policy Sciences* 21: 129-68.

Schimank, U. (2001) 'Funktionale Differenzierung, Durchorganisierung und Integration der modernen Gesellschaft', in V. Tacke (ed.), *Organisation und gesellschaftliche Differenzierung* (Wiesbaden, Germany: Westdeutscher Verlag): 19-38.

Schreyögg, G. (ed.) (2000) *Organisatorischer Wandel und Transformation* (Wiesbaden, Germany: Gabler).

—— and P. Eberl (1998) 'Organisationales Lernen: Viele Fragen, noch zu wenig neue Antworten', *Die Betriebswirtschaft (DBW)* 58.4: 516-36.

Schunk, D.H. (1996) *Learning Theories: An Educational Perspective* (New York: Merrill).

Schwandt, D.R., and M.J. Marquard (2000) *Organizational Learning: From World-Class Theories to Global Best Practices* (Boca Raton, FL: St Lucie Press).

Senge, P. (1990) *The Fifth Discipline: The Art and Practice of the Learning Organization* (New York: Doubleday).

Siebenhüner, B. (2002) 'How do Scientific Assessments Learn? Part 1: Conceptual Framework and Case Study of the IPCC', *Environmental Science and Policy* 5: 411-20.

Smith, J., J. Blake, R. Grove-White, E. Kashefi, S. Madden and S. Percy (1999) 'Social Learning and Sustainable Communities: An Interim Assessment of Research into Sustainable Communities Projects in the UK', *Local Environment* 4.2: 195-207.

Social Learning Group, The (2001) *Learning to Manage Global Environmental Risks: A Comparative History of Social Responses to Climate Change, Ozone Depletion, and Acid Rain* (Cambridge, MA: MIT Press).

Stagl, S. (2001) *The Role of Learning for Sustainable Development: An Evolutionary Perspective* (mimeo; Cambridge).

Swenson, L.C. (1980) *Theories of Learning* (Belmont, CA: Wadsworth).

Tews, K., P.-O. Busch and H. Jörgens (2003) 'The Diffusion of New Environmental Policy Innovations', *European Journal for Political Research* (forthcoming).

Webler, T., and O. Renn (1995) 'A Brief Primer on Participation: Philosophy and Practice', in O. Renn, T. Webler and P. Wiedemann (eds.), *Fairness and Competence in Citizen Participation* (Dordrecht, Netherlands: Kluwer): 1-16.

——, H. Kastenholz et al. (1995) 'Public Participation in Impact Assessment: A Social Learning Perspective', *Environmental Impact Assessment Review* 15: 443-63.

Wilkesmann, U. (1999) *Lernen in Organisationen: Die Inzenierung von kollektiven Lernprozessen* (Frankfurt am Main: Campus Verlag).

6

What role for politics in the governance of complex innovation systems?
NEW CONCEPTS, REQUIREMENTS AND PROCESSES OF AN INTERACTIVE TECHNOLOGY POLICY FOR SUSTAINABILITY

K. Matthias Weber

ARC Systems Research, Austria

For more than a decade, the concept of sustainable development has influenced the debates about new technology and innovation. While being initially focused on the environmental dimension, we have seen a shift towards the joint consideration of economic, environmental and social aspects of sustainable development. Although it is increasingly recognised that there is a need to give direction to innovation processes, direction in the sense of contributing to sustainable development, the dominant concepts for dealing with innovation and technology policy are still geared towards growth objectives. What are needed, however, are system innovations and a transition to a new technological regime that helps reorient our production–consumption systems and guides the future evolution of our science, technology and innovation systems in the direction of sustainable development. Such transitions can hardly be brought about by market forces alone because long-term issues of direction, of uncertainty and institutional change are involved. The problems we are facing are not only more complicated than in the past, but show complex characteristics with unpredictable long-term consequences. Understanding and subsequently managing transitions is currently an important research topic that is still in its infancy (Kemp and Rotmans 2005).

In parallel, confidence in the traditional top-down and linear approach to public policy-making and implementation has declined. New ways are required to deal with problems resulting from the development and use of technology, and to respond to the new demands for more transparent, accountable and participatory modes of policy-making. Currently, new models of governance mechanisms are being tested in many areas touching on innovation and new technology.

Finally, there have been changes taking place in the patterns of innovation itself. Most relevant with respect to governance is the observation that the relationships between science, policy, industry and the public in innovation systems have undergone a major transformation. This happened partly in response to the aforementioned changes in problem perception, but was also driven by the recognition that new scientific and technological insights need to be embedded in an application context that is shaped by user needs, societal requirements and institutional conditions in order to generate successful innovations. Concepts such as 'Mode 2 of knowledge production' or 'post-normal science' have been suggested to describe these new patterns of scientific inquiry, underlining in particular the need to involve a broader range of actors in the knowledge-generating process (Gibbons *et al.* 1994; Funtowicz and Ravetz 1993).[1] Other important developments, as recognised in recent literature, can be summarised as follows:

- Innovation processes are increasingly systemic, characterised by intense interactions between a growing range of actors, technologies, competences and institutions, which shape the emergence of innovations.

- The dynamic patterns of innovation and diffusion processes and the fundamental uncertainty associated with them have been dealt with in the context of evolutionary economics (Dosi *et al* 1988; Saviotti 1996), and more recently in the literature dealing with complex phenomena in innovation networks (Pyka and Küppers 2002).

- Historical and socioeconomic studies of technological development have led to the recognition that technological change is of a path-dependent nature. Different concepts have been coined to describe this: for example, technological trajectories and paradigms (Dosi 1982), large (socio-)technical systems (Mayntz and Hughes 1988) and others.

- The role of institutional and organisational frameworks for innovation has been analysed and recognised prominently in the context of the innovation systems literature, addressing national, regional or sectoral characteristics of innovation systems (Lundvall 1992; Edquist 1997b; Breschi and Malerba 1997; Braczyk *et al.* 1998) recognising the importance of institutional and organisational frameworks.

- Growing emphasis is also put on processes of mutual learning, interaction and adaptation, both between disciplines (interdisciplinarity) and between science and practice (transdisciplinarity).

- Innovation systems are regarded as multi-level settings where actors at different levels are interconnected by formal hierarchical and market structures as well as by informal networks.

---

1   The arguments raised by these authors question the argument regarding a growing differentiation of society into functional (sub)systems in order to cope with growing complexity (Luhmann 1988). Instead, they see a tendency towards new forms of co-operation and interaction across functional systems in the knowledge-producing process.

- As a consequence, the role of policy and of policy-making process in innovation is changing in line with the emergence of a new governance paradigm. Policy is regarded as part of the problem area, with a mediating/facilitating rather than a steering role (Scharpf 1993; Sorensen 1999).

These new insights about innovations processes in connection with the new normative implications raised by an orientation towards sustainable development and by the decline in confidence in government policy imply a range of new demands with respect to the governance of innovation systems:[2]

- The underlying conflicts about values and risk perception related to innovation and new technologies require a stronger involvement of a wide range of stakeholders in the policy decisions leading to and enabling new technologies to emerge.

- Due to the growing extent of interactivity of innovation processes, research work needs to become application- and practice-oriented much earlier than in the past. New policy frameworks are needed to stimulate the emergence of transdisciplinary and interdisciplinary practices.

- Different kinds of incentive and structure are needed to ensure the goal-orientation of large parts of R&D work towards sustainability (without denying the need for bottom-up exploratory research).

- Policy strategies for enabling sustainability-oriented system innovations under conditions of uncertainty, complexity and ambiguity are therefore needed, paying more attention to the exploration of future options and the development of scenarios as a foundation for policy-making.

- This implies a growing need for strategic anticipation and intelligence, in order to inform action to respond to high problem pressure, to uncertainty and to conflicts between strategic action and lack of confidence. New analytical (e.g. benchmarking, evaluation) as well as interactive (e.g. foresight, scenario development) methods are needed to provide strategic input to policy.[3]

Although these demands are widely regarded as pertinent to the development of a sustainable innovation and technology policy, they are hardly taken into consideration in innovation theory. One of the reasons for this deficit is the lack of a consistent conceptual foundation for dealing with both innovation and sustainability jointly, a deficit that I would like to address in this contribution. Such a foundation should also take into account the aforementioned new role of government and other stakeholders with respect to innovation, but also build on the advances made in innovation research over the past decade. Therefore in the next section I will first highlight key requirements that a conceptual framework for dealing with innovation and sustainability should meet. Then some recent streams in innovation research will be pointed out on which I

---

2   Governance is understood here as the rules and institutions guiding the process of transformation of social, and here in particular of innovation, systems. Obviously, our particular interest is in the role of politics as part of governance.

3   See for example Tübke *et al.* 2001 for a review.

will build when formulating a conceptual framework ('complex innovation systems') for dealing with governance and innovation policy in support of sustainability objectives. The conceptual framework will finally be used to formulate a number of specific requirements for the governance of innovation systems and the role of politics.

6.1 Towards complex innovation systems: analytical perspectives

Before formulating a conceptual framework, it is useful to be very specific about the key features it should have and the key requirements it should meet. This will be done in the subsequent section, before pointing to the main research streams on which I will build for formulating the complex innovation systems approach.

6.1.1 Requirements for a conceptual framework

The new characteristics of innovation processes in conjunction with the governance demands as formulated above can be translated into requirements for a conceptual framework to deal with the governance and innovation policy for sustainability:

- More attention needs to be devoted to the *technical specificities and requirements* of the technologies and innovations in question.

- This issue is of particular importance when it comes to the *second* requirement that our framework needs to be able to deal with, namely that of the *direction of change*. This implies that the framework should be able to describe and understand system innovations and how they occur.

- It is necessary to *broaden the range of actors* considered in the framework. The conceptual framework sought needs to be able to take such multi-level network-type of structures into account.

- A consequence of considering a broader range of actors as part of the innovation system is that *policy actors need to be understood as integral parts of the innovation systems*. This has conceptual consequences for the role of policy and politics in coping with growing complexity, uncertainty and ambiguity in a multi-actor context.

- When discussing policies to induce transition processes in innovation and technology systems, it is indispensable to take a *multi-level perspective and multi-domain perspective on innovation*. Most approaches have either a structural or a behavioural bias. However, from a complex systems research perspective it would be indispensable to look at the interactions between behavioural and structural level and how the complex mechanisms characterising this interaction shape the transformation path.

- One of the main difficulties of current approaches is the lack of understanding of the *dynamic mechanisms* underlying the evolution and transformation of innovation systems, and in particular the non-linear, often complex dynamics that innovation processes show.

- Obviously, given the interest in policy and governance issues, these aspects need to be core elements of the conceptual framework. In particular multi-level governance issues related to innovation and sustainability need to be dealt with. It is widely recognised that, in order to direct innovation efforts towards sustainability, concerted policy efforts at several levels are necessary.

6.1.2 Current approaches and their limitations: innovations systems, science and technology studies and complexity

Over the last ten years *systems approaches* to innovation have been quite popular and have almost come to dominate the debates about innovation and technology policy (Lundvall 1992; Edquist 1997b). Initially developed to describe the set of national institutions and structures framing innovation processes, they have subsequently been adapted to deal with regional or sectoral systems as well. However, in view of the aforementioned requirements, they show several shortcomings. In particular, the role of policy and regulation is reduced to that of an external factor. Infrastructures, which represent a vital element of sociotechnical systems, are under-represented, and the cultural dimension of sociotechnical transformations is reduced to that of institutions.

Science and technology studies have paid more attention to the detailed processes and actors involved in the shaping of new technology and innovation, and in particular the cultural aspects in this context (see, for a recent review, Sorensen and Williams 2002). The same applies with respect to the role of political processes and structures for the shaping of innovations. Governance and politics have been research issues in political sciences for many years but started to influence the political debates about innovation and technology policy only recently, when their importance for the ideological underpinnings of the dominant policy approaches was recognised.

A third line of research on which I will draw in the following deals with the *dynamics of innovation* systems. Apart from descriptive approaches that build on phases and stages of innovation processes, there are not many generic approaches available for capturing dynamics. Evolutionary concepts—for example, in the context of evolutionary economics—have provided valuable insights into the micro-foundations of innovation dynamics. The basic mechanisms of variation, selection and stabilisation represent the main elements to explain how non-linear dynamic processes emerge. The evolutionary approach relies also on an actor model that is characterised by rule-guided behaviour and learning by accumulation of knowledge.[4] Complexity and complex systems research has also given rise to models for explaining the dynamics of innovation phenomena.[5] In particular, the concept of self-organisation, i.e. the emergence of struc-

---

4 This is obviously a very brief characterisation of what evolutionary economics is all about. For a more detailed introduction see, for instance, Dosi and Nelson 1994.
5 The term 'complex systems research' is used here in a comprehensive sense, i.e. comprising a wide range of more specific concepts, such as synergetics, self-organisation, self-reference, etc.

tural patterns from the micro-behaviour of diverse actors, has inspired innovation research (e.g. Pyka and Küppers 2002).

These different lines of research will not be discussed in further detail, but it is important to point to the origins of the complex innovation systems framework that will be introduced subsequently.

6.1.3 Complex innovation systems: from static to dynamic analysis

The approach of complex innovation systems combines elements of the lines of thought discussed above (i.e. innovation systems, science and technology studies, evolution and complexity) and integrates them in a consistent framework to guide policy-oriented, applied research. It provides the basis for a heuristic for investigating concrete innovation phenomena and how they could be tackled by policy.

A systems approach will be used as the basis for formulating such an integrative framework in a consistent way, i.e. as a platform for connecting different streams of research work.[6] There are three main reasons why this appears to be a promising inroad. First of all, the systems language has already been used in several approaches to the study of innovation and thus facilitates compatibility with earlier work. Second, a systems language does not presuppose any specific theoretical perspective, but allows us to use different theoretical arguments to establish the relationships between the constituent parts of the system. Third, the approaches for dealing with innovation dynamics mentioned (i.e. evolutionary and complexity concepts) are usually formulated in a systems language as well, and can thus be integrated in the complex innovation systems framework more easily.

A complex innovation system is defined as an open, multi-level sociotechnical system, embedded in a wider social context or system environment. In order to structure a complex innovation system internally three levels are distinguished: (i) the structural level of the innovation regime (i.e. structural characteristics, institutions and paradigms); (ii) the behavioural level of actors, interactions and networks; and (iii) the societal knowledge base in terms of knowledge, concepts and visions regarding the innovation domain in question. The approach is formulated in a sufficiently neutral way to be applicable to national and regional as well as to sectoral examples or case studies.

6.1.3.1 The static picture

Delimiting system and system environment
One of the most difficult tasks in any systems research is the delimitation of the system under study. National boundaries of innovation systems have often been chosen in the

---

6   There is a long-standing debate about what constitutes a 'system', which cannot be outlined here. I start from a very simple definition saying that a system is composed of elements and the relationships between them. These elements can be actors or technologies or other entities relevant to innovation processes. A key problem consists of defining the limits of a system. Especially with respect to social systems, this delimitation is far from obvious and needs to be justified in each empirical case, depending on the research question addressed as well on pragmatic arguments.

past, mainly based on the argument that the key institutions framing innovation processes are defined at national level. For any specific problem, this definition of system boundaries needs to be checked and will depend on the characteristics of the innovation field in question. This also implies that system boundaries are not fixed during a process of system transformation. New actors and furthermore a far broader range of actors may join the innovation arena, e.g. as a consequence of the increasingly interactive character of innovation or as a result of creating new supra-national regulatory frameworks.

The system under study draws resources from its environment and is subject to external pressure to which it needs to adapt. This pressure can be due to, for instance, lack of resources or new societal demands, leading to innovative responses and selection decisions within the system, at various levels. These decisions and responses are interpreted as collective choices, negotiated among a range of relevant actors.

Consequently, the system should be delimited from its environment such that the impact of the 'wider world outside' is taken into account while feedback effects from the system on the environment are minimised. Only in this case, the analytical distinction between system and environment makes sense. We know of several historical examples where factors external to an innovation system have exerted a major influence on its evolution. In energy supply, for instance, the oil price shocks, or societal opinion about nuclear power have deeply affected innovation processes. They would not be regarded as part of the sectoral innovation system of energy supply, but as exogenous environmental factors.

The levels of a complex innovation system

In complex systems, at least two levels of analysis are distinguished: first, the level of observable patterns or structures and, second, the level of underlying mechanisms driving and determining these patterns. Usually, the patterns or structures of a system change only very slowly whereas there may be a high intensity of interaction underlying this apparent stability. There may, however, also be phases of comparatively fast structural change, that can be explained only on the basis of 'non-linear' or self-reinforcing mechanisms, resulting from the complex interplay between these two (or possibly more) levels.

In innovation research, for instance, the terms 'technological paradigm shift', 'technological regime shifts', 'creative destruction' or 'system transformation' are used to denote the corresponding empirical phenomena. The interactive and interdependent character of innovation processes has been identified as being at the origin of such phenomena. This explains also the importance of user–producer interactions or science–industry relations in recent innovation research. However, the dynamics of concepts and knowledge has also been identified as one of the reasons for the non-linear, path-dependent and complex character of innovation. Therefore, the complex innovation systems approach is based on a three-level model, with the level of concepts, knowledge and visions complementing the structural and behavioural levels.

The **innovation regime** can be defined as the technological, economic and political structures, infrastructures, institutional settings and rules, the mental frameworks or paradigms that guide and frame the behaviour of actors, i.e. their innovation behaviour in terms of research and development, investment, co-operation and use in a complex innovation system.[7] This level is usually characterised by a comparatively slow pace of change, compared with the level of actor behaviour. However, this does not exclude phases of fast and revolutionary change. In fact, phases of rapid change of usually stable characteristics are of particular interest from a complex systems perspective on innovation because it is actually in spite of rigidities at the regime level that fundamental changes and transformation can occur in innovation systems (e.g. the information technology revolution).

The level of **actors, interactions and networks** focuses on patterns of interaction and the individual decision-making processes of actors. Most innovation studies have concentrated on firm behaviour at the micro level, even if growing attention has been paid in recent years to other actors such as users, while policy was mostly regarded as an external factor. In complex innovation systems, a broader range of actors is taken into account, comprising political actors as well as different types of intermediary organisation and stakeholder.

These actors participate in innovation processes using highly diverse mental framework and guiding rules sets for their behaviour. To put it in different words, innovation activities and systems exist at the intersection of different functional systems of society.[8] The interaction between different functional systems might be supported on the one side by actors operating at the borders between functional systems or by border-crossing networks of actors.

The third level of **concepts, knowledge and visions**, sometimes also referred to as the societal knowledge base, captures the idea that, beyond the organisations and actors in which knowledge is stored, it is also necessary to dispose of a representation entirety for the knowledge on which an innovation system is able to draw. Scientific research findings, while sometimes contradictory, are widely accessible, as are assessments of current innovations. Obviously, other pieces of knowledge are proprietary to individual actors, but the public or semi-public debates about innovations rely on pieces of knowledge from what we call the societal knowledge base.

In other words, this societal knowledge base represents the totality of concepts, knowledge and visions about the different aspects or dimensions of an innovation. These may also be hypothetical statements and expectations about the future state of a technology, both positive and negative ones. These 'innovation hypotheses' compete for support by different actors in the social realm (Ahrweiler 1999), either to persuade other actors of their beneficial character or of the contrary. They can represent very broad visions of the future, including not only the technical and economic aspects, but also the necessary support networks for an innovation to be realised. In fact, an innovation hypothesis can be regarded as a comprehensive sociotechnical image or scenario of the future. The more 'radical' a new technology is and the more system-wide implications it has, the more comprehensive will be the associated innovation hypotheses. In fact, you may need to have 'a guiding vision' or 'paradigm' of how the entire future

---

7 Cf. the concept of technological regime as defined by Kemp *et al.* (1994) which is more specifically focused on *technological* innovations, whereas the notion of innovation regime can also be used to analyse, for instance, policy innovations.

8 This formulation reflects ideas similar to those expressed in Luhmann's theory of social systems, where he distinguishes different functional systems of society (e.g. economy, politics, science, etc.) with their specific codes (Luhmann 1988).

system (e.g. of energy supply) would look if the new technology was introduced on a larger scale.

The aspects covered by an innovation hypothesis reflect the different issues or problem dimensions that are of particular relevance to the actors involved. For example, a profit-maximising agent would tend to formulate his or her problem in terms of economic benefit. Often problem/issue dimensions are assessed differently by different actors (e.g. assessment of long-term environmental impacts), and their importance can be valued differently as well (e.g. economic versus environmental benefits). In other words, each actor contributes his or her perspective to the societal knowledge base, but each values the assessment dimensions differently. As a consequence, it is sometimes difficult to determine whether two actors still support the same innovation hypothesis or whether they actually have different ideas in mind. However, the fuzziness of innovation hypotheses is an important issue when it comes to building a support network.

6.1.3.2 The dynamic picture

We will now move towards the distinctive dynamic aspects of complex innovation systems. Complex innovation systems have been conceptualised as a three-level model (i.e. innovation regime; actors and interactions; concepts, knowledge and visions). The dynamics of complex innovation systems are driven by the interactions between and within the three levels. These interactions give rise to complex phenomena. The aim of this highly structured way of dealing with dynamism is to understand and describe major transformations of sociotechnical systems, so-called transitions based on system innovations. In order to capture the complex dynamics, it is necessary to look into the interplay between these levels.

Descriptive dynamics and driving forces of change

Transformation processes of complex innovation systems can in the first instance be captured in a descriptive way, by distinguishing phases of transformation and by analysing the aggregate, macroscopic features of the system. Phase or wave models remain essentially at this descriptive level.

Transitions and system innovations can be described as processes of change that may originate in niches and may be followed by a shift in the dominant innovation regime, i.e. of structures, institutions and dominant mental frameworks (Geels 2002). The real challenge is to relate the structural changes systematically to the underlying behaviour of actors and to the knowledge, concepts and visions they draw on.

A second, often complementary inroad to capture dynamics is to look at 'driving forces', i.e. at factors that induce processes of transformation. Scientific discovery has for long been regarded as a major driving force of change. While the importance of science is certainly not to be neglected, a number of additional requirements need to be met to realise innovations on a larger scale. These are obviously market-related factors but in many cases science and market alone are not sufficient to drive innovation and diffusion forward. In particular with regard to environmental innovations, where a regime shift would in principle be needed, additional factors come into play. Regime shifts can also be driven by problems and by the inability of the dominant regime to address these (Geels 2002). The perception of the problems and challenges by actors can lead to new initiatives, pioneered either by private actors, by government or by other stakeholders.

Underlying processes driving the dynamics of complex innovation systems

Any attempt at political intervention requires a deeper understanding of the dynamics, and this is where complexity research promises the most useful insights. In the end, macroscopic transformation processes need to be traced back to the behaviour of actors, decisions, perceptions and interactions at the micro level and—as we suggest here—to changes at the level of concepts, visions and knowledge. These linkages need to be understood in terms of feedbacks or circular causalities (Küppers 2001) as the characteristic features of complex innovation systems. These circular causalities are at the origin of self-reinforcing (or self-delaying, stabilising) mechanisms that drive system change, and help explain why and how collective choices in innovation systems take place.

In other words, self-organisation is used as a key concept to capture the mechanisms that underlie the evolutionary, but sometimes also revolutionary processes of system change that can be observed at macroscopic level. In the following, we will distinguish three aspects of dynamics that can be regarded as co-evolving in a complex innovation system. They correspond roughly to the three levels of the complex innovation systems framework:

- The formation of innovation hypotheses
- The formation of actors' opinions and decisions
- The transformation of the innovation regime

The formation of innovation hypotheses

Both problem pressure and opportunities can trigger search procedures for new, innovative solutions by actors. Problem pressure may emerge as a result of external developments in the system environment (e.g. societal concerns about environmental degradation, shortage of resources, etc.), but also as a result of perceived inefficiencies within the system (e.g. bad performance indicators). In terms of opportunities, one may consider also new scientific findings as factors standing behind the search for new solutions. Such an innovation hypothesis may be related to a particular concern or issue dimension. Other actors may look at the same innovation hypothesis from different perspectives, related to the issue dimension they are particularly concerned with.

Once an actor comes up with a novel innovation hypothesis it cannot in most cases be implemented immediately, but requires the support and co-operation of other actors. This is at least what most theories about the growing importance of innovation networks would argue. In the course of the interaction process, the innovation hypothesis is complemented by additional information regarding other issue dimensions in order to make it match the concerns and perspectives of other actors. The innovation hypothesis becomes thus refined and starts to be regarded as a real alternative to the dominant technology. If it has far-reaching implications for the system as a whole (e.g. a radical or architectural innovation), then this adjustment and learning process can take a long time (or even never be finished at all!). In this case, the innovation hypothesis not only represents a promising option for certain application niches, but embodies a projection or vision of a new and comprehensive alternative system.

In many cases, there are several alternative innovation hypotheses under discussion that relate to the same problem area. The confrontation of these hypotheses can be a very fruitful process that gives rise to new, integrated innovation hypotheses. By combining the views of different actors, innovation hypotheses become more complex and sophisticated and can get more widespread support. This can have the consequence that many actors will regard it as superior and then initiate actions to enable its wider application (e.g. through new regulatory adjustments). By this mechanism, opportunities open up to replace the dominant technology.

However, support for innovation hypotheses does not automatically mean that the new technology also replaces the dominant one in the real world. Actors are not necessarily rational; there are non-linear effects, etc. This process of translating ideas into decisions cannot be dealt with in detail.[9] However, what we would need is a decision model that takes into account the perception of innovation hypotheses by actors, their interpretation/evaluation and their decision and interaction rules.

So far, we have been dealing only with concepts and ideas. However, once first niche applications are implemented, they are confronted with many problems and obstacles. Even very careful planning cannot prevent such problems. Learning processes need to take place in different ways: systematic scientific learning, learning by doing/using, etc. These experiences may further improve the knowledge base. Owing to the growing complexity of the problems to be addressed in our modern societies, and the multitude of perspectives that have to be taken into account in order to make a new innovation hypothesis acceptable, network-like structures for learning about innovation hypotheses are particularly suitable.[10]

The formation of actors' opinions and decisions
Actors form their opinions about different technologies and/or innovations. Building on the selected set of issue dimensions they are interested in, they have to make up their minds about different options, once the problem pressure or the opportunities they are confronted with make it necessary to choose from the decision options at stake. This can be regarded as a first individual selection step about adopting or not adopting different innovation hypotheses. Individual positions or opinions about innovation, adoption and policy options are taken on the basis of several factors: objectives and priorities, financial resources, the individual knowledge and competence base, interactions and exchange with others, guiding paradigms and mental frameworks, the information 'filters' and routines applied, etc.

Opinions are hardly ever formed in an isolated way, but are always preceded by interactions with others. These interactions can be regarded as taking place in the innova-

---

9   See, for example, the understanding of decision-making proposed by Clark and Juma (1991). It builds on information theory and elements of evolutionary economics such as the routines concept. Also the concept of adaptive agents and their rule-guided behaviour comes into play. The emergence of culture and language are further aspects to be considered which some authors have tried to understand as a non-genetic evolutionary process. Birchenhall (1999), for instance, suggests using the notion of memes instead.

10   This is actually one of the main arguments put forward in the Mode 2 approach (Gibbons *et al.* 1994).

tion, information and/or policy networks. The importance of these interaction arenas is obvious for political decisions, but they matter a lot also for the other types of decision: for example, when a company negotiates with a client about tariffs or prices.

Different means of interaction can be distinguished: for example, in terms of money, law, information and technological hardware. The ability of at least some members of a network to use these means is important for the success of the technology they support and that best matches their interests.

The final decisions to implement an innovation hypothesis (and thus transform it into an innovation) can be regarded as a second, often collective selection step. The actual decisions made affect and transform the functional realm (e.g. by constructing new types of power plant) but they can also have an impact on organisational and social structures (e.g. through the creation of a new regulatory authority or other institutions) that govern the social realm. In other words, the decisions made by the actors in the different networks affect all realms of the system: the functional, the social, and, by way of making new experiences in the transformed system, also the conceptual. This should be kept in mind, even if we focus on the functional realm in the following.

The transformation of the innovation regime
Actors' decisions are the processes by which an innovation hypothesis is transformed into changes in the real world. This is not a straightforward process, but characterised by many feedbacks and non-linearities. For example, first adoption decisions of a new technology already start to transform the system structure, but only in a minor way. However, the first experiences made in technological niches are decisive for reinforcing or weakening the support for the innovation hypothesis which is represented by this technology. This learning-from-experiments process is a typical reinforcement mechanism that feeds back into the next innovation stage, and affects, for example, how far further political support can be created.

The replacement of an old technology by a new one (technological succession) is thus a multifaceted process which builds on several mechanisms. There are interdependences between the patterns of social organisation and technical realisation, path dependences and feedback loops in operation.

Basically, 'old' and 'new' models co-exist as both innovation hypotheses and as realised technologies. The issues of the aforementioned path dependence and technological succession can thus also be addressed for both realms, i.e. real-world and innovation hypotheses. Actors in the networks subscribe to old or new technologies as well as to old or new system views.

The complexity of system transformation means that it is not possible any more just to 'invent' and then introduce a new technology. In fact, to achieve the diffusion of an innovation that has wider systemic implications, it is necessary to 'reinvent the system'. This obviously requires the contribution of a large number of different actors, and the activation of their competences and influence

Self-organisation and the dynamics of complex innovation systems
It is important to highlight the central role of the concept of **circular causalities** (i.e. of reinforcing, delaying or stabilising feedback mechanisms) for our interpretation of innovation system dynamics. 'Circular causalities' is a term that has been used to explain

the origin of emergent properties in self-organising systems.[11] This concept can be applied to the three levels of complex innovation systems: that is, both within each of the three levels (e.g. horizontal relations between actors) but in particular also between them (e.g. vertical relations between regime and actor level).

Emergent properties at the *regime level* are, for instance, the organisational structures, the diffusion patterns and the regulatory frameworks. They 'emerge' from the interactions among the different types of interrelated network and/or actor, and are in turn perceived by these actors and translated into expectations, preferences and decisions.

As an example of a *vertical* circular causality, actors perceive the situation and the changes in that part of the environment that is relevant to them. Based on the issue dimension of most importance to them, they look at and interpret their respective environments. The perception of this external world, the interactions with others and also their own experiences contribute to their learning and thus to the expansion of the societal knowledge base. In line with their perceptions and assessment of the different available systems (innovation hypotheses), they select them for their potential decisions. These decisions then shape the emerging structures and regime elements of the innovation system.

An example of a *horizontal* circular causality is certainly mutual learning between users and suppliers of a technology, but also the interactions between users and regulators that not only enable adjustments of the regulatory rules but also adjustment of users' decisions to the adjusted context.

Circular causalities can also be interpreted in evolutionary terms, i.e. as being at the origin of variation, selection and stability. The joint operation of reinforcing and delaying mechanisms, applied to different technology options, gives rise to a *selection* process. For example, a circular causality of the learning-by-experimenting type reinforces, if successful, the transformation process in a favourable way for the technology in question. It favours its selection by users, manufacturer and policy-makers. If in parallel the competing options are disfavoured, for example by unsuccessful experiments, a selection pattern emerges as a result of the combination of these circular causalities.

The situation is more complicated with respect to *variation*. New combinations of elements from the societal knowledge base, possibly combined with elements from new fields of scientific knowledge, represent new innovation hypotheses. These potential combinations mostly lie 'dormant' but can be picked up or composed by individual actors and brought into the social interaction processes. In many cases, their new suggestions will be rejected and remain irrelevant. Innovation in this interpretation is a process of picking new combinations from a pool of knowledge,[12] but at the same time feeding back new insights into the knowledge pool. The search for such new combinations can be triggered by different impulses: problem pressure, new fundamental opportunities or new incentive mechanisms in a new regulatory framework.

These processes of variation and selection can be *stabilised* by several mechanisms. Technological (e.g. sunk costs) and organisational rigidities (e.g. centralised organisa-

---

11   For further information on the basic principles of self-organisation, see, for example, Küppers 2001.

12   However, we should not forget that variation is not blind but guided by paradigms and routines in a kind of internal selection process.

tions) or interdependences (e.g. a grid network) are examples of them, but also the inertia of dominant paradigms and mental frameworks. They tend to be based on path dependences, which can also be interpreted as circular mechanisms. For example, once new institutions and organisations are created that accommodate a new technology and are compatible with its characteristics (e.g. decentralised organisational units), the interest in and the benefits of the new technology increase, leading to a strengthening of the complementary organisational context. Obviously, such interdependences not only stabilise the dominant innovation regime, but their creation also offers good opportunities to reinforce the establishment of a new regime and new technologies.

6.1.3.3 The direction of innovation

A better understanding of how system transformations and regime shifts take place is an important step forward, but it does not yet tell us very much about whether the direction is right, and whether individual innovations actually contribute to the desired direction change. Probably, it is even impossible to know in advance whether this is the case or not, due to the high degrees of uncertainty, ambiguity and complexity associated with future system innovations.

However, this does not mean that today's decisions cannot be intelligibly informed about the direction of change and whether it is in line with current societal and policy objectives. First of all, criteria can be put in place to assess emerging innovations with respect to their compatibility with policy objectives (e.g. sustainability) and thus inform priority-setting in STI (science, technology and innovation) policy. While it is often very difficult to formulate substantive criteria for the assessment of technologies and innovations that are still in the making, the most recent research programmes in the field of sustainable development aim to establish more procedural criteria to be applied to individual research activities in order to make sure that the perspectives of various stakeholders are taken into consideration early on in the research process (Whitelegg and Weber 2002). Second, the incentive structures in the innovation system may be geared in a way to favour developments that are compatible with the objectives, e.g. by means of taxes and regulations. And, finally, the development of shared societal visions can contribute to co-ordinate different actors and align their activities.

Moreover, there also need to be mechanisms in place that ensure the continuous adaptation once new and better knowledge about emerging innovations becomes available. In other words, mechanisms are needed to make sure that new knowledge from the societal knowledge base is continuously fed into the decision-making process. Assessments nevertheless differ due to differences in objectives and values of actors. Therefore, mediating this adaptation process and defining the sets of commonly agreed criteria and objectives could thus be regarded as a key role for government in complex innovation systems. The objectives and criteria may contribute to defining a corridor for innovation.

Overall, the combination of process criteria for research, vision building and incentive structures, embedded in a process of continuous adaptation and learning, provide the ingredients for the *soft* steering of the emergence of innovation and system trajectories. In the next section, I will discuss the necessary capabilities and inputs to policy needed to perform such a mediating function.

6.2 Requirements for governance and the role of politics

Assuming that the theoretical framework described above represents an accurate description of how innovation and policy-making processes interact, and that additional conditions are raised by the necessity to orient innovation processes towards the goal of sustainability, a number of implications and requirements with respect to governance and politics can be raised.[13]

First of all, the complex innovation systems framework implies a number of obvious changes for the role of politics and policies with respect to innovation. Politics is regarded as an integral part of the innovation system. In other words, government actors ought to be regarded as one type of actor among others contributing to systemic innovation processes. One may nevertheless argue that public policy-making has a key role to play because it is expected to fulfil certain key functions in innovation systems, not least to ensure that structural transformations of innovation systems are oriented towards sustainability. More specifically, this has further implications for the type of policy that government can sensibly implement in complex innovation systems:

- Government agents can no longer assume a directive role but rather a moderating function with respect to the different relevant actors in an innovation system. Their special responsibility for the overall co-ordination of political processes can rather be compared with that of managing a network of decentralised and highly autonomous actors ('decentralised network governance').

- In spite of disposing of a special legitimation by being elected democratically, there are limits to what governments can do, especially in terms of giving direction to transformation processes. Other actors' decisions and value positions—either at international level or nationally—constrain the possibilities of governments. It also constrains their ability to steer system transformations towards sustainability. In line with the notion of decentralised network governance, the definition and enforcement of processes (i.e. also participatory processes) thus become a key role for policy-making. Politics, in the sense of informal lobbying and participation, becomes dissolved in such semi-formalised processes and networks.

- In addition to the use of many conventional policy instruments (regulations, finance, infrastructures, S&T [science and technology] policy, etc.), this new role requires the use of new ones as well, such as the stimulation of processes of networking and knowledge exchange, the initiation of processes of vision-building in order to give orientation to a spectrum of actors. Jointly they should allow government to play a co-ordinating role in a process of system transformation or transition.

In other words, this new modulating role still allows government to exert a wide range of instruments and policies, but they are defined and specified in different settings

---

13   Governance of innovation systems are defined here as the rules, structures, processes and institutions guiding the interactions between a broad range of actors who exert an influence on innovation processes.

from the formalised, mostly constitutionally defined structures or the informal lobbying processes. A new form of intermediate governance processes is required.

A second important issue is due to the multi-level character of governance in Europe in particular. National policy-making is embedded in European and international politics and often frames regional processes. A new division of labour emerges also with respect to innovation and innovation systems. Renn (2002) argues with respect to foresight-processes that mainly 'epistemological' discourses—that is, debates about 'potential opportunities and risks based on a common vision and the likely developments that we can foresee without relying on pure speculation'—should be conducted at EU level, whereas debates about assessments of trade-offs and values require a stronger participation from the bottom up and the consideration of local specificities. The sustainability orientation of innovation systems will in many cases have to be addressed at several levels simultaneously. However, we should also be aware that this argument may have to be differentiated with respect to different problem areas, because in a highly internationalised or Europeanised field (e.g. climate change or aeronautics, genetic technology), the appropriate level for assessments and value discourses may well differ from, for instance, regional development issues.

A third consideration has to do with the time- and path-dependent character of complex transformation processes. It implies that the appropriate role of policy may change over time, and that governance settings and politics need to be tuned in such a way as to enable the time-sensitive use of policy instruments. For instance, as shown for the case of transport technology policy, the appropriate role for EU policy changes in the course of the innovation processes, and key policy roles needed, may move down to lower policy levels or may even be taken up by actors outside the realm of government (van Zuylen and Weber 2002). Moreover, time is also a critical factor in the complex innovation systems perspective because of the necessity to exploit time windows of opportunity (Erdmann 2005).

What does this now imply for *governance structures and processes,* meant to support system transformations towards sustainability? Governance structures and processes need to guarantee certain key capabilities in complex innovation systems, in particular in the following respects:

- The capability to integrate technological, economic, political and institutional knowledge: that is, to enable the participation of an appropriate range of actors and stakeholders in network-based processes of preparing policy decisions

- The capability to adapt to new emerging challenges (e.g. environmental, social security systems). This requires the ability to change the structural characteristics of the system. This flexibility needs to be balanced with stabilising elements, but in general the problem of the multi-level system lies rather in their rigidity

- The capability to make use of reinforcing mechanisms and trigger system changes, as part of the need to be not just reactive and adaptive, but also proactive in shaping future transformation paths

- The capability to manage the process of transition and system transformation, based, for instance, on niche management approaches as an example of collective and co-operative learning process, guided by shared visions and operationalised in the form of concrete policy agendas

- The capability to change the role of politics and policy (and thus also of other actors) in the course of the innovation process and the system transformation

6.3 Conclusions

This chapter began with a conceptual framework for describing the complex dynamics of innovation systems. This with the idea in mind that moving towards sustainable development requires us to understand and guide politically the future transformation of innovation systems. The framework was used as a foundation for suggesting new requirements for the governance of transformation processes of innovation systems and the corresponding role of politics.

It still remains to be tested how far such an approach can contribute to improving policy-making, in the sense of moving towards more sustainable innovation systems. The complex systems framework points to a number of inroads that science, technology and innovation should consider. For instance, the notion of timing of policy interventions to benefit from reinforcing or delaying mechanisms in complex innovation systems becomes crucial. Similarly, vision building as an orienting and focusing device for actors and interactions would be seen as a more important ingredient than in currently dominant policy approaches. It is also key to giving innovation processes direction towards sustainability. Finally, a forward-looking and adaptive approach to policy-making is suggested by the complex innovation systems framework, informed by a continuous monitoring process about innovation hypotheses, actor perspectives and changes at the level of the innovation regime.

While these may be critical ingredients and principles for policy approaches aiming to combine innovation and sustainability objectives, a clear methodology of how to arrive at appropriate policy initiatives is still missing. What needs to be done next is to develop a methodology that allows us to develop concrete forward-looking innovation policy strategies in a way that is compatible with the governance principles outlined above.

A key enabling element of such a methodology would be the improvement of the forward-looking, exploratory and evaluative capabilities of policy-making at different levels. Taking into account the more decentralised nature of decision-making, it will be decisive to devise structures and processes to make use of the 'distributed intelligence' in our innovation systems (Kuhlmann 2001). This is where the main challenge for politics lies because it implies a radical departure from former politics practices in two respects.

References

Ahrweiler, P. (1999) *Conceptual Framework for CHP Simulation* (SEIN Working Paper; Bielefeld, Germany).

Birchenhall, C. (1999) *SEIN: A Memetic Framework?* (SEIN Working Paper; Bielefeld, Germany).

Braczyk, H.-J., P. Cooke and M. Heidenreich (eds.) (1998) *Regional Innovation Systems* (London: UCL).

Breschi, F., and F. Malerba (1997) 'Sectoral Innovation Systems: Technological Regimes, Schumpeterian Dynamics and Spatial Boundaries', in C. Edquist (ed.), *Systems of Innovation: Technology, Institutions and Organizations* (London: Pinter): 130-53.

Clark, N., and C. Juma (1991) *Long-Run Economics: An Evolutionary Approach to Economic Growth* (London: Pinter).

Dosi, G. (1982) 'Technological Paradigms and Technological Trajectories: A Suggested Interpretation of the Determinants and Directions of Technological Change', *Research Policy* 11: 147-62.

—— and R.R. Nelson (1994) 'An Introduction to Evolutionary Theories in Economics', *Journal of Evolutionary Economics* 4: 153-72.

——, C. Freeman, R. Nelson, G. Silverberg and L. Soeto (eds.) (1988) *Technical Change and Economic Theory* (London: Pinter).

Edquist, C. (1997a) 'Systems of Innovation Approaches: Their Emergence and Characteristics', in C. Edquist (ed.), *Systems of Innovation: Technology, Institutions and Organizations* (London: Pinter): 1-35I.

—— (ed.) (1997b) *Systems of Innovation: Technology, Institutions and Organizations* (London: Pinter).

Erdmann, G. (2005) 'Innovation, Time and Sustainability', in K.M. Weber and J. Hemmelskamp (eds.), *Towards Environmental Innovation Systems* (Heidelberg: Springer): 195-208.

Funtowicz, S., and J. Ravetz (1993) 'Science for the Post-Normal Age', *Futures* 25: 735-55.

Geels, F. (2002) 'Understanding Technological Transitions: A Critical Literature Review and a Pragmatic Conceptual Approach', paper for the workshop *Transitions to Sustainability through System Innovations*, University of Twente, Netherlands, 4–6 July 2002.

Gibbons, M., C. Limoges, H. Nowotny, S. Schwartzman, S. Scott and M. Trow (1994) *The New Production of Knowledge* (London: Sage).

Kemp, R., and J. Rotmans (2005) 'The Management of the Co-evolution of Technical, Environmental and Social Systems', in K.M. Weber and J. Hemmelskamp (eds.), *Towards Environmental Innovation Systems* (Heidelberg: Springer): 33-55.

——, I. Miles and K. Smith (1994) *Technology and the Transition to Environmental Stability: Continuity and Change in Technology Systems* (research report; Maastricht, Netherlands: MERIT).

Kuhlmann, S. (2001) *Management of Innovation Systems: The Role of Distributed Intelligence* (Antwerp, Belgium: Maklu-Uitgevers).

Küppers, G. (2001) 'Complexity, Self-Organisation and Innovation Networks: An Introduction', in G. Küppers (ed.), *SEIN Project Final Report* (Bielefeld, Germany: SEIN).

Luhmann, N. (1988) *Die Wirtschaft der Gesellschaft* (Frankfurt am Main: Suhrkamp).

Lundvall, B.-A. (ed.) (1992) *National Systems of Innovation: Towards a Theory of Innovation and Interactive Learning* (London: Pinter).

Mayntz, R., and T.P. Hughes (eds.) (1988) *The Development of Large Technical Systems* (Frankfurt am Main: Campus).

Pyka, A., and G. Küppers (2002) *Innovation Networks: Theory and Practice* (Cheltenham, UK: Edward Elgar).

Renn, O. (2002) 'Foresight and Multi-Level Governance', paper for the conference *The Role of Foresight in the Selection of Research Policy Priorities*, Seville, Spain, 13–14 May 2002.

Saviotti, P.P. (1996) *Technological Evolution, Variety and the Economy* (Aldershot, UK: Edward Elgar).

Scharpf, F.W. (1993) 'Coordination in Hierarchies and Networks', in F.W. Scharpf (ed.), *Games in Hierarchies and Networks: Analytical and Empirical Approaches to the Study of Governance Institutions* (Frankfurt am Main: Campus): 125-66.

Sorensen, K. (1999) *Providing, Pushing and Policing. Towards a New Architecture of Technology* (INTEPOL Project Report; Twente, Netherlands: University of Twente).

—— and R. Williams (2002) *Shaping Technology, Guiding Policy: Concepts, Spaces and Tools* (Cheltenham, UK: Edward Elgar).

Tübke, A., K. Ducatel, J.P. Gavigan and P. Moncada Paternò-Castello (2001) *Strategic Policy Intelligence: Current Trends, the State of Play and Perspectives—S&T Intelligence for Policy-Making Processes* (research report; Seville, Spain: IPTS/ESTO).

Van Zuylen, H., and K.M. Weber (2002) 'Opportunities and Limitations of European Innovation Policy in Transport', *Technological Forecasting and Social Change* 69: 929-51.

Whitelegg, K., and K.M. Weber (2002) *National Research Activities and Sustainable Development* (research report; Vienna/Seville: ARC/ESTO).

7
Gender mainstreaming
PATHWAY TO DEMOCRATISATION?

Claudia von Braunmühl

7.1 The concept of gender mainstreaming

Ever since gender mainstreaming travelled from the 1995 Fourth International Women's Conference held in Beijing to find accommodation in the European Treaty of Amsterdam signed in 1998, it spread all over the continent. With surprising speed it consolidated in a wide range of legal stipulations, standing orders, guidelines, checklists, monitoring, evaluations, quality control devices and the like (von Braunmühl 2001a). In its communication on gender mainstreaming the European Community defines gender mainstreaming in the following way:

> Gender mainstreaming involves not restricting efforts to promote equality to the implementation of specific measures to help women, but mobilising all general policies and measures specifically for the purpose of achieving equality by actively and openly taking into account at the planning stage their possible effects on the respective situation of men and women (gender perspective). This means systematically examining measures and policies and taking into account such possible effects when defining and implementing them . . .
>
> Action to promote equality requires an ambitious approach which presupposes the recognition of male and female identities and the willingness to establish a balanced distribution of responsibilities between women and men . . .
>
> The promotion of equality must not be confused with the simple objective of balancing the statistics: it is a question of promoting long-lasting changes in parental roles, family structures, institutional practices, the organisation of work and time, their personal development and independence, but also concerns men and the whole of society, in which it can encourage progress and be a token of democracy and pluralism . . .
>
> The systematic consideration of the differences between the conditions, situations and needs of women and men in all Community policies and actions: this is the basic feature of the principle of 'mainstreaming', which the Commission has adopted (European Community 1996).

The very title of the communication, *Incorporating Equal Opportunities for Women and Men into all Community Policies and Activities,* speaks to the origins of EU attention to gender asymmetries as being situated in the world of work and employment and, some fear, contained therein. Indeed, when the European Commission embarked on adopting the strategy in 1996, reference to the labour market could not be avoided as the legal foundation of the Treaty of Amsterdam was not yet available at the time. However, the European Commission made it quite clear that 'Gender mainstreaming must go beyond the spheres of employment and structural policies, it should be extended to all policies that affect in one way or the other the lives of European citizens—women and men' (Gradin 1999). Some will justifiably point to the fact that equal opportunities is a far cry from gender democracy and the gender-just policy results demanded in the Beijing Platform of Action.

Yet, looking more closely, the definition of gender mainstreaming spelled out in the communication can easily be read as an institutionalisation of the *perspectives* and the *objectives* of the international women's movements. This, in fact, is the reading guiding the present-day understanding of gender mainstreaming strategies on the part of many feminists and women's organisations:

> Gender mainstreaming aims to offer an answer to the problem of enabling the machinery of the state to deliver gender sensitive policy. It is an expression of the institutional establishment of a world wide women's movement which intends to fundamentally transform the definition of the situation (Woodward 2001: 1).

What are the reasons forwarded for this understanding?

- Men and women experience different life situations and as a consequence have different needs. It is an issue of human rights as well as of equality in citizenship status that these differences do not result in differentials and asymmetries irreconcilable with gender justice and gender democracy. Gender mainstreaming is based on this perspective and therefore holds transformative potential.

- Gender mainstreaming requires the integration of the aims and objectives of equality and of gender-sensitive institutional action into the organisational mandate, thereby binding hierarchically structured institutions and bureaucracies to act accordingly. The top-down approach can be an extremely powerful complement to the bottom-up approach of the women's movements.

- With gender mainstreaming forming part of the institutional mandate and mission, institutionally marginalised und under-resourced women's or gender desks may be liberated from the role of policy ghettos with exclusive responsibility for gender-relevant action. By the same token the pervasive tendency of agencies to keep abreast of attention to gender issues by shifting the job to these units can be rightfully challenged. Conceptually, ownership is relocated from the margins to the centre (Jahan 1995).

- Gender mainstreaming acknowledges that the myth of gender neutrality systematically privileges men and works to the disadvantage of women. It exposes the hidden mechanisms of asymmetrical, power-structured gender regimes and requires gender-differentiated analyses of policies (content), polities (organisational structures) and politics (processes). By implication it calls for a gender-sensitive reconceptualisation of citizenship as a prerequisite for gender democracy.

- Gender mainstreaming is an innovative strategy. In fact, when adopted in Europe no adequate instruments for implementation were readily available. However, this must not necessarily be considered a handicap. On the contrary, the very process of developing the instruments required may very well reinforce the strategy. The elaboration of gender-differentiated data and methods to generate them, indicators for identifying and measuring gender imbalances, instruments for impact monitoring of action taken and the like has to engage the entire organisation in the effort. This process is likely to have a potentially powerful effect on sensitisation and gender awareness.

The international debate to a great extent focused on the capacity of gender mainstreaming to impact favourably on gender-just results. In Europe greater emphasis was placed on its potential to enhance democracy. Two factors contribute to this perspective. The ongoing debate about the fate of democracy in the process of the deepening and broadening of the European Union provided a natural environment for such concern. In later years the women's movement and particularly the Green parties entertained a vivid discussion on gender democracy. Gender mainstreaming had to position itself within these debates.

The following reflections will retrace the evolution of gender mainstreaming within the United Nations and within development co-operation, the domains in which it was originally conceived, analyse its adoption in Europe, and explore its democratisation and transformation potential.

7.2 The evolution of gender mainstreaming

When in the early 1970s in the US and in Europe the newly emerging women's movements turned to the field of development co-operation, they confronted development agencies with serious charges:

- Women do not have equitable access to the resources and benefits of development and aid (equity).

- Development projects and programmes overlook women to the detriment of the effective impact they desire (efficiency).

- Aid agencies have to recognise and overcome the inbuilt mechanisms constituting gender blindness.

The 'Women's Decade' 1975–1985 declared by the United Nations generated an enormous amount of information on women and their sociopolitical conditions of life. Women began to claim their share in the promises of modernisation—unquestioned as such—by seeking integration into development. Aid agencies were lobbied into the creation of special units, WID (women in development) desks and elaborated WID policies and methodologies.

The final Conference of the Decade held in Nairobi in 1985 came to rather disappointing conclusions. While undoubtedly remarkable achievements have been made in making the 'invisible women' (Scott 1979) visible, resources committed to redressing the disadvantaged situations uncovered were minimal, action was guided more by its legitimatising or aesthetic value (women's group in exotic attire dancing to the arrival of VIPs) than by either efficiency or equity considerations. As a consequence, the WID approach came under heavy criticism for its implicit acceptance of prevailing development strategies and for its systematic silence on the most decisive barrier to equitable and just development, the structural oppression and subordination of women. Moreover, experience had it, conceptualising gender imbalances as *women's issues* inevitably obscured the role of men and released them as well as society at large from responsibility and accountability.

Feminist epistemological critique had since progressed beyond the mere distinction between sex and gender and begun to analyse the social construction of gender and its inherent power relations. The change from WID (women in development) to GAD (gender and development) was to accommodate the resultant shift in focus and critique. At the same time the dominant development paradigm and its strategies came under attack from different corners, influenced by considerations of social justice and/or ecological sustainability. Under the impact of the social devastation brought on by structural adjustment, these initially different schools of thought feeding into the critique of WID over time merged into a fundamental questioning of the model and the strategy of modernisation and development and the gender regimes prevailing in it.

In Nairobi the network Development Alternatives with Women for a New Era (DAWN) from the South introduced the concept of empowerment into the debate (Sen and Grown 1987). Empowerment offered a vision of individual autonomy at the same time that it challenged the given set of societal gender regimes and called for their fundamental transformation. Development policy now was challenged not to merely support women in their ascribed roles and functions but to design programmes and projects with the core objective of women's empowerment in mind. The integration of gender into development debate brought about significant shifts. Gender analysis allowed a much broader grasp of social reality and began to lay claim to the revision of departmentalised WID/GAD policies as well as of gender-blind development interventions.

Thus the stage was set for the introduction of gender mainstreaming. The term as such was actually coined by the United Nations Fund for Women (UNIFEM). Originally centred on development interventions, it soon graduated to the larger arena of development where 'the time has come for women to move beyond being on the agenda to start setting the agenda' (Anderson 1993: 2). Gender mainstreaming framed as targeting for 'fundamental gender equality' was defined ambitiously. 'Mainstreaming, understood as agenda-setting, highlighted the need for fundamental change in the development paradigm, in the structures of the institutions that are involved in development planning and programming, and in the actual strategies, processes and outcomes of development' (Anderson 1993: 8). Within development discourse the strategy continued to push its claim for gender justice and full participation of women from project to programme to macro-economic and political levels. By the time of the Fourth UN International Women's Conference in Beijing in 1995, all major development agencies presented themselves with far-reaching definitions of gender mainstreaming professing to aim for agenda setting and for impact on projects and programmes, but also on macro-economic decision-making levels.

On an epistemological level, the category gender is to inform any analysis and decision leading to relevant development action. At the same time it has to retain the aspect of agenda setting and therewith its transformative capacity and mission. In implementation terms gender mainstreaming is defined as a dual two-pronged strategy. Gender issues are to be identified and taken into account on all levels of development action at the same time that women-specific projects should continue to overcome the barriers and constraints pertaining particularly to women and which have been brought to the fore through gender analysis. At the same time the category gender is not to be reduced to identifying given gender regimes, but to expose inherent repressive mechanism with the transformative policy intention of dismantling them.

While the aims and objectives of what was now referred to as the gender approach were systematically woven into the rhetoric of aid agencies, the numerous evaluations and academic reflections on institutional experiences produced on the way to the Beijing Conference brought to the fore two major constraints (Jahan 1995; Kabeer 1994; MacDonald 1994; Staudt 1997; Goetz 1995, 1997; Longwe 1997).

7.2.1 The direction of the mainstream

The social effects of neoliberal structural adjustment and corporate-led globalisation have proven to be of devastating impact on women and on gender relations. In line with the neoliberal creed of lean government and the benign effects of a private sector largely unencumbered by social or environmental considerations, governments withdraw dramatically from the provision of basic services and shift them into private households where prevalent gender arrangements heap them on the shoulders of women. The phenomenon has been dubbed 'feminisation of poverty' or 'feminisation of responsibility'; its systematic critique formed the basis for the rise of feminist economics (Elson 1991; Palmer 1994; Bakker 1994; Sassen 1998; Wichterich 2001). Under these circumstances an opportunity structure for the unfolding of meaningful empowerment strategies does not exist. Empowerment is married to poverty alleviation and redefined as the capacity to survive under most inclement conditions.

7.2.2 The patriarchic structure of bureaucracy

Gender mainstreaming demands organisational ownership of the gender mandate and integration of gender justice into the objectives, mechanisms, procedures and professional ethics of agencies. Using the insights of organisation sociology, administration theory and state theory and its feminist critique, the process has been closely observed and analysed by feminist academics and has been diagnosed as a case of 'continuing indifference, ambivalence and active resistance' (Moser 1993: 180). The dynamics of decision-making within institutions and their operating mode is deeply entrenched with and shaped by the patriarchal gender order. Hidden, at times however quite outspoken, gender hierarchies mould prevalent norms, criteria for bestowing legitimacy, procedural requirements, career patterns, achievement criteria, expectations and informal cultural mores. The African sociologist Sara Longwe sarcastically speaks of 'the evaporation of gender in the patriarchal cooking pot' (Longwe 1997). In short, mainstreaming of the gender approach in terms of its institutionalisation in structures and procedures as well as the professional self-image and standards of organisations appears to be a near to unattainable target (Jahan 1995; Goetz 1995, 1997; Razavi and Miller 1995a, b; Staudt 1997, 1998; von Braunmühl 1997, 1998).

These sobering findings were very well known when in Beijing gender mainstreaming was woven firmly into the Action Platform. There were solid reasons for this apparent disregard. It was all too clear that the 4th UN Women's Conference would constitute a climax of attention to gender matters on an international level. Therefore, it was crucial to secure achievements with whatever serious limitations remaining in order to have them as a legitimising point of reference when continuing the transformative struggle for gender justice and equality on regional and national levels.

As development debates moved on to the global debates transported by the UN Conference series of the 1990s, the needs-based debate entertained in the development community on basic needs and gender needs evolved into a rights-based debate. The international women's movements in turn engaged in a discourse on women's rights as an integral part of human rights. Over many years and many stages—critique of the concept and the articulation of universal human rights as eurocentric, andocentric, biased towards middle-class women—the human rights discourse established itself as the frame of reference serving the struggle of women from local to global levels and by the same token serving as a frame of reference for coalition building on all levels (von Braunmühl 2001b).

7.3 The Treaties of Maastricht and Amsterdam

When in 1994 the Treaty of Maastricht was up for revision, it took the untiring lobbying of the European Women's Lobby (EWL) to bring about the results achieved. In Article 2 and 3 of the Treaty of Amsterdam, signed in October 1997 and ratified in May 1999, 'equality between men and women' (art. 2) is elevated to the level of a core objective of the Community, and gender mainstreaming is the binding strategy to reach this aim. At the end of a long list of Community activities, Article 3 states: 'In all the activities referred to in this article, the Community shall aim to eliminate inequalities, and to promote equality between men and women.'

Starting even earlier, in January 1996 action had been taken to commit Union policies and strategic instruments such as structural funds and framework programmes to gender mainstreaming. Action programmes were formulated with a view to redressing gender imbalances within the Commission and expert groups, gender-differentiated reporting was made mandatory, sectoral programmes adjusted accordingly, and the like. At the end of the decade, evaluations, impact assessment and parliamentary hearings documented the first results of the new strategy.

All evaluations concur in underlining the potential of gender mainstreaming to produce gender-just results and to contribute to substantial equality. Emphasis is also placed on the importance of tools development for gender mainstreaming as a powerful vehicle to transport gender concerns. Some actions are profiled as commendable best practice.

However, disappointment and serious misgivings predominate. These can be summarised in recurrent observations:

- Gender mainstreaming is instrumentalised in order to dismantle the elaborate women's machinery existing in the Europe of the 1990s at the same time as precious little is done about genuine gender mainstreaming.

- Additional resources for implementation are not made available. Sectoral strategies are equipped with facile references to empowerment and equality without these being attributed any value of their own.

- Agenda setting stands little chance. In line with the predominant neoliberal agenda, achievement of gender-just results is crowded out by opportunity defined in individualised terms.

- Critique of patriarchy and the formulation of transformative policies and politics lose ground in favour of a perspective of equality in given system structures ('Add women and do NOT stir!').

7.4 Constraints to the implementation of gender mainstreaming

At this point it may be opportune to recall the different historical settings of gender mainstreaming within the system of the United Nations and North–South politics and in Europe.

When in 1995 gender mainstreaming became the defining feature of the Action Platform, it happened at the end of a quarter of a century of debate and interaction of the international women's movements with multilateral and bilateral actors who are active in the field of development and command vital resources. Women demanded that these resources—finances as well as decision-making and implementing power—be guided by concerns of social justice and be managed more equitably, with enhanced gender sensitivity and substantive gender-just outcomes. Gender mainstreaming never ceased to be embedded in development discourse. In fact, with the critique of the social impact of neoliberal adjustment programmes consolidating into feminist economics, women's organisations became a major voice in critical development discourse.

When in 1995/1996 gender mainstreaming reached Europe, it was introduced at a time at which—with the Treaties of Maastricht and Amsterdam and their prevailing interpretation—neoliberal policies had firmly settled in all OECD (Organisation for Economic Co-operation and Development) countries. Furthermore, gender mainstreaming encountered a long since institutionalised, equality-oriented infrastructure the struggles and arguments for which lay way back in the past and do not form part of the life experience of present-day office holders. The women's movement had left the streets and turned to professionalised lobby politics. The stress put on the top-down character of gender mainstreaming in the European debate is an immediate reflection of these circumstances. The strategy is grafted on the mode of operation of hierarchical structures with the traces of an emancipatory struggle on the part of a social movement illegible to current actors. With the integration of gender mainstreaming into their institutional mandate, the political directorate and the management of institutions is expected to act in line with equality objectives and may be held accountable for gender-just results. As ownership is to shift from the marginal women's machinery centre stage to the top brass, the top-down approach can indeed be perceived as potentially powerful. However, in bureaucratic settings more often than not gender mainstreaming comes across merely as a new instrument of equality politics rather than a strategy of social transformation. Finally, the fact that the new strategy—or for that matter instrument—comes in the form of a foreign word in most of Europe does little to endear it to either women or men.

All of these sobering experiences and restrictions notwithstanding, a growing number of women and women's organisations engaged in emancipatory gender politics consider gender mainstreaming to hold considerable potential for democratisation, much more so than previous equality politics with their absence of transformative aspirations (e.g. *Femina Politica* 2002). The final section of this chapter will now discuss this position.

7.5 Democratising potential of gender mainstreaming

If pursued with sincerity and vigour, so the argument runs, gender mainstreaming may secure access to resources previously barely attainable for women. It may contribute to the re-balancing of differentials in the life situations of men and women in the private as well as in the public domain. In that way it may be a factor in achieving more equitable gender results as well as a more inclusive democracy, one that embraces gender democracy, that is. The very process of pursuing gender mainstreaming strategies by way of identifying and elaborating adequate instruments of implementation may already transport elements of sensitisation, democratisation and transformation.

For this vision to materialise, I contend, at least three prerequisites regarding the type of discourse accompanying gender mainstreaming are critical: these are participation, hybridity of women's organisations, and interaction with the public sphere.

7.5.1 Discourse and participation

With gender mainstreaming as the institutionalisation of the perspectives and objectives of the women's movements, discourses that form an essential part of these movements find themselves relocated into institutions where they encounter—in fact, clash with—entirely different dynamics and rationales. To list but a few: present-day policies are firmly framed in a neoliberal paradigm which severely infringes on social betterment. The social contract moving within that paradigm presupposes a sexual contract that puts a premium on patriarchal rights (Pateman 1988). The state as well as administrations of any sort are structured along principles of patriarchy; their culture is governed by male alliances and entrenched with masculinism (Kreisky 1999; Sauer 2001).

If gender mainstreaming is to stand a chance, the weight of these factors has to be counterbalanced somewhat by engaging in discourse with women active in movement-based gender politics. The discourse in turn has to be institutionalised in mechanisms of participation. At the same time the structures of interface and participation have to allow for a certain externality. Otherwise institutional rationales would all too easily superimpose themselves and cease to be challenged. In other words, the top-down approach of gender mainstreaming needs to be complemented with interaction with bottom-up movement impulses in order to relate to the direct representation and articulation of gender realities and demands. Introducing so-called gender budgets, more suitably referred to as gender-differentiated analysis of corporate and public budgets, could well provide a useful additional instrument to that effect.

7.5.2 Discourse and hybridity

The issue of interaction and participation raises the question of the shape the women's movement is in today. The debate on adequate forms of organisation—traditional group-based, collective movement politics versus networks of professional women individually committed to redressing gender imbalances—carries a generational bias with younger women preferring the latter. But whether action is based on organised collectives with a certain amount of continuity or on looser networks mobilised in ad hoc fashion, with gender mainstreaming, advocates of gender justice and gender democracy have to be able to master both rationales, that of administrations as well as that of social movements.

In her analysis of the Latin American experience with 'engendering democracy', Sonia Alvarez (1990, 1997, 1999), taking it from the field of cultural studies, introduced the concept of hybridity and uses it as an analytical yardstick. She conceptualises hybridity as the condition that allows women's organisations to balance bureaucratic demands and neoliberal rationale with the dynamics and perspectives of social movements in search of political, economic and social gender justice. 'De-hybridisation'— that is, the loss of that balancing grasp—will compromise the agency of women's organisations. Therefore, Alvarez insists on the need to explore the interaction between an administratively mediated system rationale and the dynamics and aspirations of the women's movements.

Such a self-monitoring strategy would be equally relevant in Europe. Much could be gained from an interface analysis that conceptualises gender mainstreaming as negotiation space between actors of different social character. Such analysis could help women's organisation and feminist professionals to identify the conditions and circumstances most conducive to the introduction of strategic gender policy aspects, at the same time as to closely monitor their own capacity to retain that difficult and delicate balance of hybridity required for gender mainstreaming. Monitoring and analysing the 'encounters at the interface' (Long 1989), to use a phrase coined in the field of development, could also contribute to more democratic interaction between citizens and public and private executive administrations.

7.5.3 Discourse and the public sphere

Institution politics is arcane politics. Experience with gender mainstreaming in development agencies has shown the many forms and fashion institutional resistance and sabotage can take and the extent to which these reactions carry personal, frequently quite intimate meanings and connotations. In fact, in concurrence with the official introduction of gender mainstreaming, unofficial, but quite consensual and highly efficient modes of resistance are being elaborated. Yet it is virtually impossible to expose carefully crafted inner-institutional blockages and to interfere with their formation at an early stage. While mobbing is by now considered a breach of law and of inner-agency peace, building counter-alliances to gender mainstreaming is not. Obligations of confidentiality will not permit recourse to the public sphere.

As a consequence, evaluations may very well reflect results, but are unable to capture the process. The decisive questions—does the top-down approach of gender mainstreaming induce a trickle-down process and, if so, what exactly is trickling down to whom, how is it received and how is it implemented?—are still awaiting answers. We know precious little about the 'filters' that may block, divert, dilute or reduce gender mainstreaming to a minor innovation that documents 'modernness' and embellishes the annual report or website. Or, rather, what we do know remains anecdotal and subject to discretion. On the one hand, this is a major impediment to meaningful participation and interaction with institutions. Any demand or recommendation originating outside of the organisation may all too easily be discarded as being out of tune with the operative modes and constraints of the agency. On the other hand, relevant experiences made within institutions are silenced and cut off from public debate. By the same token the public continues to be fed with the rhetorics of gender mainstreaming while remaining uninformed about implementation barriers, bottlenecks, the impact of informal mechanisms of resistance and the like. As a consequence, core elements of democracy—transparency and deliberation—are missing, or at least find it very difficult to be acted out. Therefore, for gender mainstreaming to unfold its democratising potential, institutional knowledge and experience have to develop modes of accountability and have to open themselves to discourse in the public sphere. In turn, this could be a substantial stepping-stone towards a more democratic society.

7.6 Conclusion

By its very nature gender mainstreaming as an institutional strategy holds a certain potential to enrich the formal structures of democracy by making institutions more inclusive in terms of equal opportunity and equal access for women, by complementing them with the formal elements of gender democracy. However, past experience shows for this democratising process to happen the implementation of gender mainstreaming has to leave the confines of discrete institutional walls and has to engage in public discourse, thus broadening the space of the political. The continued restrictions imposed on women in social, public and political life can be overcome only by embarking on a debate in the public sphere that encompasses a review and revision of the fundamental objectives and values of the given societal order. That kind of debate would indeed carry transformative dynamics.

Women's organisations in the global South actually are more concrete and more demanding in their analysis. They point to decades of experience with development models not delivering on their promises, even severely damaging the lives of women. As a consequence, they see gender mainstreaming, which aims at the realisation of at least equal opportunity if not equality of results, inextricably linked with the need for profound changes in the prevailing macro-economic and macro-political order. Because neoliberal structural adjustment and corporate-driven globalisation constantly erode social development and systematically produce gender-unjust results, gender mainstreaming of necessity will have to be embedded in a transformative critique of prevailing growth strategies.

This as it were dialectical vision contrasts somewhat with the additive approach implicitly or explicitly at work in many studies of the functioning of gender mainstreaming in Europe. Institutionalised gender mainstreaming, so the argument runs, may very well work, but will at best produce integration of women into a highly unsatisfactory status quo of social and political life. Therefore a transformative aspect, such as sustainable development, has to be *added*. It may, however, be appropriate to give more attention and more credence to the experience of women in those parts of the world that look on a much longer history of gender mainstreaming. According to that experience gender mainstreaming can unfold its meaning only to the extent that the integration and instrumentalisation of repressive gender regimes in the prevailing mode of economic and social reproduction is challenged.

References

Alvarez, S. (1990) *Engendering Democracy in Brazil: Women's Movements in Transition Politics* (Princeton, NJ: Princeton University Press).

—— (1997) 'Contradictions of a "Women's Space" in a Male-Dominant State: The Political Role of the Commission on the Status of Women in Post-Authoritarian Brazil', in K. Staudt (ed.), *Women, International Development and Politics: The Bureaucratic Mire* (Philadelphia, PA: Temple University Press).

—— (1999) 'Advocating Feminism: The Latinamerican Feminist NGO Boom', *International Feminist Journal of Politics* 1.2 (September 1999): 181-209.

Anderson, M. (1993) *Focussing on Women: UNIFEM's Experience in Mainstreaming* (New York: UN).

Bakker, I. (ed.) (1994) *The Strategic Silence: Gender and Economic Policy* (London: Zed Books)

Elson, D. (1991) *Male Bias in the Development Process* (Manchester, UK: Manchester University Press).

European Community (1996) *Incorporating Equal Opportunities for Women and Men into All Community Policies and Activities* (COM[96]67final; Brussels: European Community).

Femina politica (2002) 'Geschlechterdemokratie: Ein neues feministisches Leitbild?', *Femina politica: Zeitschrift für feministische Politik-Wissenschaft* 11.2.

Goetz, A. (1995) *The Politics of Integrating Gender to State Development Processes* (Occasional Paper 2; Geneva: UNRISD).

—— (ed.) (1997) *Getting Institutions Right for Women in Development* (London: Zed Books).

Gradin, A. (1999) 'Equal Opportunities in Community Policies: Eriksson Report on Gender Mainstreaming', speaking note, 8 March 1999.

Jahan, R. (1995) *The Elusive Agenda: Mainstreaming Women in Development* (London: Zed Books).

Kabeer, N. (1994) *Reversed Realities: Gender Hierarchies in Development Thought* (London/New York: Verso).

Kreisky, E. (1999) 'Wieder verborgene Geschlechtlichkeit: Die maskuline Unterseite politischer Gerechtigkeitsdiskurse', in A. Dornheim, W. Franzen, A. Thumfart and A. Waschkuhn (eds.), *Gerechtigkeit: Interdisziplinäre Grundlagen* (Opladen/Wiesbaden, Germany: Westdeutscher Verlag): 168-207.

Long, N. (ed.) (1989) *Encounters at the Interface: A Perspective on Social Discontinuities in Rural Development* (Wageningen, Netherlands).

Longwe, S.H. (1997) 'The Evaporation of Gender Policies in the Patriarchal Cooking Pot', *Development Practice* 7.2 (May 1997): 148-56.

Macdonald, M. (ed.) (1994) *Gender Planning in Development Agencies: Meeting the Challenge* (Oxford, UK: Oxfam).

Moser, C.O. (1993) *Gender Planning in Development: Theory, Practice and Training* (London: Routledge).

Palmer, I. (1994) *Social and Gender Issues in Macro-economic Advice* (Eschborn, Germany: GTZ).

Pateman, C. (1988) *The Sexual Contract* (Stanford, CA: Stanford University Press).

Razavi, S., and C. Miller (1995a) *From WID to GAD: Conceptional Shifts in the Women and Development Discourse* (Occasional Papers 1; Geneva: UNRISD).

—— and —— (1995b) *Gender Mainstreaming: A Study of Efforts by the UNDP, the World Bank and the ILO to Institutionalize Gender Issues* (Occasional Papers 4; Geneva: UNRISD).

Sassen, S. (1998) 'Towards a Feminist Analysis of the Global Economy', *Indiana Journal of Global Legal Studies* 4: 129-45.

Sauer, B. (2001) *Die Asche des Souveräns: Staat und Demokratie in der Geschlechterdebatte* (Frankfurt/New York: Campus Verlag).

Scott, G. (1979) *Recognising the Invisible Woman in Development: The World Bank's Experience* (Washington, DC: World Bank Publications).

Sen, G., and C. Grown (1987) *Development, Crisis and Alternative Visions: Third World Women's Perspective* (London: Earthscan Publications).

Staudt, K. (1997) *The Bureaucratic Mire* (Philadelphia, PA: Temple University Press).

—— (1998) *Policy, Politics and Gender: Women Gaining Ground* (West Hartford, CT: Kumarian Press).

Von Braunmühl, C. (1997) 'Mainstreaming Gender oder von den Grenzen, dieses zu tun', in M. Braig, U. Ferdinand and M. Zapata (eds.), *Begegnungen und Einmischungen: Festschrift für Renate Rott zum 60. Geburtstag* (Histoamericana 4; Stuttgart: Akademischer Verlag).

—— (1998) 'Gender and Transformation: Nachdenkliches zu den Anstrengungen einer Beziehung', in E. Kreisky and B. Sauer (eds.), *Geschlechterverhältnisse im Kontext politischer Transformation* (Politische Vierteljahresschrift 38. Jg. Sonderheft 28).

—— (2001a) 'Gender Mainstreaming Worldwide: Rekonstruktion einer Reise um die Welt', *ÖZP* 30 (2001/2): 183-201.

—— (2001b) 'Zur Universalismusdebatte in der internationalen Frauenbewegung: Konzepte einer transnationalen Genderpolitik', *Feministische Perspektiven in der Politikwissenschaft. Femina politica: Zeitschrift für feministische Politikwissenschaft* 10.2: 129-41.

Wichterich, C. (2001) *The Globalised Woman: Reports from a Future of Inequality* (London: Zed Books).

Woodward, A.E. (2001) *Gender Mainstreaming in European Policy: Innovation or Deception?* (Discussion paper; Berlin: WZB)

8

Governance and participatory approaches in Europe*

Angela Liberatore

European Commission, Directorate General for Research, Belgium

Participation is a fundamental, and sometimes controversial, aspect of the European debate and experience of governance. Since governance is not an exclusive domain of governments and other public actors, the question of who participates in governance processes and institutions is a truly crucial one. Is direct participation of civil society in policy development a threat or a complement to democratic representative institutions? What is, actually, 'civil society'? Does participation increase 'the intelligence of democracy' (Lindblom 1965), or lead to privatisation of government by economic and other non-state actors? Does participation enhance both 'input and output legitimacy' (Scharpf 1996), that is, both policy process and policy outcomes, or does it expand the first at the expenses of the other? Can participation help early identification and resolution of conflicts? These questions are at the core of debate on governance and participation. Some of them were tackled during the formulation of, and responses to, the European Commission's White Paper on Governance (EC 2001a); participation also emerged as important during the debate on the EU constitutional treaty.

Recent developments seem to point to some shifting from informal to formal approaches to participation. For example, the setting of minimum standards of consultation (EC, COM[2002]704final) is an explicit attempt to respond to the quest for more transparency over who participates, when and how in EU policy-making. At the same time, informal venues of pressure and lobbying remain an important feature of multi-level (from local, to national, European and global) policy formulation. Are we witnessing a new 'co-existence' between formal and informal approaches to consultations, and what are the implications?

Participation has been a founding feature of discourses and practices of sustainable development, from the focus on communities' participation in the Brundtland Report (WCED 1987) to the experience of Local Agendas 21 (Lafferty 2001). At the same time, governance—and the role of participation—remains an often 'implicit pillar' in policy statements that acknowledge the ecological, economic and social dimension of sustainable development (EC 2001c). Such an 'implicit pillar' is, however, at the core of

---

* The views expressed in this chapter are those of the author and do not necessarily represent the view of the European Commission.

proposals for policy frameworks and instruments and for institutional reform, and came to focus on the occasion of the World Summit on Sustainable Development held in Johannesburg in September 2002. Environmental advocacy organisations, among the pioneers in demanding and helping to achieve more participation of non-governmental actors in policy-making, raised the question of whether the private sector was taking ownership of the sustainable development agenda. Here, some of the questions raised above, such as the relations between participation and democratic representations, prove their specific as well as general relevance: that is, their relevance to a specific area of policy development and, at the same time, their significance for other policy areas and beyond Europe, at the global level.

The analysis offered below starts with an overview of participatory approaches and practices in Europe with a focus on the European Union context and policy-making process and continues with some reflections on their impacts and prospects. The main conclusion of the analysis is that participation is increasingly presented as a key factor to address legitimacy and effectiveness problems; however, it provides increased legitimacy and effectiveness only under specific circumstances of accountability, balance, relevance and transparency. In short, participation improves both policy processes and outcomes if the balance between different interests, forms of knowledge and values is achieved, if participation is seen as and proves to be relevant to the tackling of issues of genuine concern, if the participation process is sufficiently transparent to allow for democratic scrutiny, and if responsibilities can be identified.

8.1 Participatory practices

Participatory procedures have been implemented in Europe (in different ways, frequency and depth) in several areas, including technology and risk assessment, environment, consumer and health protection, research policy, development of transport infrastructures, trade agreements and product regulation. Some procedures focus on specific levels of debate and decision-making (from Local Agenda 21 initiatives to consultations on European policy proposals or the involvement of civil-society organisations in the context of global environmental and trade negotiations). Even with such specification, most participatory procedures address issues of concern and are decided on across many geographical areas and levels of responsibility.[1]

Procedures can be mainly 'issue-based' (e.g. participatory technology assessment [PTA]) or 'generic' (e.g. citizens' juries); however, this is mainly a matter of 'starting point' rather than of diversity in substance. For example, PTA procedures address a specific area for debate on policy options and decisions—that is, those involving the development or application of certain technologies—but at the same time link with several other (non-technological) issues ranging from behaviours and attitudes to economic or

---

1   Within the rich literature on participatory approaches in Europe, some research with an explicitly comparative dimension is worth mentioning: for example, the projects EUROPTA (Klüver et al. 1999), PESTO (Jamison 1999), ULYSSES (Jaeger et al. 1999), VISIONS (Rotmans et al. 2001), PARADYS (Bora et al. 2001) and TRUSTNET (Dubreuil et al. 2000).

legal matters. It must also be noted that participatory procedures can be seen as including a continuum between 'passive' and 'active' participation, between 'purely consultative' and 'fully interactive'. While the passive and purely consultative side tends to prevail, different circumstances (from access to political and legal systems, resources and others discussed later in this chapter) can determine more active and interactive participation.

Participatory procedures can put the general public in focus (while, of course, involving 'samples' either pre-selected by the organisers or self-selected by those intending to participate) or target specific 'stakeholders' from the start. Internet-based consultations (e.g. on green and white papers by national and European institutions), consensus conferences, citizens' juries and focus groups tend to involve 'the public'. Other procedures—for example, scenario workshops—target specific actors (policy-makers, groups targeted by policy initiatives and experts). Many procedures are organised on an ad hoc basis, while others are provided for in legal texts: for example, consultations within the framework of environmental impact assessment (EIA) legislation, or related to the authorisation of deliberate release of genetically modified organisms (GMOs). More generally, some participatory procedures have a formal nature (through legal and administrative instruments) while others are informal (from lobbying to social mobilisation). Participatory procedures can be initiated by institutions (e.g. public hearings by parliaments, local and national governments), by interest groups and by advocacy groups.[2]

While some procedures aim at consensus, at least in their name, most procedures tend to identify major areas of agreement and disagreement (e.g. by making explicit minority views), and to prevent or mitigate acute conflict through debate and argumentation. In this regard, participatory procedures can be seen as mechanisms for social conflict resolution; issues of inclusiveness, timeliness, and of real—rather than 'cosmetic'—debate are crucial for participatory procedures to be able to fulfil such a task.

The role of the mass media and of the diffusion of information technologies (IT) cannot be underestimated when examining participatory procedures. The media are powerful vehicles for the voices of diverse interests and opinions, as well as agenda setters by selecting or ignoring and framing specific issues in terms of risk, responsibility and other aspects that can prompt state, economic and/or public advocacy actors to initiate formal or informal participatory procedures. As to IT, the various declensions of '*e*' (*e*-government, *e*-democracy, *e*-participation, etc.) are currently used to indicate the pervasiveness of these technologies in organising 'interfaces' between public authorities and citizens (see, for example, the Electronic Democracy European Network[3]). At the same time, the notion of 'digital divide' indicates that such pervasiveness is by no means universal and symmetrical in terms of power relations and economic and social conditions. For example, problems of seriously imbalanced inputs to Internet-based consultation on green or white papers were noted by the European Commission in areas such as regulation of PVC and others (EC 2001b).

---

2   For example, petitions, requests for referenda, assemblies and other initiatives by employers' and employees' associations, and by consumers', environmental, human rights, patients', students' and women's organisations among others.

3   See europa.eu.int/information_society/activities/egovernment_research/doc/project_synopsis/syn_eden.pdf.

In short, there is an extensive, diverse and dynamic experience with participatory practices in Europe. Their implications for governance and democracy can also be seen as extensive, diverse and dynamic.

8.2 Participation, governance and democracy

When examining the implications of participatory procedures for governance (and, in turn, the implications of changing governance modes for participatory procedures), a first issue that comes into focus is the reconfiguration of the relations between public and private actors. Answering the question 'who governs' is no longer easy (in case it ever was). Since governance is not the exclusive competence of states, the forms and impacts of involvement of non-state actors is the 'novelty' to be analysed. This leads to the question of who is entitled to participate, how, why, and under which conditions.

The variety of definitions of 'civil society' does not seem conducive to answering the question of who participates with any precision. Such definitions range from including as civil society all non-state actors, from grass-roots groups to transnational corporations (ECS 1999), to considering civil society as distinct from both state and market (Crouch *et al.* 2001). While the second approach has the merit of singling out the specific feature of economic interests compared with other social actors, it is still necessary to seek further specifications of actors involved in governance. A useful typology of 'holders', persons and organisations that possess some quality or resource that entitles them to participate, was developed by Philippe Schmitter (2002) within the broader framework of analysis of participatory governance. The quality or resources of 'holders' include: rights (for citizens), spatial location (for residents), knowledge (for experts), share (for owners), stake (for those affected by a decision, both beneficiaries and victims), interests (for private- or public-interest spokespersons) and status (for representatives of economic, social or political groups).

With such distinction in mind, we get closer to the identification of major issues involved in designing and implementing participatory approaches. Different 'holders' can participate in different ways and configurations; having the resources that entitle them to participate in governance does not mean they will indeed participate, or that they will do so on equal footing. The main determinant of who participates and how, the design and implementation of participatory procedure, depends to a great extent on the reasons for initiating and for getting involved in a participatory procedure. Such reasons vary from seeking legitimacy (e.g. through inclusiveness in the process) and effectiveness (including at implementation stages) of policies, to democratising institutions, improving the credibility and image of those involved (as open, reliable, etc.), to stabilising or changing power relations (e.g. within and between levels of governance, or within and between public and private sectors). These motivations lead to a number of options with regard to 'holders' participation. For example, for governance to be inclusive and legitimate, the variety of 'holders' needs to be as broad as possible; for governance to be effective and efficient, the 'holders' having a specific capacity or stake should be privileged; for governance to be democratic, the role of citizens and representative institutions must be in focus.

In current debate on European governance, issues of legitimacy and effectiveness are focused on, as well as their relation to the issue of (further) democratising the European Union (EC 2001a; Joerges *et al.* 2001; Liberatore 2004). The latter includes the debate on the development of a European public sphere, a sphere for debate on, and participation in, decisions, taking into account the specificity (and greater diversity) of the European context compared with national ones (Giorgi *et al.* 2002; Koopmans 2002; Risse *et al.* 2003; Strath *et al.* 2002). In this context, it is necessary to turn to the question of whether and how participatory procedures can 'deliver' in terms of legitimacy, effectiveness and democratisation.

This depends on a number of specific conditions, including balance and resources, relevance, accountability and transparency. For example, broad but extremely imbalanced participation will not lead to inclusiveness and legitimacy; actually, broad but merely 'cosmetic' participation is likely to result in disenchantment of participants, and in lower legitimacy and credibility of the initiators. A too narrow selection of 'holders' might seem efficient in terms of monetary or time resources, but will miss the input of competences and the full understanding of stakes that are essential to deliver effective decisions. Also, losing sight of the role of representative institutions within a generic notion of participation would lead to decreasing scrutiny and legitimacy, while an exclusive focus on representative institutions could lead to the neglect of forms of direct participation that are vital for democratic debate. On the basis of such examples and reasoning, it is necessary to provide for some balance to avoid the 'capture' of participatory procedures by some 'holders' with more resources. It is also necessary to find provisions for transparency so that it can be possible in principle to trace who was involved, at what stage and how.

In all cases, it is fundamental to establish accountability so that, whatever the shape of participation, it is possible to identify who is ultimately co-responsible (both public and private actors) for the formulation, implementation or evaluation of a certain measure. Of course, these are and remain procedural safeguards that will never lead to the abolition of lobbying and co-optation 'behind closed doors'. What they can offer is to interpret in a 'governance' perspective the normal checks and balances of liberal democracies; and they can enhance procedures of deliberative democracy that are doomed to irrelevance in case accountability is not clear, or to failure in case of imbalanced or non-transparent processes. As to substantive democracy, it is increasingly clear that rights are not only political but also social and economic (as recognised in the European Charter of Fundamental Rights); participatory governance can help to find the balance between them when conducted within a democratic framework.

8.3 Participation and sustainable development

As this chapter is part of a broader reflection on governance and sustainable development, it can be useful to examine the specific implication of participation for sustainable development. The Brundtland report (WCED 1987) as well as Agenda 21 and Local Agenda 21 adopted at the UNCED (UN Conference on Environment and Development) of 1992 stressed the importance of participation in the pursuit of sustainable development. Procedures for EIA and more recently sustainability impact assessment[4] also emphasise the need to involve local populations and other actors. A basic argument in this regard is that the search for ecological, economic and social compatibility requires that all views can be put 'on the table' and that decision can be checked and challenged. Indeed, such argument needs to be tested against a number of issues. These are briefly indicated below.

Does participation help in overcoming 'sectoralisation' of policy? This is a basic ingredient for tackling the complexity and interdependence of environmental, economic and social processes. It is also a challenge to current governance modes where sectoral policies, administrative structures and political agendas tend to exclude 'cross-cutting' issues from consideration, or prove incapable of handling them if such issues succeed in emerging.

Also, is participation improving the managing of public goods? Clearly 'who participates' is especially important here. Concerns are often expressed about an increasing influence of the private sector in public decisions that might lead to disregard for, or inappropriate management of, public goods such as water or health. Corporate social responsibility schemes aim at responding to such concerns, with different degrees of success.

The influence of participation in tackling distributive aspects should also be examined. The possibility of avoiding distributive conflicts and accommodating everybody by simply 'expanding the cake'—for example, uncontrolled use of natural resources or postponement of decisions (e.g. on pension schemes) to later generations—is not feasible. Equitably 'sharing the cake' becomes then an issue that cannot be shifted or postponed and that involves important governance and participation issues: for example, the balanced representation of interests within and between countries, and between generations (who represents or participates on behalf of future generations?).

The latter point is also very important with regard to the need to avoid 'short-termism' in policy-making. Electoral and investment cycles, which are crucial when deciding on issues such as infrastructures, tend in fact to be too short to deal with long-term changes and to take care of future generations as sustainable development principles prescribe.

Finally, does participation improve the development and diffusion of knowledge? The development and use of knowledge and 'expertise' is a key feature of governance and of sustainable development as many complex issues need to be tackled that require scientific as well as practical knowledge. Expertise itself needs to be 'democratised' to contribute to public debate and decision-making. This is especially the case when, as in many sustainable development issues, 'minority views' may prove more accurate in anticipating risks or where local and indigenous knowledge is crucial to the identification of both problems and solutions.

These issues, suggested as a sort of analytical 'checklist' to examine the implications of participation for sustainable development, rather than to provide answers that

---

4   Proposed by WWF in the 1980s (WWF 1986), sustainability impact assessment (SIA) was endorsed by the European Commission, Directorate General for Trade, in 1999: europa.eu.int/comm/ trade/sia/pro60203_en.htm. Interestingly, SIA raises the important issue of participation also of 'stakeholders' from non-European countries, namely from developing countries, in trade agreements and measures.

would require much longer discussion, point us to the question of the impacts of participatory procedures for European governance.

8.4 What impacts of participatory procedures, and what prospects?

In conclusion, does participation matter, and how? Table 8.1 tries to visualise various features of participatory procedures, including possible impacts, from a generic perspective. With regard to the specifics of the European Union context, several policy initiatives indicate that participation is by now considered a 'matter of fact' that characterises European governance. Such initiatives, namely the Communications issued as follow-up to the White Paper on Governance, deal with a number of issues strongly related to, or involving, participation. These are: the formalisation of consultation (COM[2002]704 final, Communication on minimum standards of consultation), the need for partnership between local, regional, national and European authorities (COM[2002]709 final, Communication on tripartite contracts), the need for argumentation and impact assessment of policy proposals (COM[2002]276 final, Communication on impact assessment), and the need to extend the notion of expertise to include practical knowledge (COM[2002]713 final, Communication on the collection and use of expertise).

Such initiatives show that participation is considered as an important element to address legitimacy (e.g. standards for consultation) and effectiveness (e.g. impact assessment). They might lead to significant impacts in terms of policy process and outcomes, on the changing of initial conditions and on actors' perception and behaviour. More specifically, more transparent procedures for consultation and better involvement of local authorities and communities can enhance policy legitimacy. Breadth of expertise and inclusion of practical knowledge in impact assessment and various stages of policy-making can increase policy learning and effectiveness including in relation to sustainability objectives. In addition, measures to improve access and transparency and the requirements to provide stronger argumentation, also based on inputs through participatory procedures, of policy and legislative proposals, can lead to a stronger sense of involvement by citizens in European matters. Finally, a new 'co-existence' can be developed between formal and informal procedures of consultation, with formalisation possibly empowering some less resourceful actors if balance is properly taken into account.

Implementing the above-mentioned Communications will involve tackling issues such as possible trade-offs between participation and time efficiency or budgetary resources, changes in administrative culture (e.g. in the European Commission) and in political cultures predominantly nation-based, diversity of experience with participatory approaches in an enlarging European Union, and other factors. With regard to this last aspect, the usefulness of participatory procedures in early identification and mediation of conflicts should not be underestimated as diverse economic, social and cultural situations may increase the likelihood of distributive and other conflicts. In short, the potential for extending participatory approaches that might improve policy legitimacy

Participatory features	Examples of participatory procedures			
Why?	*Increase legitimacy*	*Increase effectiveness*	*Identify and resolve conflicts*	*Change power relations*
How?	*Formal:* e.g. hearings, consultations on legislative proposals, referenda, EIA procedures	*Informal:* e.g. ad hoc groups, unsolicited inputs, lobbying	*Restricted:* e.g. expert advisory committees; focus groups	*Broad:* e.g. Internet-based consultation (language might restrict)
Where?	*Policy fields:* technology/risk assessment, environmental, employment, industrial, regional, science, trade policies, etc.	*Levels:* local (e.g. LA21) regional (foresight exercises), national (referenda), European (consultations on green/white papers)	*Space:* physical (for face-to-face meetings), virtual (e.g. IT); related to levels and 'how' aspects	
When? (what policy phases; often not linear sequence)	*Problem definition* (e.g. foresight, scenario workshops)	*Policy formulation* (e.g. consensus conf., consultation on green papers)	*Policy implementation* (e.g. EIA, consensus conf.)	*Evaluation, monitoring* (e.g. ad hoc panels)
Who?	*Initiators:* local communities, national governments, European institutions, advocacy groups, experts, media	*Core participants:* initiators of some procedures can be core participants in others in various configurations (depending on how/where features; see above)	*Mediators:* mass media (as vehicles of voice, pressure, lobbies), intermediary institutions (e.g. between science, policy, public)	*Peripheral participant:* actors involved in related issues or levels but not directly in the one(s) at stake
What conditions?	*Access and transparency:* to/of political and legal systems	*Balance (and related resources):* time, knowledge, money, space	*Accountability:* tracking back and identifying responsibilities	*Relevance:* of issues for participants
What impacts?	*On policy process:* legitimacy, inclusiveness, democratisation, learning	*On policy outcome:* effectiveness, implementability, sustainability	*On initial conditions:* access, resources, relevance	*On actors':* behaviour, perceptions, status, relations

TABLE 8.1 Features and impacts of participatory procedures

and effectiveness is significant; its transformation in reality will require strong commitment from all actors of European governance—from citizens to the political and economic elite at various levels and in various areas of public life.

References

Bora, A., *et al.* (2001) PARADYS: *Participation and the Dynamics of Social Positioning. The Case of Biotechnology: State of the Art Report* (DG Research Key Action 'Improving the Socio-economic Knowledge Base', 5th FP; Brussels: European Commission, www.uni-bielefeld.de/iwt/paradys).

Crouch, C., K. Eder and D. Tambini (eds.) (2001) *Citizenship, Markets, and the State* (Oxford, UK: Oxford University Press).

Dubreuil, G.H., *et al.* (2000) *The Trustnet Framework: A New Perspective on Risk Governance* (DG Research, Nuclear fission safety programme, EUR 19136; Brussels: European Commission).

ECS (1999) 'Economic and Social Committee, Opinion of 22/9/1999', *Official Journal of the EC* C 329 (17 November 1999): 10.

EC (European Commission) (2001a) *White Paper on European Governance* (COM[2001]428, 25 July 2001; Brussels: EC).

—— (2001b) *Democratising Expertise and Establishing Scientific Reference Systems: Report of the Working Group 1b for the White Paper on Governance* (Brussels: EC; europa.eu.int/comm/governance/areas/index_en.htm).

—— (2001c) *A Sustainable Europe for a Better World: A European Strategy for Sustainable Development* (COM[2001]264 final; Brussels: EC).

Giorgi, L., *et al.* (2002) *A European Public Space Observatory: Assembling Information that Allows the Monitoring of European Democracy* (Key Action 'Improving the Socio-economic Knowledge Base', 5th FP; Brussels: European Commission, www.iccr-international.org/europub).

Jaeger, C., *et al.* (1999) ULYSSES: *Tools for Citizens Participation* (DG Research, Environment Programme, 4th FP; Brussels: European Commission).

Jamison, A. (1999) PESTO: *Public Engagement and Science and Technology Policy Options, Final Report* (DG Research: TSER Programme, 4th FP; Brussels: European Commission).

Joerges, C., Y. Meny and J. Weiler (eds.) (2001) *Mountain or Molehill? A Critical Appraisal of the Commission White Paper on Governance* (Florence and Harvard Law School: European University Institute).

Klüver, L., *et al.* (1999) EUROPTA: *European Participatory Technology Assessment, Final Report* (DG Research: TSER Programme, 4th FP; Brussels: European Commission).

Koopmans, R. (2002) *The Transformation of Political Mobilisation and Communication in European Public Spheres* (Key Action 'Improving the Socio-economic Knowledge Base', 5th FP; Brussels: European Commission; uropub.wz-berlin.de).

Lafferty, W. (ed.) (2001) *Sustainable Communities in Europe* (London: Earthscan Publications).

Liberatore, A. (2004) 'Governance and Democracy: Reflections on the European Debate', in B. Abraham and S. Munshi (eds.), *Good Governance in Democratic Societies* (London: Sage).

Lindblom, C. (1965) *The Intelligence of Democracy: Decision Making through Mutual Adjustment* (New York: The Free Press).

Risse, T., *et al.* (2003) 'Europeanization, Collective Identities and Public Discourse', www.iue.it/RSCAS/Research/Tools/IDNET.

Rotmans, J., *et al.* (2001) *Visions: Integrated Visions for a Sustainable Europe: Final Report* (DG Research, Environment Research Programme, 4th FP; Brussels: European Commission).

Scharpf, F. (1996) 'Democratic Policy in Europe', *European Law Journal* 2: 136-55.

Schmitter, P. (2002) 'Participation in Governance Arrangements: Is There any Reason to Expect it Will Achieve "Sustainable and Innovative Policies in a Multilevel Context"?', in J. Grote and B. Gbikpi (eds.), *Participatory Governance: Political and Societal Implications* (Opladen, Germany: Leske & Budrich).

Strath, B., A. Triandafyllidou *et al.* (2002) 'Representations of Europe and the Nation in Current and Prospective Member-States: Media, Élites and Civil Society', improving-ser.sti.jrc.it/default.

WCED (World Commission on Environment and Development) (1987) *Our Common Future* (Oxford, UK: Oxford University Press).

WWF (1986) *An Effective Multistakeholder Process for Sustainability Assessment: Critical Elements* (Geneva: WWF).

9

Partnerships and networks in global environmental governance
MOVING TO THE NEXT STAGE*

Jan Martin Witte and Thorsten Benner
Global Public Policy Institute

Charlotte Streck
Global Public Policy Institute and Climate Focus BV

After the protracted preparatory process, most delegates to the 2002 World Summit on Sustainable Development (WSSD) had few illusions as to the eventual outcomes. Yet even these modest expectations went unfulfilled.

Simply decrying the failure of formal summit diplomacy to advance state commitments to sustainable development, however, misses the new and remarkable element of the Johannesburg process. The transition from pure intergovernmental conference diplomacy to a broader notion of 'environmental governance', involving not only governments and international organisations but also businesses and non-governmental organisations (NGOs) for the first time took a world stage.

Few would deny that the debate on the greater role for public–private partnerships (or, in UN jargon, 'Type II outcomes'[1]) was the most striking and novel element of the Summit held in Johannesburg in September 2002. Yet there is broad disagreement on whether this new development is positive. Many find fault in the risks associated with the 'jazzier dance' of partnerships and multi-sectoral governance. Critical NGOs regard the new partnership lingo as a shrewd effort by governments to abdicate their responsibility in promoting sustainable development through new binding commitments. They argue that the partnership approach may undermine formal intergovernmental

---

* This chapter was prepared as part of the Global Public Policy Institute's Research Program in late 2002. This project was financially supported by the Hans Böckler Foundation and the Heinrich Böll Foundation. For more information on the Global Public Policy Institute, see our website at www.globalpublicpolicy.net.

1 As opposed to 'Type I outcomes', which refer to intergovernmental agreements and declarations, such as the Johannesburg Political Declaration and the Johannesburg Implementation Plan of Action (WSSD 2002a, b).

processes through a 'privatisation' of the United Nations. Critics opine that much of what may be perceived as corporate environmentalism is merely 'greenwash': an attempt to achieve the appearance of a social and environmental conscience without corresponding substance. In addition, a coalition of developing countries lobbied until the very end against the adoption of partnerships as an official outcome of the Summit. Their mistrust was based on the fear that the introduction of partnerships would lift pressure from industrialised countries to provide additional resources for sustainable development.

This criticism and concern is a consequence of the failure of the WSSD to clearly define the partnership concept. No comprehensive understanding was developed of what to expect from partnerships and what role various actors should play. On a broader level, it also remained unclear how 'Type II outcomes' were to relate to the official intergovernmental process and the negotiation of binding commitments during the Summit. The result was that the two processes co-existed but without substantial interaction or an exploration of their complementarities.

Simply embracing or completely discarding these new forms of networked governance out of hand appears short-sighted. Instead, we need a forward-looking and critical assessment of the potential role as well as the limitations of collaborative partnerships in promoting sustainable development.

9.1 Conceptual framework: how to analyse and categorise partnerships

During the preparatory process for the Johannesburg Summit, government delegates agreed on a preliminary and vague definition of partnerships, stating that they are 'specific commitments by various partners intended to contribute to and reinforce the implementation of outcomes of the intergovernmental negotiations of the WSSD and to help achieve the further implementation of Agenda 21 and the Millennium Development Goals' (Kara and Quarless 2002). They also produced a long list of recommendations for how partnerships should be organised and how they should be operating. Irrespective of these preparations, the approach taken by the delegates was so broad and unfocused that it resulted in an anything-goes policy for partnerships in the WSSD context. The 228 'partnerships' listed to this date on the WSSD website[2] feature a broad range of organisational forms, procedural rules and objectives, making it almost impossible to compare across cases and to establish benchmarks for best practice.

At this early stage in the development of environmental governance, a case can be made for a proliferation of different types and forms of partnership. At the same time, wanton creation of partnerships without concern for impact, accountability or ethical behaviour might result in worse-than-nothing outcomes. Thus, there is an urgent need for a better conceptual understanding of partnerships in order to assess their potential

2   Accessible at www.johannesburgsummit.org/html/sustainable_dev/partnership_initiatives.html (accessed 7 November 2002).

as well as their limitations and to initiate a framework to guide partnership formation in a direction that is both effective and ethical.

Various observers have suggested that partnerships are part of a phenomenon that has attracted growing attention in recent years among researchers and policy-makers, known as 'global public policy networks' (Reinicke *et al.* 2000). Indeed, the global public policy framework can bring much-needed clarity and helpful guidance to the debate on partnerships. In fact, we believe that taking this framework as a basis for further discussions on the future of Type II outcomes in the WSSD is critical to move the debate to the next stage, and to arrive at a balanced assessment of the potential as well as the limitations of partnerships as a part of the overall system of global environmental governance.

9.1.1 Key properties of global public policy networks

Global public policy networks have emerged over the past two decades in response to the growing pressures to find practical solutions to complex global problems that cannot be effectively addressed by individual actors alone. The absence of a centralised governmental and rule-making structure and attendant bureaucratic procedures has provided space for innovation and experimentation. In many cases, multi-sectoral networks have developed in response to the failure of traditional state-centred governance solutions to complex problems.

Networks bring together actors from various sectors. Spanning socioeconomic, political and cultural gaps, networks manage relationships that otherwise degenerate into counterproductive confrontation.

We suggest that the Type II outcomes of the WSSD process should be analysed and interpreted in the same conceptual framework as global public policy networks. Similar to the problems they were developed to tackle, networks as well as partnerships require commitment by all participants, monitoring and assessment in order to be effective. While there are important differences in the scope and scale of political commitment and involvement in partnerships and networks, they all require substantive and sustained investment in management and process on the part of all participants.

The idea that partnerships are simple, technocratic 'production mechanisms' suitable to addressing the implementation crisis in global environmental governance is misguided. Both implementation of solutions and development of solutions through partnerships require sustained involvement and monitoring by all parties. We should trade the 'mechanistic' understanding for a political conception of partnerships. Not only would this allow us to understand the significance of the partnership phenomenon in the broader context of global environmental governance, but a political conception also highlights critical issues such as democratic control and power sharing, which so far have not received adequate attention.

Although networks tend to come in as many flavours as the problems they address, there is a set of overarching characteristics that they share. Some ideal-type characteristics have been developed for global public policy networks that clearly differentiate these institutional innovations from traditional, hierarchical organisations.

9.1.1.1 Interdependence

Co-operation in networks is based on the premise that individually no single group can address and solve the issue at stake. Multi-sectoral networks, however, are able to build bridges that transcend national boundaries between each of the sectors: the public and private sector and civil society. Multi-sectoral networks are able to reflect the changing roles and relative importance of each of the actors involved in combining resources to solve a particular problem.

9.1.1.2 Flexibility and learning capability

Networks come in various forms and organisational types that can also evolve through the process of co-operation, particularly as there are few binding constraints on the role of each participant. Networks structures are able to update and evolve in response to input from successes and failures. Furthermore, their evolutionary character and flexible structure allows for openness—accommodating new players during the process and tying them into the network, and letting go of partners whose tasks are completed. In the evolution of the network, old links break and new links form as required.

9.1.1.3 Complementarity

Networks profit and are sustained by the diversity of their constituency. Through their 'strength of weak ties', networks are able to handle this diversity of actors precisely because of the productive tensions on which they rest (Granovetter 1973). As a result, networks facilitate the discussion of controversial issues and provide a favourable framework for political deliberation, which is often not possible in the, at times, highly charged, aggressive diplomatic negotiations among states.

9.1.2 Different types of network

Networks come in a wide range of forms and perform a multitude of functions, and so do partnerships. So far, no clear-cut typology of networks has been developed. Yet preliminary empirical research suggests three ideal types, summarised in Table 9.1. These types should not be seen as mutually exclusive; some networks encompass more than one type or may have characteristics that overlap between two types. These ideal types should be viewed as a loose categorisation for understanding the potential roles and types of networks.

Table 9.1 emphasises one crucial point: different types of network have different implications for concerns about legitimacy, accountability, transparency and power asymmetries. There is no one-size-fits-all solution for a rules-based framework for partnerships; nor are there generic answers to the concerns outlined above. The issue area and the scope (national versus transnational) of the network dictate the modus operandi.

For example, the most difficult and contentious function a network can fulfil is facilitating the setting of global norms and standards. Global **negotiation networks** have developed in complex issue areas such as transnational money laundering and global

	Negotiation networks	Co-ordination networks	Implementation networks
Goal	Negotiating global norms and standards	Facilitating joint action strategies	Facilitating implementation of intergovernmental agreements
Building on existing environmental treaties	Not necessarily	Not necessarily	Yes
Equal representation of stakeholders	Important	Less important	Potentially important
Number of actors included in network	Limited	Unlimited	Limited
Transparency	Important	Less important	Important
Balancing power asymmetries	Important	Less important	Potentially important
Equal financing	Important	Less important	Less important
Example	World Commission on Dams	Roll Back Malaria Initiative	Clean Development Mechanism

TABLE 9.1 Ideal-type forms of network

water management.[3] In those instances, questions of legitimacy (who is allowed to sit at the table), accountability (who is accountable to whom?) and the distribution of power are of utmost importance.

In contrast, simple **co-ordination networks**, where actors from all sectors come together to co-ordinate action strategies in order to pool their resources, do not demand the same degree of inclusiveness. Driven by new information technologies, co-ordination networks facilitate broad-based knowledge exchanges between governments, international organisations, NGOs and the private sector, and thereby help to identify common goals and the development of co-ordinated action strategies. As a result, co-ordination networks help to improve the allocation of scarce resources and avoid duplication. Such networks function according to the principle of comparative advantage and are usually open to any group willing to contribute resources to solve a specific problem. Examples include the Roll Back Malaria Initiative (RBM) or the Global Water Partnership (GWP).

Implementation networks are hybrids, multi-sectoral alliances that come together to promote international environmental treaties negotiated by governments. In some cases, they build on consensual knowledge and simply help to address the implementation challenge. In other cases, an implementation network may also take on different parallel functions, renegotiating some of the underlying standards for implementation, or building coalitions for a revision of existing treaty norms.

---

3   For a thorough treatment of all cases mentioned in this chapter, see Reinicke *et al.* 2000 as well as our institute's website at www.globalpublicpolicy.net.

9.2 Improving coherence, accountability, evaluation and learning: critical management challenges for networks and partnerships

Analysing partnerships through the global public policy lens brings tremendously important new perspectives to the current debate on how to move forward. First and foremost, the discussion above highlights the need for a set of basic rules for the practice of partnerships to enhance their impact and accountability.

Governments and international organisations need to act on three fronts to avoid a sustained popular backlash against partnerships and to create adequate structures and rules to take advantage of the potential of partnerships.

1. They have to create a systematic global framework to integrate partnerships into the overall system of global environmental governance.

2. Governments need to ensure that there are commonly accepted ground rules for partnerships to which all actors adhere.

3. Governments and international organisations need to put in place a mechanism for monitoring, evaluation and learning.

9.2.1 Promoting coherence: linking 'Type I' and 'Type II' outcomes

During the Johannesburg Summit, the Type I and Type II processes appeared to be almost entirely disconnected. It remained unclear what types of role governments envisioned for partnerships in the overall context of global environmental governance. On the one hand governments emphasised the 'additionality' of partnerships, yet on the other they failed to provide an overall global framework by setting meaningful global goals.

Governments have to recognise and emphasise the symbiotic relationship between Type I and Type II outcomes. Partnership approaches to governance on their own will never form a substitute for binding international commitments by governments. Nor would that be desirable. The success of partnerships depends to a large degree on the willingness of governments to set ambitious binding targets. Partnerships can be one means through which such targets can be effectuated. But partnerships will not develop outside of such a nurturing context precisely because they have no legitimacy in their own right; they draw their mandate from the participation of national governments or international organisations.

Furthermore, it is important to link partnership efforts more directly to the official intergovernmental agenda. The decentralised nature of partnerships is part of their strength, but there should be an overall framework specified possibly by the UN on the areas in which partnerships would be useful in order to channel efforts in the right direction.

The development of a guiding framework requires the strengthening of institutional capacity within those parts of the UN system directly responsible. In the same way that we recognise the need for accountability in corporate financial reporting or banking regulation, there should be a reliable and effective framework for partnerships.

9.2.2 Setting ground rules for partnerships: accountability, capacity building and evaluation

Participation in partnerships is voluntary in nature. But in fact, as has been amply demonstrated by various empirical studies, the success or failure of partnerships is contingent on the existence of trust among partners, the level of transparency and the way partnership initiatives deal with power asymmetries—all of which depend on the effective application of a minimum set of rules (see Nelson and Zadek 1999; Reinicke *et al.* 2000; Nelson 2001 for case studies).

Governments and international organisations are not the only players that have to respond to this pressing agenda. Business and civil-society organisations are equally challenged to work with the public sector to apply basic rules to their activities and to monitor and enforce good behaviour. Yet governments and international organisations have a particular responsibility *vis-à-vis* their citizens. An overall value framework for partnerships, developed in a multi-sectoral negotiation process, combined with a powerful and innovative incentive mechanism monitored and enforced by international organisations are important steps in the right direction.

A value framework for partnerships should reflect the concerns and opinions of all stakeholders, and set out the basic rules for partnerships in the field of global environmental governance while accounting for the fact that partnerships come in different forms and fulfil varying functions. The process through which such a value framework should be developed could be modelled on the experience of the World Commission on Dams (WCD). The UN as the most universal international organisation could be the convener for such a multi-sectoral process.

Many observers have called for an intergovernmental treaty to set out the basic rules for partnerships, as well as a binding framework for overall corporate behaviour in the global marketplace.[4] However, such binding rules would be exceedingly difficult to negotiate, given that such negotiations even on a national level are difficult and rare. In addition, it is not clear whether this would be the best means to achieve ethical and environmentally sound behaviour of a company, as binding rules would be inflexible and difficult to adapt to changing conditions.

9.2.3 Accountability

As emphasised above, partnerships are meant to complement national policy-making and intergovernmental co-operation. They can facilitate the negotiation of global norms and standards, co-ordinate resource use and help to close the 'implementation gap', but they do not legislate. Therefore, it is evident that elections or direct hierarchical accountability structures are not suited for these decentralised processes.

---

4   See, for example, the discussions on a binding international framework for corporate social responsibility in the European Union (document collection accessible at forum.europa.eu.int/irc/empl/csr_eu_multi_stakeholder_forum/info/data/en/csr%20ems%20forum.htm, accessed 6 November 2002). See also the 'Resolution: People's Action for Corporate Responsibility', signed by more than 100 NGOs during the 'Corporate Accountability Week' held in Sandton, South Africa, in August 2002 on the eve of the WSSD (accessible at www.globalpolicy.org/reform/business/2002/2002action.htm, accessed 6 November 2002). See also Friends of the Earth 2002.

However, the lack of a mechanism for political oversight of partnerships should not be taken as an excuse to ignore the implications of new networked forms of governance for democratic legitimacy. If they do become a constant and significant feature of the overall system of global environmental governance, citizens around the world should have the right and the opportunity to review partnership participants, processes and results. But, given the lack of any single clear principal or any one electorate, to whom should partnerships be accountable?

National governments and international organisations should advocate a pluralistic system of accountability. The basis of this system would be the natural checks and balances provided by the participation of diverse actors and incentive mechanisms designed to generate compliance with a broad set of rules. Mechanisms of accountability should include:

- **Professional/peer accountability.** Partnership actors from a similar sector (e.g. experts, NGOs, business, governments) should be subject to peer accountability by other NGOs, experts or members of the business community.

- **Public reputational accountability.** 'Naming and shaming' is important in this context; actors in partnerships are accountable to the public for their actions and face reputational costs.

- **Market accountability.** Participants in partnerships who are also market participants might be rewarded/punished by other market participants/consumers for their actions.

- **Fiscal/financial accountability.** Partnerships and their participants have to account for the use of funds in the partnership according to a widely recognised set of accounting standards.

None of these mechanisms alone will be sufficient in ensuring the accountability of partnerships. Rather, the individual components work together in a self-reinforcing way. As a result, there is no single straightforward strategy to foster the accountability and legitimacy of partnerships. Instead, governments and international organisations should ensure that all of the elements of a pluralistic system of accountability are nurtured and strengthened (Benner *et al.* 2002).

9.2.4 Rules, sharing of resources and capacity building

There can be no doubt that partnerships are characterised by strong power asymmetries. However, as already indicated by the above depiction of partnerships as a diverse rather than a uniform phenomenon, the scale as well as the significance of power asymmetries vary across cases.

There are two basic strategies to address power asymmetries in partnerships. First, actors can be empowered to participate effectively and to make their voices heard. This could be accomplished through capacity building and resource endowment. Second, rules can be set to ensure that those who do not have access to financial or other resources are not disadvantaged in the partnership process. On both strategies, governments and international organisations can make important first steps.

Without doubt, the task of empowerment can only succeed as part of a decentralised strategy of capacity building. There is no global institution that would have the resources—financial or otherwise—to function as a central capacity-building institution. In fact, the only suspect for such a role—the United Nations—is most likely in need of capacity building itself. National governments and international organisations, however, can make a start in providing funding and other resources for capacity building and could also promote capacity building through the creation of a partnership resource network.

Capacity building and the establishment of a global resource network are important, yet most likely medium- if not long-term projects, whereas setting out the rules governing partnerships is more important for addressing power asymmetries immediately. Various measures are needed to counteract the domination that differential resource endowments have on partnership outcomes. For example, tough transparency rules for partnerships might make the exercise of financial superiority by companies more difficult. Correspondingly, it would make it easier to 'name and shame' those who abuse their power. Increased transparency would not only help to ensure greater accountability and thereby legitimacy overall, but it would also help to address the power imbalances by giving the weaker partners a larger voice for their concerns, thereby allowing them greater exercise of their moral authority in influencing partnership processes and outcomes. Another approach to tackling power asymmetries is to mandate clear cross-sectoral staffing of any partnership bodies or institutions entrusted with facilitating the partnership process or with implementing results. In this way, individuals from all sectors would be equally integrated into formal partnership structures regardless of their financial resources. Such multi-sectoral staffing may help weaker partners to maintain some control over the process and allow them to have direct access to all critical information.

9.2.5 Monitoring and evaluating partnerships

Monitoring and evaluation mechanisms need to be put in place to endow the legally unbinding rules framework with sufficient strength to accomplish its mandate. In the absence of top-down sanctioning mechanisms, effective monitoring and evaluation are key factors for ensuring compliance. It is here that governments and international organisations will have to make their greatest effort to ensure the viability of the partnership approach to sustainable development.

Evaluation and monitoring are critical for a number of reasons. Both, if properly managed, facilitate learning from experience. Many observers have questioned directing crucial resources such as time, money and personnel, towards process-heavy governance mechanisms that do not promise hard and fast results. Proper evaluation is needed to assess whether a partnership is the correct as well as necessary governance mechanism, and when it simply contributes to waste. Monitoring and evaluation also help to improve the transparency of partnership proceedings, and are therefore the most important—if not the only—instrument to allow outsiders to arrive at informed judgements on the legitimacy, effectiveness or efficiency of a given partnership. Finally, monitoring and evaluation help to identify 'free-rider' and 'rent-seeking' behaviour within partnerships.

In particular, the following dimensions of partnerships should be part of an overall monitoring and evaluation strategy.

- **Category and function of partnership**. What kind of partnership is evaluated? Have function and form of the partnership changed over time? Are they likely to change in the future?

- **Equity**. Who participates? Is representation of stakeholder interests equitable? Who decides who may sit at the table? Who has made the selection rules?

- **Procedural rules**. How are decisions being made in the partnership? What types of decision-making rule are employed? Who has set the rules?

- **Costs and benefits**. Who benefits from the partnership? What kinds of benefit are distributed? Is distribution equitable? Who bears the costs? Who finances the partnership? Are there unintended costs?

- **Stability of partnership**. How stable is the partnership? What determines stability, instability? Who/what is instrumental in ensuring the stability of the partnership?

- **Degree of formalisation**. To what extent has the partnership been 'formalised', i.e. have partners agreed to sign a written contract, create a secretariat, etc.?

- **Results**. Do partnerships define verifiable results? Do partnerships use milestones? How do partnerships control for results? Did the partnership finally realise/arrive at the self-defined results?

Proper evaluation and monitoring first of all require a sound understanding of the partnership at hand. Also, despite the fact that we can build on a wealth of experience in the evaluation discipline,[5] thorough assessments of partnerships have only recently come on the agenda.[6] It is unfortunate in this context that the UN Secretary-General's new reform agenda emphasises the greater role and significance of partnerships for the organisation's work, but fails to recognise this important dimension (United Nations General Assembly 2002). The UN and its various specialised agencies urgently need to put proper evaluation practices in place to ensure the accountability and effectiveness of their involvement with partnerships.

---

5   Various organisations provide substantial expertise and offer high-quality services in evaluation. See, for example, the World Bank's Operation Evaluation Department (OED, accessible at www.worldbank.org/oed) or UNDP's Evaluation Office (EO, accessible at www.undp.org/eo). In addition, there are numerous national evaluation societies that provide a wealth of information.

6   See, for example, the papers presented at last year's World Bank Conference on Evaluation and Development: The Partnership Dimension, Washington, DC, 23–24 July 2001, accessible at www.worldbank.org/html/oed/partnershipconference (accessed 7 November 2002).

9.3 Conclusion

Partnerships promote change and innovation by introducing new actors, new settings and new modes of interaction to global environmental governance. If governments provide the necessary framework condition, and if partnerships get the process right, the interplay between the different sectors, between different levels (local/national/regional/global) and actors from both North and South holds great potential for policy implementation and policy learning.

Engaging in partnerships can have beneficial feedback effects for the way states, international organisations, businesses and civil-society actors conduct their business. But fruitful collaboration in partnerships can work only if all actors are willing to question formerly unquestioned routines and beliefs. Learning to operate in a highly dynamic environment, and to cope with the many pressures it generates is a tremendously complex task. For public institutions especially, both on the national and multilateral level, learning processes often seem to proceed only at a painstakingly slow pace.

The UN and the World Bank have undertaken to make partnerships and 'coalitions for change' a central part of their strategic orientation for the future (United Nations 1999; Wolfensohn 1999). Nevertheless, involvement of international organisations in partnerships remains scattered and public institutions generally lack a coherent strategy for mainstreaming engagement in partnerships into their 'normal' way of doing business. There are no processes to be selective and to prioritise, no rigorous mechanisms to determine their appropriate role in various partnerships and the kind of internal restructuring and adjustment this change in strategy would require. Increased involvement of multilateral institutions, and especially the UN and its specialised agencies in partnerships, will require bold steps in changing the organisational structures and cultures of these institutions. Equally, if not more important, it requires a fundamental change on the side of the stakeholders in these organisations: the member states.

Partnerships are by definition volatile constructs that require much attention and careful management. That is why they do not offer an easy ride. But the difficulties are well worth the risk, given the daunting challenges of a complex world with an ever-expanding multiplicity of actors, interests and issues that need to be resolved. They represent a promising medium through which states and their international organisations can achieve their mission, maintain their competence in a changing global environment, and serve their citizens in a more effective and legitimate way.

References

Benner, T., J.M. Witte and W. Reinicke (2002) 'Innovating Global Governance: Multisectoral Networks and Accountability', paper prepared for the *Miliband Conference on Global Governance and Public Accountability*, London School of Economics, 17–18 May 2002.

Friends of the Earth (2002) 'Towards Binding Corporate Accountability', FoEI Position Paper for the WSSD, January 2002, www.foe.co.uk/resource/briefings/corporate_accountability.pdf, 13 November 2002.

Granovetter, M. (1973) 'The Strength of Weak Ties', *American Journal of Sociology* 78.6: 1,361-81.

Kara, J., and D. Quarless (2002) 'Explanatory Note by the Vice-Chairs: Guiding Principles for Partnerships for Sustainable Development', *PrepCom IV*, Bali, 7 June 2002 (www.johannesburgsummit. org/html/documents/prepcom4docs/bali_documents/annex_partnership.pdf, 6 November 2002).

Nelson, J. (2001) *Cooperation between the United Nations and all Relevant Partners, in Particular the Private Sector* (Report of the Secretary-General A56/323; New York: United Nations).

—— and S. Zadek (1999) *Partnership Alchemy: New Social Partnerships in Europe* (Copenhagen: The Copenhagen Centre).

Reinicke, W., H. Francis and M. Deng with T. Benner and J. Herschman (2000) *Critical Choices: The United Nations, Networks and the Future of Global Governance* (Ottawa: IDRC).

United Nations (1999) 'A Compact for the New Century', Address of UN Secretary-General Kofi Annan to the *1999 World Economic Forum Meetings*, Davos, Switzerland, 31 January 1999 (www.un.org/ partners/business/davos.htm#speech, 16 November 2002).

United Nations General Assembly (2002) *Strengthening of the United Nations: An Agenda for Further Change* (Report of the Secretary-General A/57/387; New York: United Nations).

Wolfensohn, J.D. (1999) 'Coalitions for Change', *World Bank Group/IMF Annual Meetings* speech, 28 September 1999 (www.imf.org/external/am/1999/speeches/PR02E.pdf, 17 November 2002).

WSSD (World Summit on Sustainable Development) (2002a) *Johannesburg Declaration on Sustainable Development*, 4 September 2002; accessible at www.johannesburgsummit.org/html/documents/ summit_docs/1009wssd_pol_declaration.htm, 8 November 2002.

—— (2002b) *Plan of Implementation*, 4 September 2002; accessible at www.johannesburgsummit.org/ html/documents/summit_docs/2309_planfinal.htm, 8 November 2002.

Part 3
Actors in global governance and their changing roles

10
The role of the nation-state in environmental protection
THE CHALLENGE OF GLOBALISATION

Martin Jänicke

German Advisory Council on the Environment (SRU); Freie Universität Berlin

I have used the concept of ecological modernisation for 20 years. The core of this concept is an environmental policy approach strongly relying on the logic of innovation and its diffusion in market economies. Such an innovation-oriented environmental policy is by its very nature a national pioneer policy.

But what are the conditions of first-mover-policies in environment? Is the nation-state still able to implement a demanding environmental policy in times of globalisation?

During recent years we have witnessed more and more fears that the ability of the nation-state to set ambitious standards in fields such as environmental policy has diminished in the context of globalisation. There is also, on the other hand, the hopeful prognosis of neoclassical economists that the same globalisation would be connected with deregulation and fundamental reduction of the role of government. Neither the fear nor the hope of a withering-away of the nation-state in times of globalisation are supported by empirical research. But the subject is still highly relevant, since the debate has taught us a great deal about the role of the nation-state in the context of globalisation.

I would like to present ten theses regarding the role of the nation-state in global environmental policy. My bases are mainly cross-national studies, partly made by the Environmental Policy Research Centre of the Freie Universität of Berlin.

10.1 Globalisation has created a policy arena for pioneer countries, at least in environmental policy

Pioneering environmental policy of certain (highly developed) countries has been possible since 1970. The influence of small, innovative countries in global policy has never been as important as it is today in the field of environmental policy (Andersen and Lief-ferink 1997; Jänicke and Weidner 1997; Jänicke and Jacob 2001; Andersson and Mol 2002). This means that political competition and pioneer roles of countries have become relevant. But political competition needs an arena. The international system and especially the globalisation of environmental policy have created this policy arena. The Johannesburg Summit may be taken as an example. Here the situation has improved since the end of the Cold War (and its dichotomic policy arena). International institutions such as the OECD (Organisation for Economic Co-operation and Development) or UNEP (United Nations Environment Programme), but also global networks of all kinds provide a basis for benchmarking and competition in global environmental policy. At the core is regulatory competition giving support to domestic innovative industries or protecting the national regulatory culture against pressures to adapt to policy innovation from abroad. This countervailing mechanism against the neglect of environmental considerations in the global economy may be not strong enough, but it can be improved.

10.2 The nation-state is both the subject and the object of global environmental policy learning and lesson drawing

The national government is the subject of policy learning on how to solve environmental problems. At the same time national governments are looking for best practice, by observing other governments (Bennett 1991; Rose 1993; Kern *et al.* 2001). Successful environmental policy innovations—the introduction of new institutions, instruments or strategies—thereby are often adopted by other governments. This improvement by imitation can be conceived as **horizontal policy learning**. It is an important mechanism of global environmental policy development and policy convergence. International institutions such as the OECD, UNEP or special regimes play an important role as policy arenas for pioneers and as agents for the diffusion of environmental policy innovations. This role seems to be more important than the creation of policy innovations by the international institutions themselves. Figure 10.1 shows some examples of the diffusion of environmental policy innovations—such as environmental ministries or green plans—from pioneer countries to the rest of the world. The speed of diffusion increased in the 1990s, strongly supported by the Rio process. This may imply capacity building at the national level, even if the divergence of capacities (behind the convergent policy patterns) remains remarkable.

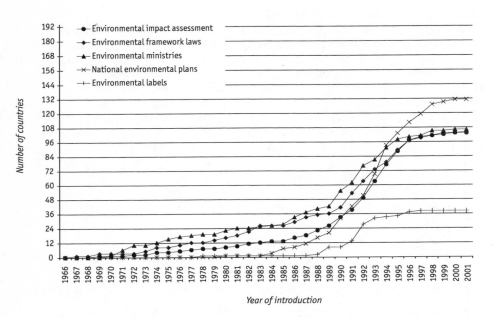

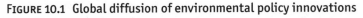

FIGURE 10.1 Global diffusion of environmental policy innovations

Source: Busch and Jörgens 2002

10.3 Policies are differently affected by globalisation

The international pressure on wages, taxes on mobile sources and social security provisions is a reality in times of globalisation (Scharpf 1998). Environmental, but also health or security standards have their own (e.g. World Trade Organisation [WTO]) rules and their own logic in international regulatory competition. The reasons why environmental policy is a special case seem to be extremely important and need special explanation:

10.4 There is no 'race to the bottom' in environmental policy: but why?

Several empirical cross-national studies have rejected the 'race to the bottom' (RTB) hypothesis (see Box 10.1). Many of the arguments are well known today (Vogel 1995; Wheeler 2001; Drezner 2001):

- 'We find no race to the bottom . . . countries with more open trade regimes have more stringent regulations' (Eliste and Fredricksson 1998).

- National environmental pioneer policy can create 'first-mover advantages' (Ashford *et al.* 1979; Porter and van der Linde 1995; Wallace 1995).

- Bangladesh, India, Indonesia and Thailand 'are fast adopting industrial pollution control standards similar to those in developed countries' (Hettige *et al.* 1996).

- Strict environmental policy is no strong incentive to de-locate 'dirty industries' into developing countries with re-imports into rich countries (Jaffe *et al.* 1995; Jänicke *et al.* 1997).

Box 10.1 No international race to the bottom

- Countries and companies that trade with countries with strict regulations tend to have stricter policies themselves (Foljanty-Jost 1997; Eliste and Fredricksson 1998); the largest markets are rather strictly regulated.

- The globalisation of environmental policy has partly changed the framework conditions of the world market (Jänicke and Weidner 1997; Vogel 2001; Weidner and Jänicke 2002).

- Regulatory competition in environment often creates first-mover advantages for national economies. This is part of global competition (Porter and van der Linde 1995; Wallace 1995) and essential to the development of 'environmental lead markets' (Jänicke and Jacob 2001).

- Strict environmental regulations (within limits) remain a possibility for protecting national industries.

- Multinationals tend to use the same standards everywhere (Wheeler 2001).

- Differences in environmental standards tend to decrease; generally they are less important than differences, for example, in labour costs or taxes.

I would like to add two arguments:

- The environmental issue has become a dimension of general technological progress: 40% of the innovations in 2010 are expected to be relevant for environmental improvement (Faucheux 2000).

- The environmental issue has become important in the international competition for innovation; there is a close correlation between strict environmental regulation and competitiveness.

10.5 Pioneer countries in environmental policy are highly competitive

The *Global Competitive Report* shows a remarkable high correlation ($R^2 = 0.89$) between ambitious environmental policy and the competitiveness of a country (WEF 2000). Other studies have revealed a similar relationship (Sturm *et al.* 2000). Of course, this is no causal proof. The causal relation can go in both directions; also a third factor, GNP (gross national product) per capita, may be important. But in the light of such a correlation nobody can any longer insist on the traditional economic argument of an imminent contradiction between competitiveness and a demanding environmental policy. The strong correlation of the 'third factor', GNP, can be explained by the observation that highly developed countries are characterised by both high perceived environmental pressure and high capacity to react.

10.6 The open ('globalised') national economy needs and is characterised by strong government, both in size and scope

This is contrary to the thinking of many neoclassical economists. There are cross-national studies showing that public expenditures in open economies in the OECD tend to be relatively higher (see Cameron 1978; Garrett 1998; Bernauer 2000). But it seems plausible to assume both a larger size and a larger scope of government activities in countries that are highly integrated into the international economy. Open economies need:

- A well-developed infrastructure for successful international competition; that means more money and more public activities in fields such as education, R&D or transport

- The compensation of distributional and other effects of rapid structural changes connected, for example, with a low degree of protection of domestic industries

- More regulatory activities of all kinds necessary to adapt to international developments (e.g. standards)

10.7 New technologies as a rule start from national 'lead markets'

The ecological modernisation of the world market depends on national lead markets for environmental innovations (Jänicke and Jacob 2001; Beise 2001). A lead market is 'the core of the world market where the local users are early adopters of an innovation on an international scale' (Beise 1999: 4). The US as lead market for the Internet, Japan as lead market for fax, or Finland as lead market for mobile phones are well-known examples. Empirically, lead markets are characterised by, for example, high per capita income, demanding, innovative buyers, high quality standards and pressure for change (see also Meyer-Krahmer, 1999).

Lead markets for *environmental* technologies, however, are characterised by two additional factors:

1. They are typically not only stimulated by higher environmental preferences of consumers in that country but also by special promotion measures, or by political intervention in the market.

2. A lead market for environmental innovations relates to global environmental needs and is—due to market failures—strongly dependent on government support, sometimes also on support from NGOs such as Greenpeace or the media.

Here again the role of the highly developed nation-state and of pioneer countries is crucial: the global economy and its multinational enterprises are still in need of locations where the risky take-off of a new environmental technology finds public support and innovative buyers who are willing to pay a higher price and accept the teething problems of that technology before it becomes cheap and effective enough to succeed on global markets. The regulators in Denmark and Germany created favourable market conditions and the customers of electricity in both countries were willing to bear the high price for wind power technology until it became competitive and profitable on the global market.

10.8 Environmental policy innovation as well as regression are caused primarily at the national level

In an expert inquiry among 20 different countries we asked the participants: What are the main restrictive sectors in environmental protection? The answer was: first the energy sector, second road traffic, third agriculture and fourth the construction sector (Jänicke and Weidner 1997). These are actually sectors that are not under rigorous global competition, even the contrary is partly true (agriculture, the power industry and the construction industry strongly depend on public or regulated demand). Many times it is again the nation-state that resists international regulation: Countries such as the US, Japan, the UK or, more recently, Denmark are examples of the double option of either being innovator or laggard in environmental policy.

10.9 The nation-state will remain the 'local hero', not least in the field of environmental protection

There is no functional equivalent to national governments as highly visible, legitimised and competent territorial actors and protectors (Willke 1992). To whom could we address our complaints on environmental disruptions or issues such as BSE if not to this actor? Governments, on the other hand, have no exit option. They need both a material and a political base. They do not react to economic pressure alone. The legitimacy they need necessitates a broader orientation. The environment is an aspect that cannot be ignored. Therefore national governments try to seek compromises between the economy and the ecology. The answer is technology. As far as technology can provide solutions for environmental problems (in many fields we need more far-reaching 'structural' solutions), the potential of national policy action is higher than is generally assumed. This solution, however, is essentially restricted not only by the general availability of technology but also to the more advanced countries.

- High visibility, 'first address' in case of complaints
- Highest competence, also as actor in the global arena
- Monopoly of coercive power
- Financial resources
- High pressure for legitimation (compared with other levels)

Box 10.2 The nation-state as 'local hero'

10.10 Global environmental governance strongly depends on both the competence and the creativity of national governments and the international system as a complex mechanism of policy diffusion and co-ordination

Of course this ('horizontal') view of the role of national governments is no alternative to the ('vertical') view of international institutions. The more interesting question is whether international regulation or the competitive role of pioneer countries represents the main motor of global environmental policy development. At the Johannesburg Summit the EU (strongly influenced by the German government), for the first time, has gone beyond the minimalist global consensus by stressing its pioneer role.

- **Consensus.** 'Governance by international regulations' (e.g. Kyoto Protocol)
    - International institutions, negotiations and regulations and their effects on national policies
    - Global consensus, often at a low level
    - 'Vertical' perspective
- **Competition.** 'Governance by national pioneer policy' (e.g. obligatory feed-in tariffs; alliance for renewable energies)
    - Influence of pioneer countries in terms of policy diffusion
    - Demonstration effects of policy innovations and best practice
    - Pressure by political and technological competition
    - 'Horizontal' policy learning and lesson drawing

Box 10.3 Two approaches to global environmental policy

Together with a large group of about 125 countries it is going to follow an ambitious policy to support renewable energies.

This chapter has underlined the role of the pioneers, of innovation and diffusion. We need a lot more research on the role of (different) national policies as well on the mechanism of political competition in the global arena to provide an answer to the question. But even if the competitive pressure (both in policy and technology) caused by pioneers in environmental policy proved to be the most effective driving force, the international institutions would still play an important role as policy arenas and as agents of diffusion.

10.11 Conclusions

This short chapter is not to be misunderstood as an optimistic picture of globalisation. In general we are not very successful in the field of environmental protection. Global economic development increases, both at the same time, the level of environmental pressure (e.g. in the field of transport) and the capacity to react to environmental problems. The race between those two tendencies may not be won by environmental policy. The question is, however, whether globalisation is the main problem.

In sum, neither the increased importance of global markets nor the globalisation of political governance has weakened the role of national governments: 'the economic dimensions of globalisation have had little, if any, impact on lowering national regulatory standards, while the social and political dimensions of globalisation have, on balance, contributed to the strengthening of national regulatory standards' (Vogel 2001). 'States in concert' have expanded and co-ordinated their regulatory powers. And it is only the state, the guarantor of diverse societal interests, that has the competence, the resources, the coercive power and legitimacy 'to regulate the actions of disparate actors who, in their pursuit of individual gain, might otherwise destroy shared environmental resources' (Raustiala 1997).

One important reservation, however, needs to be mentioned: it is the highly developed nation-state that has preserved or even increased its capacity in the context of globalisation. The situation of the less developed countries may be viewed quite differently.

Keeping this in mind, we could draw two political and normative conclusions from the above ten statements.

First, there is a remarkable potential in the advanced OECD countries to promote change by the adoption of pioneering policy, the stimulation of international competition and the diffusion of best practice. This may sometimes be more helpful than relying only on weak and/or on weakly implemented treaties (such as the Kyoto Protocol). Second, this potential of the highly advanced countries may be seen as a moral argument to assume a greater responsibility for global environmental development. The advanced nations cannot hide behind the fictive monster of globalisation, seemingly legitimising any kind of inactivity. On the contrary, it is their obligation to provide the world with better 'demonstration effects', with a better model of production and consumption overcoming the resource- and environment-intensive model of the past.

References

Andersen, M.S., and D. Liefferink (eds.) (1997) *European Environmental Policy* (Manchester, UK: The Pioneers).

Andersson, M., and A.P.J. Mol (2002) 'The Netherlands in the UNFCCC Process: Leadership between Ambition and Reality', *International Environmental Agreements* 2: 49-68.

Ashford, N.A., G.R. Heaton and W.C. Priest (1979) 'Environment, Health, and Safety Regulation, and Technological Innovation', in C.T. Hill and J. Utterback (eds.), *Technological Innovation for a Dynamic Economy* (New York: Pergamon Press): 161-221.

Beise, M. (1999) 'Lead Markets and the International Allocation of R&D', paper prepared for the 5th *ASEAT Conference 'Demand, Markets, Users and Innovation: Sociological and Economic Approaches'*, Manchester, UK, 14–16 September 1999.

Beise, M. (2001) *Lead Markets: Country Specific Success Factors of the Global Diffusion of Innovations* (Heidelberg, Germany: Physica Verlag).

Bennett, C.J. (1991) 'What is Policy Convergence and What Causes it?', *British Journal of Political Science* 21: 215-33.

Bernauer, T. (2000) *Staaten im Weltmarkt: Zur Handlungsfähigkeit von Staaten trotz wirtschaftlicher Globalisierung* (Opladen, Germany: Leske & Budrich).

Busch, P.-O., and H. Jörgens (2002) *Globale Ausbreitungsmuster umweltpolitischer Innovationen, Forschungsstelle für Umweltpolitik* (FFU Report 02-05; Berlin: Freie Universität).

Cameron, D.R. (1978) 'The Expansion of the Public Economy: A Comparative Analysis', *American Political Science Review* 72.4: 1,243ff.

Drezner, D.W. (2001) 'Globalization and Policy Convergence', *The International Studies Review* 3.1: 53-78.

Eliste, P., and P.G. Fredricksson (1998) *Does Open Trade Result in a Race to the Bottom? Cross Country Evidence* (unpublished manuscript; Washington, DC: World Bank).

Faucheux, S. (2000) 'Environmental Policy and Technological Change; Towards Deliberative Governance', in J. Hemmelskamp, K. Rennings and F. Leone (eds.), *Innovation-Oriented Environmental Regulation: Theoretical Approaches and Empirical Analysis* (Heidelberg, Germany: Physica): 153-71.

Foljanty-Jost, G. (1997) 'Die Bedeutung Japans für die vergleichende Umweltpolitikforschung: Vom Modell zum Auslaufmodell?', in L. Mez and H. Weidner (eds.), *Umweltpolitik und Staatsversagen: Perspektiven und Grenzen der Umweltpolitikanalyse* (Berlin: Edition Sigma): 314-22.

Garrett, G. (1998) *Partisan Politics in the Global Economy* (Cambridge, UK: Cambridge University Press).

Hettige, H., M. Huq, S. Pargal and D. Wheeler (1996) 'Determinants of Pollution Abatement in Developing Countries: Evidence from South and South East Asia', *World Development* 24.12: 1,891-904.

Jaffe, B., S.R. Peterson, P.R. Portney and R. Stavins (1995) 'Environmental Regulation and Competitiveness of US Manufacturing: What does Evidence Tell Us?', *Journal of Economic Literature* 33.1: 136-63.

Jänicke, M., and K. Jacob (2001) 'Global Environmental Change and the Nation State: Lead Markets for Environmental Innovations', paper presented at the Conference *Global Environmental Change and the Nation State*, Berlin, 7–8 December 2001.

—— and H. Weidner (eds.) (1997) *National Environmental Policies: A Comparative Study of Capacity-Building* (Berlin: Springer).

——, M. Binder and H. Mönch (1997) 'Dirty Industries: Patterns of Change in Industrial Countries', *Environmental and Resource Economics* 9: 467-91.

Kern, K., H. Jörgens and M. Jänicke (2001) *The Diffusion of Environmental Policy Innovations* (FS II 01-302; Berlin: Wissenschaftszentrum Berlin).

Meyer-Krahmer, F. (1999) 'Was bedeutet Globalisierung für Aufgaben und Handlungsspielräume nationaler Innovationspolitiken?', in K. Grimmer, S. Kuhlmann and F. Meyer-Krahmer (eds.), *Innovationspolitik in globalisierten Arenen* (Opladen, Germany: Leske & Budrich): 43-74.

Porter, M.E., and C. van der Linde (1995) 'Green and Competitive: Ending the Stalemate', *Harvard Business Review* September/October 1995: 120-34.

Raustiala, K. (1997) 'States, NGOs, and International Environmental Institutions', *International Studies Quarterly* 41: 719-40.

Rose, R. (1993) *Lesson-Drawing in Public Policy: A Guide to Learning across Time and Space* (Chatham, NJ: Chatham House).

Scharpf, F.W. (1998) 'Die Problemlösungsfähigkeit der Mehrebenenpolitik in Europa', in B. Kohler-Koch (ed.), *Regieren in entgrenzten Räumen* (Sonderheft 29 der PVS; Opladen, Germany: Westdeutscher Verlag): 121-44.

Sturm, A., M. Wackernagel and K. Müller (2000) *The Winners and Losers in Global Competition. Why Eco-Efficiency Reinforces Competitiveness: A Study of 44 Nations* (Chur, Switzerland: Verlag Rüegger).

Vogel, D. (1995) *Trading Up: Consumer and Environmental Regulation in a Global Economy* (Cambridge, MA: Harvard University Press).

Wallace, D. (1995) *Environmental Policy and Industrial Innovation: Strategies in Europe, the USA and Japan* (London: Earthscan Publications).

WEF (World Economic Forum) (2000) *Global Competitiveness Report 2000* (New York: Oxford University Press).

Weidner, H., and M. Jänicke (eds.) (2002) *Capacity Building in National Environmental Policy: A Comparative Study of 17 Countries* (Berlin: Springer).

Wheeler, D. (2001) 'Racing to the Bottom? Foreign Investment and Air Pollution in Developing Countries', *Journal of Environment and Development* 10.3: 225-45.

Wilke, H. (1992) *Ironie des Staates: Grundlinien einer Staatstheorie polyzentrischer Gesellschaft* (Frankfurt am Main: Suhrkamp).

11
Governance and integrated product policy

Frieder Rubik

Institute for Ecological Economic Research (IÖW), Germany

The orientation of environmental policy towards products[1] and, in turn, the degree of environmental orientation of those products, might offer new and interesting opportunities to transform the market with an environmental intention and to stimulate significant reductions of environmental burdens. However, the crucial question is the role of policy in this context. Traditionally, environmental policy has been perceived as a task of government. However, this view is changing and the debates of the 1990s regarded government as an important actor in environmental policy, but not the only one. This chapter reflects the recently arisen topic of 'integrated product policy' (IPP) and discusses challenges in influencing micro-economic decisions through policy.

The structure of the chapter is as follows. First, we report on the slow shift of environmental policy towards products (Section 11.1). Products are confronted with several problems and challenges presented in Section 11.2. This is followed by an overview of political reactions (Section 11.3), which can be subdivided into a 'traditional' path and a new path ('integrated product policy'). Sections 11.4 and 11.5 examine the possibilities for different policy regimes. The chapter ends with some conclusions (Section 11.6).

11.1 The shift towards products

'Products' in the environmental context is a topic that emerged three decades ago, but which increased in relevance during the 1990s. There are some specific reasons for this increase in the environmental importance of products:

- **Increase of the share of product-related environmental burdens**. The successes of production process-oriented environmental policy and economic

---

1   I use the term 'product' in a general sense encompassing (material) goods and (immaterial) services.

structural change implied a relative increase in product-related environmental impacts. In addition private consumption is growing and this trend is connected with an absolute increase in the importance of products.

- **Shift of site-specific emissions towards non-point and diffuse sources.** Traditionally, environmental policy has focused on relatively large, localised sources of pollution, such as industrial and power plants. There, significant results could be achieved without too much cost and effort. In the meantime, it has become clear that an effective environmental policy also needs to address smaller and mobile ('non-point') sources of pollution, such as small firms and products.

- **Consideration of the environmental life-cycles[2] of products.** Scientific methods such as life-cycle assessment (LCA) illustrate the sharing of responsibilities for environmental burdens throughout the life-cycle of products; they hint especially at the dominant role of the consumption phase in private households: for example, in the case of energy consuming durables (e.g. washing machines, refrigerators).

- **Products as 'globetrotters'.** In recent decades, the international trade of products, components and materials has increased dramatically. Few product life-cycles are restricted to one single country. Globally produced goods are traded and consumed globally; products become 'globetrotters' and visible indicators of the interdependency of economies and societies and also of ecosystems.

- **Connection between sources and sinks.** The relationships between environmental problems can be observed systemically by considering the (environmental) life-cycle of products. The view starts at the source (i.e. the extraction of resources) followed by the next stages of the life-cycle (production, trade, consumption, disposal) and ends at the final location: the sinks (e.g. the oceans). Products connect these sources and sinks directly and make burdens visible; they are sometimes also responsible for current major environmental challenges (e.g. climate change and greenhouse gas emissions from cars).

- **Product differentiation strategies in saturated markets.** Saturation has become a problem of markets and products. Businesses intend to differentiate by offering additional features without radical changes to their basic technical patterns. However, quite often this differentiation strategy is connected with increases in environmental burdens (e.g. additional small motors in cars such as electric window opening systems which need more energy).

Altogether, an integrated approach focusing on products could supplement the 'traditional' process-oriented approach. Integration encompasses the environmental life-

---

2 The *environmental* life-cycle considers a product from cradle to grave: this means from the extraction of the raw materials, through different production and distribution processes to the use/consumption of a product until it becomes waste and is treated by re-use, recycling, recovery, disposal or landfilling.

cycle of products, their economic life-cycle[3] and the information/communication flows along the chain. Product orientation of environmental policy is regarded as an approach to 'kill several birds with one stone'.

11.2 Challenges for the product approach

In general, environmental policy is confronted by the problems of identifying, controlling and influencing environmental challenges. These problems can be attributed to the complex of externalities introduced by Minsch *et al.* (1998: 93). According to Minsch *et al.*, the complex of externalities is characterised by a huge amount of different substances which increase continuously/dynamically and which are combined to form an exploding number of interactions. This complex of externalities hints at the pure diversity, dynamics and fuzziness in perception and analysis characterising present environmental policy. The area of products is additionally marked by some specialities:

- **Plethora of different products.** There is a huge amount of different products offered and bought on the markets. As a very rough indicator, we can refer to the classification of products elaborated by the statistical offices. For example, the German Federal Statistical Office applies a distinction among nine digits of goods (Statistisches Bundesamt 1995), distinguishing between 6,431 different kinds of product group.

- **Predictability of allocation processes.** There is a systematic problem causing insufficient knowledge of allocation calculations and decisions made by micro-economic actors. The state can neither theoretically nor empirically provide the necessary information on micro-economic actors on both the supply and the demand sides (see also Wegner 1995).

- **Overload of information.** Given the hypothetical assumption that all necessary information is available to the state, there would immediately arise an information overload, which could not be dealt with.

- **Secrecy.** Business is keen to defend its internal availability of information and data and often reluctant to transmit information voluntarily because of secrecy requirements.

- **Not-knowing phenomenon.** The improvement of environmental features of products along their life-cycles could not be organised centrally; therefore it is necessary to do it in a decentralised manner, involving a plethora of actors embedded in a competition for favourite solutions. This means that decentralised search processes 'organise' innovation and seek out the best solutions. And this could be substituted neither theoretically nor practically by centrally planned decisions.

3   The *economic* life-cycle consists of the product idea, product plan, the development of pilot and test products, introduction on the market, and the diffusion, saturation and decline on the market.

11.3 Political reactions

Environmental policy has not been unperceptive about the importance of products. The 'traditional' answer to the environmental challenges of products was connected with the command-and-control approach (see Table 11.1) following the policy patterns of the 1970s. This was based on the reaction to environmental problems and particular 'hot spots'. This type of policy can be described as reactive and oriented towards the government as the actor; the government should take the lead and responsibility to counteract and 'solve' these problems. The policy pattern was quite often a regulatory approach applying command-and-control instruments (e.g. prohibitions and standards). The regulations themselves considered specific environmental aspects focused on one single specific stage of the life-cycle.

Characteristics	'Traditional' product-related environmental policy	Integrated product policy
Base	Important environmental problem, sometimes political 'hot spot'	Prior product group, selected e.g. by chain analyses or LCAs
Actors	State, sometimes using initiatives of stakeholders	State, other actors and stakeholders
Instruments	Quite often regulatory prescription; command-and-control approach	Consumer-related instruments, voluntary agreements, voluntary and mandatory information, economic instruments, regulatory instruments
Co-operation	Hearing of affected stakeholders	Joint activities, networking, own contributions Shared responsibilities 'Product management'
Duties	Government-prescribed, detailed plans with standards and time schedules Theoretically no options for target groups	Agreed flexible possibilities for activities according to target setting Options for target groups
Product responsibility	Specified with regard to specific product features	Holistic or shared, with regard to the life-cycle and environmental burdens, only partly mandatory
Control, sanctions	Administrative, prohibitions, sanctions	Reporting duties, public control, loss of image, competition
Environmental actions	Specific environmental aspects of specific life-cycle stages	Along life-cycle and across environmental media
Target groups	Specific actors, mostly companies	Actors along life-cycle
Model of action	Adaptation	Innovation
Policy type	Reactive	Anticipative/proactive

TABLE 11.1 Characteristics of 'traditional' product-related environmental policy and IPP

Source: Rubik 2002: 193

Typically, governmental prescriptions were drafted and discussed at hearings together with affected stakeholders. The elaborated prescriptions were later announced containing detailed plans of implementation with clearly indicated time schedules. This process did not offer any flexible implementation options to the target groups. Intended target groups were businesses, which were perceived as the main actor 'responsible' for the environmental problems. As a consequence, control and sanction regimes have been implemented. The idea was that the target groups and especially business would respect these prescriptions and adapt to the new regulations.

A certain shift of this 'traditional' approach has been happening since the early 1990s. Product-related environmental issues that are nowadays referred to by the term 'integrated product policy' (IPP) have gained scientific attention; there has been comprehensive research both on a conceptual level and into specific questions, such as effectiveness of certain policy instruments.

The first conceptual, empirical and EU-wide research into IPP was introduced by Oosterhuis et al. (1996). A few months later Ernst & Young together with the Science and Policy Research Unit (SPRU) of the University of Sussex started their work on behalf of DG Environment analysing national and international developments with regard to product policy with a special view to the potential for a common European policy (Ernst & Young/SPRU 1998). The study was meant to propose a first conceptual draft for a European product policy. The authors also coined the term 'integrated product policy', which was defined as: 'Public policy which explicitly aims to modify and improve the environmental performance of product systems' (Ernst & Young/SPRU 1998: 33). This definition has been discussed and criticised often, especially with regard to the exclusion of services and to the emphasis on public policy. We recommend the following definition: 'Integrated Product Policy is oriented towards products and services and their environmental features during the whole life-cycle; it aims at the improvement of their environmental performance and promotes innovations in products and services' (Rubik 2002).

On the political agenda, the European Commission mentioned product policy for the first time in a progress report on the implementation of the 5th Environmental Action Plan (COM[95]624) of the European Union. The next impulse to conceptual development of product policy was given by the British consultants Ernst & Young and the University of Sussex as mentioned above. IPP was given additional stimulus by the German European Presidency during the first half of 1999. At the European Council, which took place in Weimar in May 1999, the German initiative was welcomed and supported by all ministers. Thus, IPP became part of the political agenda. Some measures at EU level were proposed in the background document prepared for the Informal Council. Today, this BMU document (BMU 1999) forms the 'common ground' within the EU. Also EU Member States (especially Denmark, Sweden and The Netherlands) have been very active in this area (an intensive overview can be found in Rubik and Scheer 2005).

In the meantime, the Commission published a Green Paper on IPP in February 2001 (COM[2001]68; European Commission 2001). This Green Paper was intended to stimulate discussion by presenting some proposals for IPP; the Commission published a 'Communication' on IPP in 2003.

Comparing this new approach of IPP with the 'traditional' product approach of environmental policy, it becomes clear that the basis of IPP is oriented more towards prior areas/product groups and not towards 'hot spots', i.e. environmental prior areas. Actors are the state, and a multitude of different stakeholders. The IPP toolkit is not restricted to 'command and control', but has a wider range of different instruments that might be used.[4] Co-operation in the sense of sharing responsibilities and networking is an important principle, whereas, 'traditionally', affected stakeholders are heard, but that is it. Altogether, the target groups of IPP are situated along the life-cycle of products and their method of action can be perceived as innovation: that is, trying to gain competitive advantages. The product responsibility is not clearly specified, but regarded more holistically with a sharing of burdens—with some mandatory prescriptions. Also the control regime seems to be 'softer', using the public as judging body. The public could change its behaviour and shift demand between competitors or judge a company negatively (loss of image); this public control is interpreted as a possible way to change markets.

These aspects characterise the approach of product policy. Altogether, the role of policy and government is restricted; we concentrate on two types of action:

- Direct product-oriented interventions of environmental policy are possible, but they are and should be restricted to some severe exceptions foreseen for preventing actual risks and problems.

- IPP (and also environmental policy) has to pursue a role of facilitating business to arrange its operational and strategic behaviour in an environmentally sound way.

Both types of action will be explained in more detail in Sections 11.4 and 11.5.

11.4 IPP as crisis management

The first type of action happens on a case-by-case basis; it is based on the paradigm of a 'strong' intervening government. This regulation type was the 'traditional' approach taken by product policy in the past. In general, we recognise that environmental hot spots with actual and considerable health or safety problems have diminished, but that the more long-term problems (e.g. eutrophication, climate change) are increasing steadily. This also means that crisis management by government is needed only rarely. But government should be able to intervene, if necessary.

Recent examples of such interventions were associated with the sudden occurrence of BSE in Germany (2001) and the knowledge of illegal feeding of animals in Germany (2002). In such cases, government must react and regulate using specific measures and prescriptions that try to 'solve' the environmental hot spots immediately. In most cases, the reaction is based on crises: that is on a high actuality or awareness among the population which urges policy-makers and public bodies to (re-)act.

---

4 This toolkit can be subdivided into several categories of instruments: namely, consumer-related instruments, voluntary agreements, voluntary and mandatory information, economic instruments and regulatory instruments.

11.5 IPP as a strategic and facilitating approach

The second type of environmental policy with regard to products, IPP, can be subdivided into two different activities. First, a general structure should be elaborated which arranges the whole area and presents the strategic framework. This *vertical* orientation has to be supplemented by a *horizontal* orientation, which is focused on selected product groups which are regarded as important.

11.5.1 Vertical orientation: general framework

Whereas the above-mentioned first type of action stresses the role of government as actor, the second type is more oriented to the future and can be embedded in a broader governance approach. The main reason for this is our belief that the strategic challenge in the field of products is *not* retrospective, but the real effort is to look for a preventative and anticipatory approach. With regard to products, this puts innovation at the centre. Innovations can be subdivided into different types with specific degrees of reducing environmental burdens; Rocha *et al.* (1999), for example, distinguish between four types of innovation: namely, product improvement, product redesign, function innovation and system innovation. The focus on innovation is based on the real dynamic processes within business and industry which continuously try to gain competitive advantages characterised by Joseph A. Schumpeter's 'creative destruction'. Innovation is up to business; government and public bodies could act when products enter the market, but the stages within enterprises are not directly influenced. But—and this is the crucial point—once a product has been produced, both the economic and the environmental life-cycles have already started by the time the product is sold and used. The life-cycles are mainly determined by the earlier steps within an enterprise. The main constituting factor is product development and this is determined by business. Pfeiffer (1983: 67) argues with the example of mechanical engineering that more than 70% of the producing costs are determined by product development. The US National Research Council (1991) estimated that more than 70% of the costs of product development, production and use are determined by the design steps of a product. It has to be supposed that a large part of the environmental burdens of a product along its environmental life-cycle are predetermined in the same way.

Therefore, the complex challenge is to influence the innovation processes of products with the intention of improving and/or increasing their environmental features. Innovation influences markets and change conditions and the available product palette. This continuous market change should be oriented towards environmental objectives. The strategy of an IPP is to stimulate environmental market changes and market transformations.

How should policy deal with these issues? In general (see, for an overview, Cleff and Rennings 1999), economics has identified three factors that influence innovation: namely, technology (technology push), market conditions (market pull) and policy/regulation (regulatory push and pull). We believe that company-internal characteristics form a fourth influencing factor. In the meantime, it is acknowledged that technology push is of importance for the first stages of the economic life-cycle of products, whereas market pull is of importance for the future diffusion of innovations on the market (Coombs *et al.* 1987: 103). These four factors encompass 'clusters' of different activities and measures influencing innovation (Fig. 11.1).

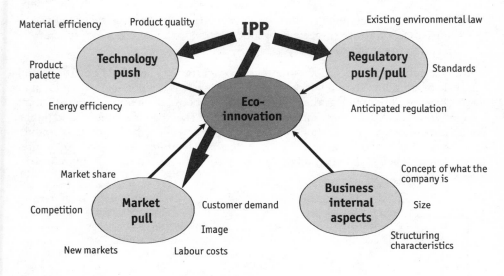

FIGURE 11.1 Determinants of product innovations

Source: Rubik 2002: 162, based on Cleff and Rennings 1999: 193

Public environmental policy and therewith IPP are able to affect three of these clusters, at least partly: namely, technology, market conditions and the regulatory framework. Company-internal conditions and aspects are not easily directly influenced by public policy. The challenge for IPP is to arrange a policy framework that influences these three clusters stimulating eco-innovation of products. Direct product-oriented interventions of environmental policy are possible, but they are and should be restricted to preventing actual risks and problems. IPP (and also environmental policy) should allow business to arrange its operational and strategic behaviour in an environmentally sound way. To do this, it should stimulate and facilitate, but not regulate. Public policy and IPP is not able to judge the decentralised search carried out by market actors on the supply and demand side for new solutions, innovations, etc.

Therefore, the role of IPP is limited to using the innovation processes of business as transmission mechanisms for environmental reorientation and restructuring in such a way that innovations are not just benign but also environmentally oriented and able to transform market(s). This also means that IPP has to address and support actors on both the supply and the demand side.

We propose to differentiate between the *political* area of governmental tasks and the area of the *real management* of products along their life-cycle at which different actors are involved. A useful orientation might be the differentiation that has been introduced in substance chain policy (see de Man and Flatz 1994):

- **Product policy** is the area of government and governmental institutions and encompasses the formulation of objectives and framework setting by selecting and implementing instruments.

- **Product management** is the area of actions and measures taken by the 'ensemble' of actors (especially producers, traders and consumers) who are involved in the life-cycle of a product.

Product policy tends to follow an integrated approach. The whole environmental life-cycle of a product should be considered. This policy is not possible without a high degree of information. In Figure 11.2, we distinguish between an information/communication flow and a flow of action. The political actor (i.e. the government) and public bodies have to receive information on the environmental impacts of a product/product group and on the management of the other actors. The other actors have to be integrated into the political 'bargaining' process by communication on objectives, instruments and knowledge.

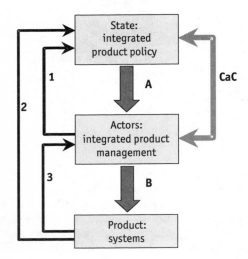

Co-operation and communication:

CaC Co-operation and communication between actors and state on objectives, priorities, measures and instruments

Flow of measures and actions:

A IPP framework by state

B Product management activities of different actors influencing the life-cycle of product systems

Flow of information:

1 Information to the state on product management of the different actors

2 Information to the state on environmental burdens

3 Information to different product management actors on environmental burdens

FIGURE 11.2 **Integrated product policy and the role of actors**

Source: Rubik 2002: 166

11.5.2 Horizontal orientation: product panels as a product group-specific approach

It is not sufficient to create a broader framework and a general interpretation of government as facilitator; additionally, policy should focus on specific cases to start and support innovations. Selected, for example, by priority lists, a product group-specific focus is necessary. This means arranging an orientation towards important issues and trying to meet the environmental challenges.

As elaborated above, this should be done by using and mobilising innovation as a transmission mechanism to extend environmental benignity. Once again, this could not be done by command-and-control approaches: that is, by regulation, for the reasons indicated above. In contrast, the idea is to involve stakeholders who influence the selected product chain directly or indirectly and to bring them together. This is also an innovation in the area of 'actors'. This approach has been practised in Denmark for many years (see Knudsen *et al.* 2001) where it is known as 'product panels'.

The initiation, realisation and 'design' of product panels and other facilitating approaches need a clarification of the contextual framework to present participants with a clear and reliable orientation. Driessen (1998: 252) lists three characteristic aspects: namely, 'the name of the game, the key players, and the playing field':

- **Name of the game.** The objective of such an approach should be clarified at the very beginning; it could be reflexive learning and also negotiation. Driessen (1998: 253) hinted at this point:

    > Most of the interaction that takes place between the parties involved in co-operative management is through consultation and dialogue. By communicating with each other, the parties gain new insight into problems: from a different vantage point, they may see some new solutions. Moreover, communication stimulates the parties to come forward with creative ideas. They 'learn' from one another how to approach environmental problems from a different . . . angle . . . On the other hand, the interaction between the parties can take the character of negotiation.

- **Key players.** Learning and negotiations with a reasonable output need a strategic choice of involved partners. We see two different possibilities: on the one hand a 'representation model' (involvement of representatives of key actors and of business associations) and on the other hand a 'change agents model' (involvement of relevant environmental trend-setters and innovators). Danish experiences favour the second model because of its incentive to change markets dynamically—starting also from market niches.

- **Playing field.** Participatory approaches are grounded on interaction processes between participants (see Chapter 9 in this volume). Mutual acceptance and a fair discourse are necessary. Driessen (1998: 258) proposed some rules:

    - Every discourse participant must have access to the knowledge needed to make validity claims and criticise others.

    - Every discourse participant must have an equal opportunity to make validity claims to comprehensibility, truth, normative rightness, and sincerity.

    - Every discourse participant must have an equal opportunity to challenge the comprehensibility, truth, rightness, or sincerity of validity claims made by others.

    - Judgement about conflicting validity claims must be made using the most reliable methodological techniques available.

    – Every discourse participant must have an equal opportunity to influence the choice of how the final determination of validity will be made and to determine discourse closure.

Besides these three aspects, some others have to be mentioned:

- **Process starters**. Often, such processes are started based on initiatives from public bodies. They should involve appropriate moderators and award some subsidies intended to start the projects.

- **Involvement of governmental representatives**. The role of government and public bodies should be very restricted towards initiation of processes and towards participation.

- **Discussed topics**. Several aspects should be treated, especially existing and planned measures and activities of government and of stakeholders in the selected area, also innovation dynamics, visions and long-term objectives, environmental successes and existing challenges, possible activities undertaken by stakeholders, identification and agreement on environmental priorities, desires and claims towards policy and voluntary agreements.

Such product panels as participatory approaches are challenges with risks of failure. Before starting such approaches the above-mentioned aspects should be considered and solved in an agreed way. The involvement of different stakeholders and actors is not a simple task. On the contrary, the composition in particular is of crucial importance. We recommend a strategic choice and involvement of change agents who are willing to transform markets—also starting from niches. If such approaches are successful, the other competitors will become aware and will perhaps try to join the process; at least they will try to imitate the results.

11.6 Conclusions

The general message of this chapter for the importance of governance is that IPP is a new way of thinking, co-operating and acting in a strategic and anticipatory pattern using (product) innovation as a transmission mechanism for market transformations.

Co-operation, information and integration are key terms of IPP. Integration is a challenge because it hints at several aspects (especially life-cycle, environmental media, actors, tools), but this can be dealt with only by accepting a shared responsibility. New ways and paths of behaviour are necessary, incorporating a paradigm shift of environmental policy-making. This is supported by business seeking deregulation, but attacked by NGOs demanding traditional command-and-control approaches.

References

BMU (Bundesministerium für Umwelt, Naturschutz und Reaktorsicherheit) (1999) 'Hintergrunddokument zum Thema Produktbezogene Umweltpolitik', *Umwelt* 6: V-XVI.

Cleff, T., and K. Rennings (1999) 'Determinants of Environmental Product and Process Information', *European Environment* 5: 191-201.

Coombs, R., *et al.* (1987) *Economics and Technological Change* (Basingstoke, UK: Macmillan).

De Man, R., and A. Flatz (1994) 'Anforderungen an künftiges Stoffstrommanagement', in S. Hellenbrandt and F. Rubik (eds.), *Produkt und Umwelt* (Marburg, Germany: Metropolis): 169-88.

Driessen, P. (1998) 'Concluding Remarks: The Scope of Co-operative Management', in P. Glasbergen (ed.), *Co-operative Environmental Governance: Public–Private Agreements as a Policy Strategy* (Dordrecht, Netherlands: Kluwer): 251-67.

Ernst & Young/SPRU (1998) *Integrated Product Policy. London: Study on behalf of DG Environment* (London: Ernst & Young/SPRU).

European Commission (2001) *Grünbuch zur Integrierten Produktpolitik* (COM[2001]68 final; Brussels: European Commission).

Knudsen, P.E., *et al.* (2001) *Evaluating Product Panels* (Working Report No. 14; Copenhagen: Danish Environmental Protection Agency).

Minsch, J., *et al.* (eds.) (1998) *Institutionelle Reformen für eine Politik der Nachhaltigkeit* (Heidelberg, Germany: Springer).

National Research Council (1991) *Improving Engineering Design: Designing for Competitive Advantage* (Washington, DC: National Academy Press).

Oosterhuis, F., F. Rubik and G. Scholl (1996) *Product Policy in Europe: New Environmental Perspectives* (Dordrecht, Netherlands: Kluwer).

Pfeiffer, W. (1983) 'Strategisch orientiertes Forschungs- und Entwicklungsmanagement: Probleme und Lösungsansätze aus Sicht der Wissenschaft', in H. Blohm and G. Danert (eds.), *Forschungs- und Entwicklungsmanagement* (Stuttgart, Germany: J.B. Metzeler/C.E. Poeschel): 124-33.

Rocha, C., H. Brezet *et al.* (1999) 'The Development of Product-Oriented Environmental Management Systems (POEMS): The Dutch Experience and a Case-Study', *ERCP '99: Sixth European Roundtable on Cleaner Production.*

Rubik, F. (2002) *Integrierte Produktpolitik: Stand, Entwicklung, Perspektiven* (Marburg, Germany: Metropolis).

—— and D. Scheer (2005) *Integrierte Produktpolitik in ausgewählten Länden Europas* (IÖW paper no. 121; Berlin: IÖW).

Statistisches Bundesamt (1995) *Systematisches Güterverzeichnis für Produktionsstatistisken* (Wiesbaden, Germany: Statistisches Bundesamt)

Wegner, G. (1995) *Wirtschaftspolitik zwischen Selbst- und Fremdsteuerung: Ein neuer Ansatz* (Baden-Baden, Germany: Nomos).

12

The role of voluntary initiatives in sustainable corporate governance

Jens Clausen

Borderstep Institute for Innovation and Sustainability, Germany

Kathrin Ankele and Ulrich Petschow

Institute for Ecological Economic Research (IÖW), Germany

The processes of liberalisation and globalisation have brought about significant changes affecting the activities of companies. These changes open up a spectrum of new possibilities but also bring about some new framework conditions, which have to be observed for continuous success in global markets. In parallel, the structure of transnational corporations (TNCs) has changed from a strong hierarchy towards a fragmented organisation, which leaves responsibilities and control nearer the production- and market-oriented units.

Furthermore, global competition has increased pressures on social concerns and environmental protection. Against this background the retention of state autonomy and power is harmful for environmental protection and sustainability. Therefore governance deficits can be witnessed that need to be addressed with new measures. Corporate self-regulation could be one possible alternative path when certain preconditions are met.

One of the most important changes in the role corporations play in global governance is coupled to their size. Through mergers and acquisitions corporations have grown bigger and, in effect, about two-thirds of the 100 biggest economic units of the world today are corporations; the remaining third are nation-states. The power and influence that the corporations have accumulated allows them to have an impact on national as well as international politics.

12.1 Transnational corporations and sustainability

As a consequence of their growing size and power, corporations are increasingly requested to take responsibility for the ecological and social impacts of their activities.

Corporations are dealing differently with these demands (Sachs 1993). The spectrum covers proactive, supporting strategies as well as defensive, reactive ones. The first can be characterised briefly as follows:

- TNCs foster the diffusion of environmental technologies and social standards, thereby environmental compliance and eco-efficiency are enhanced and compliance with at least basic social standards is attained (especially in small and medium-sized firms).

- Core companies in supply chains promote the dissemination of environmental and sustainability standards in the value chain in order to fulfil, for example, product stewardship demands they have committed themselves to.

- In order to realise positive efficiency effects TNCs apply environmental and sustainability standards company-wide, which are based on the highest requirements of all countries of operation.

The second type of strategy can be described by measures such as:

- TNCs influence the international political agenda in favour of their interests, for example in the run up to the conferences in Rio de Janeiro and Johannesburg, disregarding societal requirements.

- They use their power to impede a policy towards sustainability and environmental protection.

- They sometimes act in a way that is interpreted as greenwashing.

- The structural effect of the market-based activities of TNCs is leading to the destruction of sustainable production systems in LDCs (less developed countries).

To better understand why some companies are proactive and others are not, one should take a look at the socioeconomic context corporations are operating in and at their strategic orientation. Both shape the way in which companies address external demands.

Economic activities in modern societies are embedded in structures of social relations (Granovetter 1985; Rugman 2000[1]). Those relations generate trust and discourage malfeasance. Trust is an important resource in market economies; it supports competitive ability and legitimacy (Suchman 1995) in industrial relations within supply chains and within consumer markets (especially with regard to brand names). To maintain trust and legitimacy companies need to address concerns about their contribution to environmental and social degradation.

In this regard TNCs (and other companies) have adopted different approaches in recent years including corporate social responsibility (CSR) (see, for example, Anderson 1989; Clarkson 1995; Henriques and Sadorsky 1999), corporate citizenship[2] and

---

1   Concerning the 'embeddedness' Rugman points out that most TNCs still have a strong home base.
2   In Spring 2001 *The Journal of Corporate Citizenship* was founded with the aim of increasing and spreading knowledge on the changing relationship of business and society in a globalised economy. See also Zadek 2001.

corporate accountability (highlighted at the World Summit in Johannesburg; WSSD 2002). These approaches are characterised by a broad variety of definitions. They all have in common that they address the responsibility of corporations towards society and that they comprise management principles to handle them. CSR gained further support with the European Green Paper on Corporate Social Responsibility[3] which was published in July 2001 and complemented with a multi-stakeholder forum to exchange good practice.[4] In our view these approaches could be included in a wider interpretation of the notion of corporate governance, which includes not only the principal–agent problem concerning the financial sphere but also environmental and social concerns.

Taken seriously, these approaches will lead to strategic reorientations within corporations since external demands are addressed and active dialogue with stakeholders is initiated.

The interdependence between the corporation and its environment has been investigated in a systematic way by Kolk (2000). She developed a model that differentiates three perspectives on strategic management. In short, **outside-in** reflects external influences and pressures on companies, while **inside-in** describes corporate resources and capabilities such as interpretation of external stimuli, learning processes, development of appropriate measures, etc. The third perspective, **inside-out**, reflects the network and dependency relations of the corporation.

These three perspectives reflect the fact that a firm's strategic orientations might be influenced by a plurality of external factors and by internal structures and resources including the ability of the organisation to learn, as well as by the involvement of the firm in networks.

The inside-out perspective includes measures that are taken under the umbrella of CSR, corporate citizenship or corporate accountability. In the following section voluntary initiatives are discussed as an example of such measures. To determine whether and by which means they can contribute to sustainability they are analysed in the three perspectives of the above model.

12.2 Voluntary initiatives

In the past decade, the amounts and types of voluntary initiative have increased significantly in parallel with the expectations of politicians as well as business representatives concerning their effectiveness (for an overview, see UNEP's *Industry and Environment* journal 1998). These expectations are based on the conviction that the different types of voluntary initiative are suitable policy instruments. They also originate from the limits of regulation and the search for alternative political means. At the Johannesburg World Summit, partnership initiatives found their way into the world-

3   europa.eu.int/comm/employment_social/soc-dial/csr/greenpaper_en.pdf

4   This forum was chaired by the Commission and brought together European representative organisations of employers, business networks, trade unions and NGOs, to promote innovation, convergence and transparency in existing CSR practices and tools. Findings and conclusions are available at forum.europa.eu.int/irc/empl/csr_eu_multi_stakeholder_forum/info/data/en/csr%20ems%20forum.htm, 6 September 2005.

wide political agenda as so-called Type II outcomes. Voluntary initiatives might be targeted at the negotiation, co-ordination or implementation stages of sustainability targets (see Chapter 9 in this volume).

Concerning the relationship between partners—if there are any partners—voluntary initiatives have been categorised differently by various authors (e.g. OECD 2001; Hansen *et al.* 2002; Chapter 14 in this volume). For companies, the following three major types of voluntary initiative are of interest.

12.2.1 Codes of conduct and unilateral commitments

In a fact-finding mission on private initiatives the OECD analysed 246 private environmental and labour codes of conduct (OECD 2001). Environmental codes of conduct of firms or industry associations typically encompass a commitment to compliance, openness to community concerns, environmentally friendly products, and employee training among other issues (OECD 2001: 8). Labour codes concentrate on working environment, compliance, discrimination, compensation and child labour. Of the 96 internal codes addressing firm and employee behaviour, only 30% plan for internal monitoring, only 21% implement a whistle-blowing facility and only 19% appoint a compliance officer or committee.

Besides codes of conduct that apply to individual firms, there are initiatives by industry associations. These initiatives set out to demonstrate self-regulation in order to meet public demands and to avoid stricter regulation. Thereby standards and evaluation criteria are developed and audits are carried out to check compliance of the members with those standards. Support for the members is also provided to meet the standards (Schneider and Ronit 2000). The effectiveness of such private governance forms depends on the capacities of the association to control and sanction non-compliance and on a functioning background control by the public and NGOs (Schneider and Ronit 2000).

12.2.2 Standards and voluntary programmes

Examples of this type of voluntary initiative might be the ISO standard 14001 for environmental management systems with its 72,000 participants in 2005 (www.14001news.de), the Social Accountability Standard 8000 issued by the Centre for Economic Priorities Accreditation Agency (www.cepaa.org), the EMAS Regulation of the European Communities with about 4,000 participants in 2005 or the Responsible Care programme of the chemical industry. Each individual company is completely free to decide whether to participate in standards and voluntary programmes—unless they are forced to participate by an important customer, for example. When this happens those standards can develop an inherent dynamic and binding character. As a major difference to unilateral activities, the participating company can decide only whether it wants to participate or not; it cannot define the scope or requirements of the standard or programme. The above-mentioned activities do all contain an external certification or validation scheme which ensures compliance of the participant with the requirements of the standard or programme. The problem with this kind of voluntary initiative lies in the difficulty in measuring its effectiveness in terms of environmental protection and sustainability since the standards or programmes focus on management systems and rules and contain few material targets.

12.2.3 Negotiated agreements

Negotiated agreements are contracts between government and industry or its associations. The agreements typically fix targets and a time schedule, which must be met, and in return government usually refrains from introducing more coercive measures (Hansen *et al.* 2002). The Dutch and German governments have been actively using negotiated agreements for more than ten years and a growing number of them plan for monitoring and evaluation.[5]

In general, voluntary initiatives (should) have targets that are not (or only with extreme difficulty) achievable using command-and-control politics. Since there are plenty of such, we think that voluntary initiatives are both necessary and unavoidable for a modern sustainable policy in the business sector. But monitoring and evaluation of this type of initiative deserves some particular consideration.

12.3 Voluntary initiatives and the problem of compliance

The problem with all discussed forms of voluntary initiative is that of compliance. Compliance with national law is in some nations enforced more effectively, in others less so. Dasgupta *et al.* (2001) found differences in the stringency of national environmental law of about a factor of four between the most stringent countries such as Switzerland and Germany and the least stringent countries such as Ethiopia and Bhutan. But enforcement of compliance with voluntary initiatives is in all countries only just beginning to happen. The problem of non-compliance might therefore be more important with voluntary initiatives.

The model of Kolk offers us an opportunity to construct a link between strategic management of corporations, society and the problem of governance of voluntary initiatives. In addition to the three perspectives of Kolk (see Table 12.1), we have developed a learning cycle that:

- Comprises regulation, product market(s) and capital markets as the main direct external influences

- Adds the media as well as the NGOs as important actors in agenda setting

- Sees public discussion as the main arena, which in turn has major influences on regulation, product market(s) and capital markets

---

5   It might be added that compliance problems with negotiated agreements seem to be less severe than with the other two types. Nevertheless, many of the following arguments also apply to negotiated agreements. For more thorough facts and advice in this direction, see Hansen *et al.* 2002.

Perspectives	Aspects
Outside-in **External influences**	Industry structure (competition, markets, products, environmental risks) Main regulatory influences (in home and host countries, international) Other forms of environmental pressure (customers, societal organisations)
Inside-in **Firm**	Economic characteristics of the firm (profits, market shares, market strategy, control structure, degree of vertical integration, diversification and internationalisation) Firm-specific resources and capabilities Organisation structure Environmental impacts and risks
Inside-out **Network**	Network and dependency relationships; assessment of core firms Major environmental problems in product chain(s) and network

TABLE 12.1 Perspectives on strategic management

Source: Kolk 2000: 78

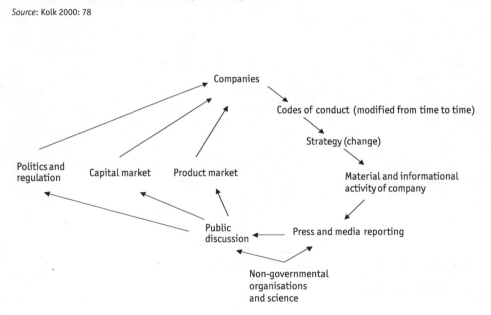

FIGURE 12.1 Civil society as actor in the governance of companies

- Ascribes an active role to corporations concerning the survey and interpretation of external influences in order to develop appropriate answers

In a dynamic perspective the problem of compliance might be overcome by actors that are interested in this field and, with this, civil society and the media might be important for the development of societal learning circles and the critical evaluation of voluntary initiatives.

Figure 12.1 is based on the above model and entails the main actors that constitute the socioeconomic context of corporations. The arrows indicate the points at which influence can be exerted on behalf of effective governance. Reverse relationships are excluded to keep the figure concise.

One should also keep in mind that this cycle is mostly triggered by external pressure from NGOs and/or the media.[6] Massive negative publicity and consumer boycotts lead to short-term measures and middle- and long-term strategic reorientations in the corporations. Since the initiation is a one-off situation, we excluded it from Figure 12.1.

The general idea behind this learning cycle remains unaffected: action as well as active information of companies directed at society will probably feed back into the firm after (and if) it has been processed in any form by the public. This feedback is likely to initiate learning inside the company. But we assume that much information that is disclosed to the public by firms remains unread because of the limited capacity of societal agents interested in corporate activities to read material from thousands of firms. We think that the often highlighted value of transparency therefore not only requires open access to company information but also calls for independent agents to collect and evaluate information about company behaviour and act as intermediaries between companies and the public. These independent agents will often be scientific organisations or NGOs; in some cases government agencies might be involved.[7] According to the functional logic of the media, company news—besides scandals or severe accidents—hardly catches their attention directly. Mostly it needs to be collected and evaluated by specialists in order to find its way into the media in aggregated form. And media attention and reporting certainly enhances the probability that societal concerns are taken seriously within corporations.

12.4 Possible governance rules for monitoring voluntary initiatives

The following paragraphs focus on the ability of individuals and their social organisation to maintain common pool resources. Most models—and most theoretical economists—are starting from the assumption that individuals are acting more or less egoistically. The personal characteristics of the economic human or *homo œconomicus* identifies him or her as a human being who is very rationally focusing on self-interest

---

6   Consider, for example, the Brent Spar case or the Nike case.
7   This is, for example, the case for the US Toxics Release Inventory, where specific information on companies is made publicly available by the national Environmental Protection Agency.

and is in continuous search of more economic means of meeting his or her needs (see, for a thorough description, Siebenhüner 2001). The most common economic assumptions about priorities of companies are quite similar: the business of business is business, as Friedman (1970) put it. As corporations are formed of human beings, these two characterisations might be not independent from one another. This point of view usually ignores societal interaction as well as institutions.

A different approach to collective action was developed by Ostrom (1999). She does not focus on experiences gained in game situations but builds her model on the observation of a broad variety of empirical examples about the management of common pool resources (CPR). Her work results in a set of rules, which can explain the formation and maintenance of successful co-operation in medium-sized groups of users of CPR. These rules should (Ostrom 1999: 241):

1. Define a group of users that have the right to use the CPR

2. Be tailored to the special attributes of the CPR in question and the respective user group

3. Be at least partially developed by the local users

4. Be monitored by persons who are accountable to the group of users

5. Be sanctioned by graded penalties

A couple of Ostrom's special findings are of particular interest. She makes a distinction between 'rational egoists' and 'conditional co-operators'. The number of 'conditional co-operators' will mount when they themselves know their number, because that makes it probable to find co-operating partners when oneself makes an offer for co-operation. Information and transparency are necessary preconditions. As an additional factor, clarity about the duration of the game (the relationship) will support co-operation.[8]

Keeping in mind that a couple of hundred TNCs are anything but a medium-sized local group there are still some aspects of Ostrom's rules that might very plausibly be observed when looking for TNC governance possibilities. The following aspects might be of importance:

- It should be clear (and easy to find out) which companies are actually active in voluntary initiatives and the group of companies should be well aware that the public knows that.[9]

- Rules for monitoring of voluntary initiatives should be developed not only by TNCs and their contract partners but also with participation of groups that might profit or suffer if the initiatives succeed or fail: in other words, stakeholders. Additionally, these rules should generally adhere to a standard procedure, which will have to be developed (see Chapter 9 in this volume).

---

8   While in the last round of public-good games different studies found up to 70% of participants to act egoistically (Ostrom 1999: 140).

9   The problem of the huge number of TNCs could partly be approached by concentrating on core firms in supply chains as potential enforcers of sustainability rules among the supply chain members (snowball effect). Associations could play a comparable part.

- Institutions in charge of monitoring voluntary initiatives should be accountable not only to TNCs but also to all other stakeholders of the voluntary initiative.[10]

- Since there are thousands of voluntary initiatives as well as TNCs involved, there should be some kind of general transparency about the achievement of targets of voluntary initiatives by individual firms, to avoid free-riding.

- Since 'graded penalties' are not an element of most voluntary initiatives, transparency about the implementation effort and status by each participant is the only penalty that society could provide for. The impact of transparency—due to its possible effect on corporate image—on the implementation effort can nevertheless be high. If international politics 'saves regulation work' by supporting voluntary initiatives, it should at least provide the means to realise transparency on the outcomes.

- In case of failure of self-regulation as well as insufficient public awareness, some kind of background threat should be maintained to be able to sanction non-compliance (legislation).

12.5 Conclusions for corporate governance

The manifold approaches of self-regulation may be an interesting starting point for the development of new forms of corporate governance in the context of global governance. It has to be pointed out that this should be interpreted as process and not as result. The target of the process should be that the firms as one main actor group in the processes of global governance take their part of the shared responsibility on the road to sustainable development. Voluntary initiatives might be practised by a single firm as well as by associations of companies. But, as the reality shows, there is a need for continuous background control of actions taken by the firms and their associations by other actors in society. To achieve long-lasting sustainable behaviour, firms have to feel that compliance with voluntary targets is as important for legitimisation as compliance with laws and regulations. Public transparency of results and a vivid critical discussion come to a central position when thinking about the possibilities of civil society to control firms' activities. External critics and feedback are also central to support learning within firms.

For the development of corporate governance systems this has the consequence that a stronger stakeholder orientation of the boards' actions is unavoidable if sustainability targets are not to be continuously jeopardised by shareholders' interests. The members of boards and management will in future have to look for win–win solutions more actively in order to realise long-term successful ventures. Management structures and visions will have to integrate this into thinking and daily routines and provide the necessary instruments, such as the sustainability balanced scorecard.

---

10   Since those institutions play an important role, they should be provided with the necessary resources.

Additionally, effective background control by institutions in society is of central importance. Such institutions must be empowered to exercise the task with the necessary resources and capabilities. And regulatory threat must be maintained as a sanction for general non-compliance on the one hand and as a safeguard for fields where no public pressure can be organised on the other hand. Therefore, powerful global institutions are needed to make corporate social responsibility a requirement for all large, or at least all global firms and to provide consistent conditions for effective and sustainable competition.

References

Anderson, J.W. (1989) *Corporate Social Responsibility* (New York: Quorum Books).

Clarkson, M. (1995) 'A Stakeholder Framework for Analyzing and Evaluating Corporate Social Performance', *Academy of Management Review* 20.1: 92-117.

Dasgupta, S., A. Mody, S. Roy and D. Wheeler (2001) 'Environmental Regulation and Development: A Cross-Country Empirical Analysis', *Oxford Development Studies* 29.2: 173-87.

Friedman, M. (1970) 'The social responsibility of business is to increase its profits', *New York Times Magazine* 13.33: 122-26.

Granovetter, M. (1985) 'Economic Action and Social Structure: The Problem of Embeddedness', *American Journal of Sociology* 91.3: 481-510.

Hansen, K., K.S. Johannsen and A. Larsen (2002) 'Recommendations for Negotiated Agreements', *Environment and Planning C: Government and Policy* 20.1 (February 2002): 19-37.

Henriques, I., and P. Sadorsky (1999) 'The Relationship between Environmental Commitment and Managerial Perceptions of Stakeholder Importance', *Academy of Management Journal* 42.1: 87-99.

Kolk, A. (2000) *Economics of Environmental Management* (Harlow, UK: Pearson Education).

OECD (Organisation for Economic Co-operation and Development) (2001) *Corporate Responsibility: Results of a Fact-Finding Mission on Private Initiatives* (Paris: OECD).

Ostrom, E. (1999) *Die Verfassung der Allmende* (Tübingen, Germany: Mohr Siebeck).

Petschow, U., J. Clausen and M. Keil (2003) *Governance und Sustainability: Die erweiterte Rolle nichtstaatlicher Akteure in globalen Steuerungsmustern* (Munich: Ökom Verlag).

Rugman, A.M.(2000) *The End of Globalization* (London: Random House Business Books).

Sachs, W. (1993) *Global Ecology: A New Arena of Political Conflict* (London/New Jersey: Zed Books).

Schneider, V., and K. Ronit (eds.) (2000) *Private Organisations in Global Politics* (ECPR Studies in European Political Science 13; London: Routledge).

Siebenhüner, B. (2001) *Homo sustinens: Auf dem Weg zu einem Menschenbild der Nachhaltigkeit* (Marburg, Germany: Metropolis-Verlag).

Suchman, M. (1995) 'Managing Legitimacy: Strategic and Institutional Approaches', *Academy of Management Review* 20.3: 571-610.

UNEP (United Nations Environment Programme) (1998) *Industry and Environment* 21.1–2 (issue on voluntary initiatives).

WSSD (World Summit on Sustainable Development) (2002) *Plan of Implementation*, 4 September 2002; accessible at www.johannesburgsummit.org/html/documents/summit_docs/2309_planfinal.htm, 1 November 2005.

Zadek, S. (2001) *The Civil Corporation: The New Economy of Corporate Citizenship* (London: Earthscan Publications).

13

Good company citizenship
DOES GOVERNANCE CHANGE THE ROLE OF COMPANIES IN SOCIETY?

Mark Wade
Shell International Ltd

13.1 Companies in a world of dramatic change

Business is facing unprecedented scrutiny, risks and challenges in the face of dramatic change sweeping the world. The powerful forces of globalisation, liberalisation and technology have brought rapid change and advancement. But the speed and scale of the impacts are posing far-reaching questions and exposing dilemmas and threats as they push the boundaries of natural and human-made systems, ethics and even humanity itself.

There are widespread calls to slow the pace of globalisation and to temper unrestricted market growth. New forms of corporate governance are emerging driven by societal expectations. There is growing recognition that companies need to move beyond being responsible to shareholders for financial performance and become accountable to stakeholders for their wider economic, environmental and societal impacts. This move reflects the evolving relationship of government, corporations and civil society.

'Today, there is growing recognition that lasting and effective answers can be found only if business joins in partnership with other actors, including government and civil society', UN Secretary-General Kofi Annan told a business audience during the World Summit on Sustainable Development in Johannesburg (2002). 'And more and more we are realising that it is only by mobilising the corporate sector that we can make significant progress. The corporate sector has the finances, the technology and the management to make all this happen.'[1]

This is particularly true in alleviating poverty. Official development assistance (ODA) from governments to developing countries has dropped significantly over the past ten years—from US$60 billion to US$50 billion per year. During the same period foreign direct investment (FDI) to these countries has risen from US$50 billion to US$200 bil-

---

1 Kofi Annan, Johannesburg, 1 September 2002. Speech at 'Business Day', organised by Business Action for Sustainable Development.

lion a year. But this has not been evenly spread, with 12 developing countries receiving 75% of the investment and the 40 least developed countries getting only 5% of the total.

But at the same time that business is being seen as part of the solution, its integrity is coming under question by many who are deeply suspicious of its motives. Companies are facing ever-greater scrutiny with calls for more transparency and openness. In the last decade, such demands centred on environmental and social performance, but since the collapse of high-profile companies such as Enron and WorldCom, the spotlight has broadened to include financial reporting and the rigour of corporate governance. Shell has experienced the downside of this over the events of Brent Spar and Nigeria in the mid-'90s and, more recently, the recategorisation of oil and gas reserves.

At Johannesburg a group of leading non-governmental organisations, including Friends of the Earth and Christian Aid, called for global regulations on corporate accountability. Such calls are part of society's fast-changing expectations, very much a consequence of the social and technological changes that had their roots in the 1950s and 1960s and have multiplied since.

It is the very speed of change that is placing tremendous demands on companies and civil society. New technologies, such as genetic engineering and gene mapping, are putting our societies under stress and many are questioning the definition of humanity itself. Demands for natural resources, such as fish and timber, are testing the ability of the Earth to provide.

These stresses are driving the call for new rules, new ways of controlling market forces so that we can get the benefits of globalisation rather than the drawbacks. The key to all of this is in how people connect with each other. At the international level some are searching for global solutions to global problems, such as climate change and poverty. At the local or regional level people are celebrating in their diversity, in the vitality of their different cultures. They are saying that they are more interested in local, rather than global solutions—ones that are more fitting for their region and culture.

Society's changing expectations are important to business, especially how society views the role of companies. There are demands for companies to be responsible to a broader group of people than only their shareholders. Companies need to be accountable to their other stakeholders (interested parties) for important aspects of their environmental and social impacts too.

13.2 Shell and society's changing expectations[2]

In 1996 we conducted a major engagement exercise at Shell to understand how society's expectations were changing. One of the key pieces of learning that came out of it identified a move from the 'trust me' to the 'show me' world. In other words there is a breakdown in people's trust in established authority.

2 The companies in which Royal Dutch Shell plc directly or indirectly owns investments are separate entities. In this chapter the terms 'Shell', 'Group' and 'Shell Group' are sometimes used for convenience where references are made to Group companies in general. Likewise, the words 'we', 'us' and 'our' are also used to refer to Group companies in general or those who work for them. These expressions are also used where there is no purpose in identifying specific companies.

People are less willing than they were in the past to take the assurances of authorities such as government, scientists and companies on trust. There is an increasing call for corporations to show what it is they are doing. And in the absence of trust—something that characterises the modern world—there is a demand for independent verification of what is being shown. This shift from the 'trust me' to the 'show me' world is summarised in Figure 13.1.

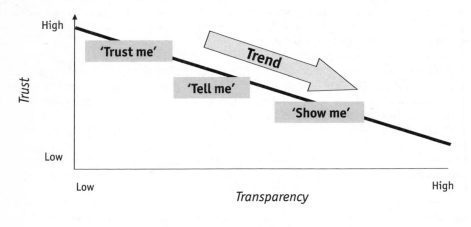

As trust diminishes, the demand for transparency
in the form of assurance mechanisms increases

FIGURE 13.1 The move to the 'show me' world

Businesses are increasingly under scrutiny. People are concerned not just with how much money companies make but also with *how* they make that money. For example, do they do it in a way that is responsible to the environment? Are they concerned about human rights and labour rights in the workforce, either in their own organisations or in contractors or subcontractors in developing worlds?

If people don't believe that companies behave ethically, then they are more likely to vote with their wallets and make their protest known by boycotting products or services. This is sometimes referred to as 'consumerism being the new democracy'.

The process that leads to regulation is also changing. The traditional model of experts of an elected government (in the civil service) working with company experts using a risk assessment approach to setting regulation is fast being overtaken by events. We are now seeing governments often running fast to catch up with changes in social expectations and to bring legislation into line with popular views.

At the same time we have witnessed much experimentation around the roles of the state and the private sector. This has been expressed differently in each region of the world, but the most obvious manifestation was the tide of privatisation of formerly government-owned businesses (telecoms, utilities, etc.) in the 1980s and 1990s. In the USA and UK this went as far as privatising prisons and schools.

In the developing world, many governments are struggling to provide their citizens with the basic social services because they are either too poor or face endemic corruption. Lack of such services creates a vacuum, because human need does not disappear simply because it is unmet. This is why many in the international community argue for business to fill the void, for companies to provide the essential social services not provided by government. After decades of being seen as sinners, companies are now being viewed in certain circles as potential saviours.

But companies must not assume the role of governments. The key question is how far should they extend their actions in partnership with governments and civil society in addressing social needs. The answer has to be determined on a case-by-case basis and by talking to people (multi-stakeholder engagement).

Multinational companies have been stereotyped as exploiters of the developing world. Clearly there have been cases to answer, but, within the global change outlined above, there is an opportunity for business to be part of the solution. Much depends on how well companies can govern themselves and the value systems and principles that their governance is based on.

Many organisations have attempted to devise codes of conduct to govern the behaviour of multinationals. Figure 13.2 gives some idea of the bewildering array of codes, standards, frameworks and conventions that a wide range of interested parties have formulated. These codes reflect two trends in regulation, one voluntary and the other statutory. The European Union has adopted a precautionary approach combined with calls on companies to comply on a voluntary basis. In the USA, though, the approach has been more compliance-driven. This is seen especially in environmental legislation but also more recently in the legal response to the Enron and WorldCom scandals.

Government
- UK Ethical Trading Initiative
- UK FCO+: Landmines
- EU Green Paper on CSR
- US FCPA

Intergovernmental organisations
- OECD Guidelines for MNEs
- ILO Declaration of Principles and Rights at Work
- ILO Labour Standards
- UNDHR
- UN Global Compact

Academic
- Charter of Common Responsibilities in Business (University of Friborg)

NGO
- Global Sullivan Principles
- Global Reporting Initiative (GRI)
- CEP SA 8000
- AA 1000
- ECCR/IRRC/TCCR Principles for Global Responsibility
- NEF/CAFOD Open Trading Initiative
- InterAction Council: UDH Responsibilities
- International League for Human Rights: Human Rights Auditing Standards and Procedures Projects
- Amnesty International Human Rights Guidelines for Companies
- CERES Principles
- Consumers International: Consumer Charter for Global Business
- The Interfaith Declaration on International Business Ethics

Industry
- Caux Round Table Principles for Business
- International Code of Ethics for Canadian Business
- ICC Rules of Conduct on Bribery and Corruption
- ICC Charter on Sustainable Development
- Corporate Social Responsibility
- ICC International Code of Advertising Practices

FIGURE 13.2 **Codemania**

Non-governmental organisations are calling for binding international legislation to force companies to behave in a certain way. Such calls—and the various codes—are a response from a society that is clearly yearning for a better order.

How can companies respond to these demands to be better equipped for the modern world? We offer some reflections here from Shell's experience. Each company has to decide on its appropriate route—there are no absolute truths and no rules. We have made some progress, but we are still learning and do not pretend to know all the answers.

A good place for any company to start is in the articulation of its own values and core purpose. This is helpful, otherwise you are rudderless in a sea of conflicting demands and expectations. Once the principles are in place, a governance framework of policies, standards and assurance processes can be set. These will reflect the business principles and be set within an understanding of the broader societal expectations.

This is what Shell does. We use our values, imbued in the Shell General Business Principles, to give us a direction. It also helps in deciding which code we support. We use the codes—all those in Figure 13.2—as both a convenient stimulus to drive our thinking and as a benchmark to judge our performance and to check our progress.

But companies should consider going one step further and use key performance indicators (KPIs), or measures of performance. The emphasis here is on 'key'. There is a call from certain circles for companies to report against a vast array of metrics. However, it is unrealistic to expect companies to report against a huge range of indicators everywhere and all the time. Reporting needs to be fit for purpose and cost-effective.

Companies, working with others in business and their stakeholders, need collectively to pick the most important indicators. The Global Reporting Initiative (GRI) may provide the process by which this can be achieved. This is an independent effort, backed by NGOs and the business community, to establish standards of reporting on company contributions to sustainable development. Shell supports the GRI and contributes our learning by doing into the process.

13.3 Governance in Shell

Figure 13.3 describes the way governance is viewed in Shell. It is seen as comprising a number of distinct orbits, which start wide—reflecting the society of which we are an integral part—and becomes more focused as we move into the business processes.

The outer orbit ensures that we consider society's values and expectations, which sometimes means that we choose to go beyond compliance. We then ensure that we comply with the prevailing laws and regulations in the different countries in which we operate or indeed international conventions. After that we set our policies and standards that govern our everyday actions. Individual managers have the freedom to run their part of the business within this governance framework.

We are a values-based organisation. Our strategy is to be a world leader in energy and petrochemicals. Every action we take is based on our core values of honesty, integrity and respect for people. These values have been part of the Shell organisation for decades. Our Business Principles are an extension of our values and a codification

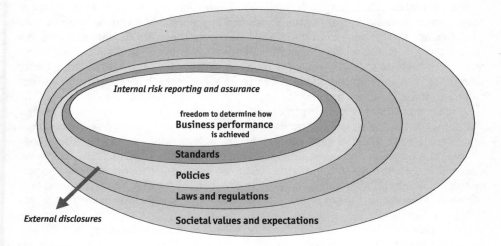

FIGURE 13.3 Governance in Shell

of how we do business. The Principles—revised in 1997 to reflect changes in social expectations—commit us to contribute to sustainable development and respect human rights. They define our responsibilities: ranging from our economic imperative to make an acceptable return on investments to the need to retain high standards of business integrity and to ensure the safety and health of those who work for Shell. Furthermore, our principles prevent us from making party political donations and specifically commit us to being a no-bribe company.

We use our business principles as our code of ethics. We expect all of our employees to adopt the principles in every country of operation, in all business dealings large or small. Shell's approach to governance is informed by an understanding of society's expectations, values and laws. Our governance process has three main elements: policies, standards and guidelines. And there is an assurance process that makes sure the policies are followed and the standards are adhered to.

13.4 Assurance processes in Shell

The **policies** are built into our thinking and demand a common approach right across the Shell Group, which operates in 140 countries. Examples of policies include our Business Principles and our Health, Safety and Environment (HSE) Commitments. Shell has HSE management systems in place in all countries of operation and environmental components of those systems have been certified to international standards in all major installations.

The **standards** clarify how the policies are implemented or set the expectations on other important matters that require a common approach in the way we run our business. Examples here range from standards that govern the way we treat our brand, our financial controls, the security of our installations and the decisions we make before testing products on animals, as we are required to do by law. **Guidelines** are adopted where the risks may not be high enough to justify a policy or standard, but we still believe that they are very important.

To make sure that the policy framework is followed we have an assurance process that comprises two letters of assurance. First, we require our country chairs (the senior representatives of Shell in each country where we operate) to report on how Shell upholds the Business Principles while managing its activities. Second, the executives who run our operations in a particular business sector must report on how they are upholding Group policies and standards. They report by letter to our Executive Committee and then to the Board of Royal Dutch/Shell plc. The process is verified by our Group auditors.

We also have a Social Responsibility Committee that comprises Non-executive Directors of the Board. This committee reviews the assurance processes relating to business principles and HSE management.

We have found that it is of little use having such a comprehensive framework of principles, standards and guidelines unless you promote them within the organisation. We do this through continuous training and awareness raising throughout the different management levels. We also produce what we call management primers on issues such as human rights, child labour, and bribery and corruption. These are written in a straightforward business style and are sent to relevant managers throughout the world to help them understand these difficult issues and to explain why—as business executives—they have to manage them well.

We have worked hard to understand our role as a business in upholding human rights. This is an important issue for us because we operate in many parts of the world where such rights hold a high profile. We have produced what we call a responsibilities map (Fig. 13.4), which helps managers put the issues into perspective. Our map—and the management thinking process—starts at what we see as the centre of human rights for our business: employee rights. The map shows our spectrum of concern and possible actions, including the Group speaking out in support of human rights.

These types of action go well beyond our legal obligations, which is consistent with our broader outlook of gauging society's expectations and aligning our actions where this makes sense to do so. This means we also go beyond compliance by supporting a number of the international codes of conduct we mentioned earlier. These include the UN Global Compact (we were an early signatory), the OECD Guidelines on Multinational Enterprises, the Global Sullivan Principles and the ICC Charter.

Shell has adopted a rigorous approach on climate change, because we believe that the consequences could be dire for the world if we as a society fail to grasp the potential enormity of the issue. We believe it is consistent with our Principles and the right thing to do.

We have already reduced our carbon dioxide emissions by 10% (from 1990 levels) and we will keep our emissions to 5% below 1990 levels for the rest of the decade while still growing the business. We include the potential cost of carbon in investment decisions for all major investments. This improves our competitiveness and encourages us

1. Employee rights
- Health and safety
- Equal opportunity
- Freedom of association
- Pay and conditions
- Personal development
- ILO Declaration
- Diversity and inclusiveness

2. Security
- Policy
- Standards
- Training

5. Advocacy
- Speaking out
- Silent diplomacy
- Education/training
- Identifying and sharing issues; engaging stakeholders

3. Community rights
- Indigenous people
- Local people
- Local HSE quality
- Social security
- Right to development

4. National rights
- Foreign direct investment/UN Global Compact/ Sullivan Principles
- Social equity/capital development
- Force for good by example

FIGURE 13.4 Human rights business responsibilities map

to invest in more efficient technologies that reduce both cost and environmental impact. Nobody is forcing us to do this but we can anticipate a time when governments will impose a cost for carbon emissions and we want to be prepared. We are also looking at carbon sequestration—finding ways to fix or store carbon so that it is not emitted to the atmosphere—and growing our solar, wind and hydrogen businesses.

We firmly believe in openness and transparency and one of the ways we demonstrate this is through our annual report to society, called *The Shell Report*. This comprehensive document reports on our contribution to sustainable development and I will expand on this later.

13.5 Sustainable development commitment and organisation in Shell

But why is Shell committed to contribute to sustainable development? The world has many major challenges to meet; extremes of poverty and wealth, environmental degradation, climate change and unsustainable patterns of production and consumption are some of the most pressing. We are part of society; we share the same agenda. Furthermore, legitimate business cannot succeed in failing societies. Business best prospers in healthy, thriving societies. Companies are composed of people and we share the same planet, breathe the same air, have the same hopes and expectations as anyone else. It is therefore in our own interest as people and as Shell to contribute to human development and to make sure that the way we run our business contributes to a cleaner, safer, better world.

Society has expectations of business—as discussed earlier. We at Shell believe the concept of sustainable development is both helpful and provides the best guidance for understanding society's changing expectations and making progress. It helps us align our business aspirations with society's broad expectations. This helps make us more competitive. In this way—by being profitable—we can sustain our success and contribute to a better world.

Of course this does not happen overnight. To make progress, we suggest that companies have to be very committed to the idea of sustainable development. For Shell, this means imbedding the ideas across our business and this requires well-designed management and governance structures. Figure 13.5 shows how we organise decision-making at the highest level.

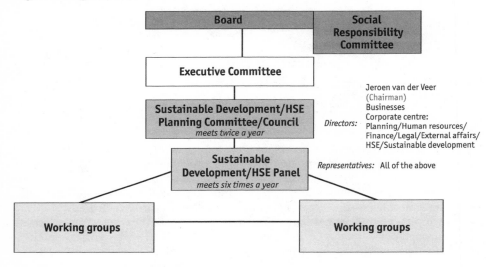

FIGURE 13.5 Sustainable development leadership

Our Executive Committee, chaired by Jeroen van der Veer, sets objectives and develops strategy for the Group. He also chairs the Sustainable Development and HSE Planning Committee/Council three times a year where the sustainable development and health, safety and environmental (HSE) agenda is reviewed and plans are put in place for concerted actions across our business. We also have a Sustainable Development and HSE Panel that meets six times a year with representatives from each of the businesses. The Social Responsibility Committee comprises Non-executive Directors of the board. They take a very keen interest in our progress.

Sustainable development to us is all about integrating the economic, environmental and social aspects involved in decision-making. It is about balancing the short-term priorities with the longer-term needs, which is a really tough challenge. Furthermore, it involves engaging with stakeholders to better understand the context in which you make decisions. This engagement helps improve decision-making because it is inclusive and also demonstrates that you are prepared to be accountable for your actions.

Once the framework is established—as shown in Figure 13.6—it has to become an integral part of your management systems and processes. We insist, for example, that any new project proposal presented to senior management must include sustainable development considerations. This is what we term 'hard-wiring'; if the proposal ignores the sustainable development aspects, then it will not go forward.

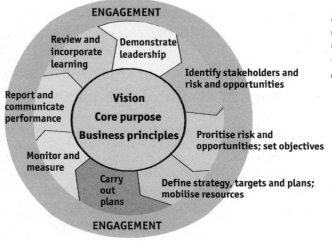

Engagement is a key characteristic of the framework allowing us to develop a shared understanding and trust with our people and stakeholders.

We take economic, environmental and social considerations into account in everything we do.

FIGURE 13.6 Sustainable development management framework

Managers need tools to help them do their business in a way that contributes to sustainable development. They also have to be convinced it is the right thing to do, right for them and right for the business. We have developed a sustainable development management framework, which encapsulates that thinking and is based on our core purpose. There are many similarities between this framework and others, but the primary difference is that it is informed by stakeholder engagement. The framework has become an integral part of our decision-making process.

To help managers further, we have also developed seven principles of sustainable development that provide guidance—a convenient checklist—to help managers in their decision-making. The principles, in brief, are:

1. Generate robust profits

2. Deliver value to customers

3. Protect the environment

4. Manage resources

5. Respect and safeguard people

6. Provide benefits to local communities

7. Consult with stakeholders

Shell has found that contributing to sustainable development is good for business on a number of levels. It benefits your reputation—which has to be defended at all times—but more importantly it is also good for your ability to compete. These benefits might show at different times.

13.6 The business case for sustainable development

When we first started out on this course, most of our effort was on risk and reputation management, particularly after the Brent Spar incident in 1995. But we saw that we had to get sustainable development into our systems and processes, and into people's hearts and minds. In this way we could gradually begin to generate business value. But we didn't expect that value to be delivered overnight; it takes time, as Figure 13.7 shows.

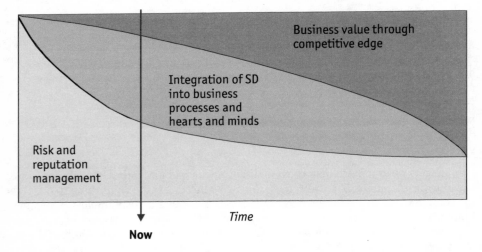

Business value through competitive edge

Integration of SD into business processes and hearts and minds

Risk and reputation management

Time

Now

FIGURE 13.7 Business value from sustainable development

What, then, is the business case for sustainable development? We see these seven points as making a compelling argument. Conducting your business in the way we have described helps to:

1. **Attract and motivate top talent.** People want to work for companies that share their values and contribute to a better world.

2. **Reduce costs through eco-efficiency.** This means making more from less, and saving money in the process. Longer-term this means turning waste into something useful.

3. **Reduce risk.** When you set out to consider a broad range of issues and consult with your stakeholders you will gain an understanding that helps to reduce your business risks.

4. **Influence product and service innovation.** Changing expectations demand new, innovative products and services that are clean, safe and ethically produced; an open and inclusive approach helps you understand the needs of the market.

5. **Influence business portfolios for the future.** Having a better understanding of the trends that influence markets helps you plan for the future. For example, we have a clear idea of how gas will provide a bridge between oil and the new forms of energy such as wind and solar, and we can arrange our business portfolio accordingly.

6. **Attract more loyal customers.** People are more likely to stay loyal to your products and services if they feel the company is acting honourably and satisfying their needs.

7. **Enhance reputation.** A good reputation opens new opportunities and cements relationships.

A critical part of our programme is to report annually on our progress. We want our business partners and the public to judge how we are doing. We report on our performance versus our targets, we discuss where we stand on challenging issues and we provide case studies as examples of how we operate around the world.

The Shell Report is integrally linked to the management cycle. These links ensure that it is a credible document that reflects our progress, means something and informs our decision-making. We also go to great lengths to verify the contents of *The Shell Report*. Financial verification has been evolving for the past 100 years. Verifying environmental information is a much more recent activity and far more complex because there are many more units, standards and definitions. But we, working with our Group auditors, have made good progress over the past 15 years and feel confident that our health, safety and environmental data are sound.

Verifying social and socioeconomic information is far more complex because the ideas are difficult to pin down and there are few standard definitions. Classic auditing procedures derived from financial auditing are just not up to the job. Verification is about developing trust and we need another approach to provide independent assurance in the social arena.

We verify at the local level, to provide assurance on issues such as the acceptability of environmental performance and the quality of engagement in the communities. This has been done in a structured way. We have reviewed the systems, processes and data and used our Group auditors to do this. An external review of stakeholder perceptions has been completed and this information fed into a tailored template approach that involves a team of international and local experts who give their judgement on how effective we are.

13.7 Practical examples

How is it working in practice? Here are three examples from different parts of the world.

The Malampaya gas to power project in the Philippines involves a major investment to reduce the country's imports of coal and oil. We set up a sustainable development council at the project planning stage, involving people from labour unions, government, academia and other stakeholders to inform and monitor our progress. We undertook environmental and social impact assessment studies and we based our planning on this data and a wide spread of stakeholder engagement. We looked for ways to enhance local employment opportunities and made tremendous efforts to protect the environment. The key difference between this project and others that we had done in the past was the presence of that sustainable development council which has been successfully monitoring and informing our decision-making.

In Nigeria, our community development programme uses a combination of local and international stakeholders—as well as traditional auditing procedures—to verify that we are meeting our objectives. Regular stakeholder engagement workshops are held, our Group auditors provide an independent audit of the management systems, and international agencies, such as the World Bank, ProNatura, UNICEF and Nigerian government agencies, provide a review of the programme's outcomes. In this way, we get assurance not only of the effectiveness of the internal control systems but also what people feel about the quality of the impacts in their communities.

Another example is our oil sands project in Athabasca, Canada, where we have set a goal of producing the oil while emitting 6% less greenhouse gases than the imported crude oil it replaces, by 2010. To see that we meet this and a number of other goals, we have established an independent panel of environmental and community experts. The panel also monitors environmental and social impacts and has assisted in drafting Shell Canada's climate change strategy.

We clearly have some way to go in refining this new approach but here are some of the benefits we can identify at this early stage. Because of local involvement, the projects retain their licence to operate. People are happier to choose us as their partners, both for business and as their neighbours in the community. With the help of the community we bring our projects in on time and to budget. Investors are noticing too, especially those highly selective fund managers who follow the socially responsible investment indexes such as the Dow Jones Sustainability indexes.

13.8 Conclusions

Does governance change the role of business? The key role of business remains as the engine that generates prosperity. We suggest that good governance does not change this. But it does fundamentally alter the way a company operates and how it relates to the society around it, as can be seen from the examples quoted above. These show that companies with governance systems similar to Shell's see society as the centre of their world and the company as one of many important actors. This differs from the traditional business model where companies saw themselves at the centre of the universe and somehow more important than the other actors.

In other words, we believe Shell goes around the sun, rather than the other way round. Once that essentially humble relationship is understood, we feel companies are in a much healthier position not only to meet the challenges of a fast-changing world but also to contribute to solutions.

It has already been mentioned that companies and their investments play a role of increasing importance in transferring money from industrialised countries in the form of foreign direct investment to developing countries; yet the focus is on only a few of them. Governments of the least developed countries need to ask why this is. At least part of the answer lies in the fact that companies need to reduce their investment risks and choose those countries that have sound governance, good infrastructure, the rule of law and where bribery and corruption is under control.

This demand for the rule of law belies the myth that companies are against regulation and legislation. Business is doing very well in regulated markets because the rules are well defined. We do ask, though, that rules are sensible and based on emerging best practice. For this reason we feel it would be premature to encourage international binding legislation in the emerging area of corporate responsibility, and certainly counterproductive at this early stage. Legislation would be a blunt instrument and prevent innovation. It might be effective at forcing some action from those who refuse to acknowledge change, but it would not drive best practice. Without best practice there would be little progress.

It is better to encourage business to follow voluntary codes rather than to impose binding agreements through an international convention. Openness and transparency are essential components of voluntary agreements and these can be highly effective if you include stakeholder verification, such as that described here. If you understand and respond to the expectations of society—and make this part of your everyday business—there is less need to attach a formal verification process at the end. This is because trust is established along the way.

In other words, governance and actions become one and the same thing.

There are web links via www.shell.com and www.shell.com/shellreport.

14

The UN Global Compact and Global Reporting Initiative
WHERE PRINCIPLES MEET PERFORMANCE

Cornelis T. van der Lugt

UNEP Division of Technology, Industry and Economics (DTIE), France

Those who look back at the outcomes of the 2002 World Summit on Sustainable Development (WSSD) with a sense of scepticism tend to underestimate the immensity of the agenda we tackled. The sceptics also undervalue the many small but significant events that took place during the preparatory process and the Summit itself. Two such significant events were those of the United Nations Global Compact (GC) and the Global Reporting Initiative (GRI), both principles-based initiatives that advance an *open-learning* and *communicating-progress* approach to corporate responsibility. In Johannesburg the newly institutionalised GRI launched its 2002 revised *Guidelines for Sustainability Reporting*. The UN Secretary-General hosted a high-level multi-stakeholder dialogue of the GC on the theme 'Growing Sustainable Business in the Least Developed Countries (LDCs): Supporting Sustainable Entrepreneurship'. This presented the first occasion for some heads of state to join a multi-stakeholder panel with representatives from business, labour and the NGO community to discuss the role of business in sustainable development. The GRI event, among others addressed by UNEP Executive Director Klaus Töpfer and Human Rights Commissioner Mary Robinson, reminded its diverse audience of the role the apartheid struggle played during the 1980s in raising the international debate on the societal responsibilities of corporations.

By 2005 a global network of over 2,000 companies, international trade unions, over two dozen international NGOs and supportive networks of CSR organisations and business schools have become engaged in the effort under the UNGC to advance corporate citizenship globally. At the time of the fifth anniversary of the Compact during a Leaders Summit in June 2005, the 300 high-level participants took note of a call by leading investment firms for corporate responsibility principles to be integrated in performance evaluation and financial decision-making.

When UN Secretary-General Kofi Annan first proposed the GC at the World Economic Forum in January 1999, he warned of a backlash against globalisation. One of the reasons he cited was the fact that the benefits of globalisation were distributed highly unequally (see Ruggie 2001: 3-4). As global wealth is rising but the income gap grows wider, his warning remains as valid as ever. This was clear in discussions at WSSD in 2002 and again in 2005 when world leaders met at the UN World Summit to assess progress made in meeting the Millennium Development Goals.

Under the GC, business leaders have been challenged to enhance shared values for the global market and promote responsible corporate citizenship globally. They have been reminded that the global market needs to be embedded in a broader framework of shared values and objectives. The term 'corporate citizenship' also served as a reminder that the corporation, like any citizen, has both rights and duties. When in 2004 the International Organisation for Standardisation (ISO) started a process to develop an international standard for 'Social Responsibility', it was also clear that all organisations—both private and public—are challenged to display societal responsibility in internalising both rights and duties.

For all organisations the process of internalisation requires effective management and communication systems. This includes measuring and reporting results, which is where the guidelines of the GRI provide a valuable tool for private and public organisations alike. Often cited as a prime example of a so-called 'global public policy network', the GRI has involved hundreds of organisations since 1997 in a multi-stakeholder effort to advance sustainability reporting. By the time of the launch of the GRI as a permanent institution in April 2002, more than 110 pioneering companies from around the world have undertaken sustainability reporting using the GRI Guidelines. By the end of 2005 there were close to 700 self-declared GRI reporters worldwide. Its significance was noted in a report by the World Business Council for Sustainable Development (WBCSD) entitled *Sustainable Development Reporting: Striking the Balance* (2002), in which it confirmed that companies are coming under increasing pressure from society and stakeholders to make their activities more transparent. Shock events in the form of corporate scandals and collapses only strengthened the case for reporting as investor and wider societal trust in major corporations was powerfully eroded (SustainAbility/UNEP 2002: 4). The most recent UNEP/SustainAbility *Global Reporters Benchmark Survey* (SustainAbility/UNEP 2004) confirmed that leading reporters from diverse industry sectors are using the GRI Guidelines. Analysis also showed that investors are enjoying growing attention in company sustainability reports, a trend influenced by the growth in socially responsible investment funds and increased interest of some mainstream investors in corporate citizenship issues (SustainAbility/UNEP 2004: 26).

Today the GRI secretariat, a UNEP collaborating centre in Amsterdam, continues the process of revising and improving its sustainability reporting guidelines. This includes user feedback and the involvement of experts from all regions and diverse stakeholder groups.[1]

---

1   The most recent Structured Feedback Process of the GRI was launched in 2003 with over 80 companies. The development of the 'third generation' (G3) of the GRI Guidelines is engaging over 100 experts in technical working groups to refine, update and improve the Guidelines for release of the third revised version in October 2006.

14.1 Business and sustainable development

It is clear that both the UNGC and the GRI have had widespread impact since the seeds of their development were planted in the late 1990s. The most obvious indicator of growth for both has been the number of leading companies and other participants involved. At the same time, growth in quantity has been accompanied by a growing debate about quality. In the case of the GC it is a debate about the quality of implementation by companies of the core principles. In the case of the GRI it is a debate about the usability of comprehensive sustainability reporting. Behind both debates lies the question of how to deepen, measure and communicate the contribution of business to sustainable development.

The GC and GRI are topical items in ongoing discussions on the role of voluntary initiatives as a means of improving the sustainability performance of companies and supporting the implementation of internationally agreed principles. UNEP has been involved in the development and creation of a number of international voluntary initiatives at the sectoral level since the early 1990s.[2] Although they are not part of the intergovernmental process, these initiatives have at their basis UNEP principles and goals (UNGA 2001: 25). They also serve, on a sectoral basis, to advance the goals of the GC and GRI as umbrella or cross-sectoral initiatives.

An important consideration in these initiatives is the credibility of the UN agency in providing a multi-stakeholder platform with global reach.[3] The role of the UN agencies is supported by the fact that public institutions are key actors when externalities and harmonisation need to be addressed at the global level. These international voluntary initiatives complement intergovernmental processes and help to fill the gaps in global governance. As was noted in the *Business UNusual* partnerships report prepared for the 2005 World Summit, voluntary partnership initiatives to develop norms and standards 'often respond to the failure of traditional governance mechanisms to come up with effective, binding frameworks'. The report added that 'voluntary codes of conduct or guidelines have (in many instances) also become the tool of choice because they provide more flexible and adaptable means to influence behaviour' (UNGC with GPPi 2005: 30).

The *Business UNusual* report confirmed the necessity for a reforming UN to partner with civil society and business in order to deliver on sustainable development goals. This message has long been in the making. 'Business and sustainable development' was the theme of the 2002 GC Policy Dialogue, co-organised by UNEP and the GC Office. Chosen in anticipation of WSSD, discussions under this theme were inspired by calls for business engagement coming from the 1992 Earth Summit. Chapter 30 of Agenda 21 called on industry and business associations to 'encourage individual companies to undertake programmes for improved environmental awareness and responsibility'. The call for responsibility was addressed by Environment Ministers at UNEP's first

---

2   These include voluntary initiatives with the banks and insurance industry, tour operators, information and communications technology, advertising, automotive manufacturing and the building and construction industry sectors (see 'Business and Partnerships' under www.unep.fr and Nelson 2002: 89-93).

3   Cf. Nelson 2002: ch.4 on the related challenges.

Global Ministerial Environment Forum (GMEF), held in Malmö in May 2000, when they discussed the private sector and the environment. The Malmö Ministerial Declaration asked for a greater commitment by the private sector 'to engender a new culture of environmental accountability'. The Declaration also welcomed the GC for providing 'an excellent vehicle for the development of a constructive engagement with the private sector'.

Discussions in Malmö were based on a paper prepared by UNEP with the title 'Private Sector and Environment: Preparing for the Twenty-first Century' (UNEP 2000). Looking at the role of the private sector in sustainable development, it posed the following key issues:

- **Corporate purpose and objectives.** Is shareholder value the goal of a company or simply the means to achieve a higher purpose?

- **Corporate governance and accountability.** What are the responsibilities and obligations of companies to societies?

- **Incentives.** How can corporate objectives and environmental or societal objectives be more closely aligned?

- **Public governance.** How can public authorities and institutions at all levels help unleash the power of companies to achieve societal and environmental goals?

These questions echoed in debates at the WSSD on corporate responsibility and accountability, with some NGOs campaigning for the creation of a new international convention on this topic. It was therefore no surprise that the Johannesburg Declaration called for private-sector corporations 'to enforce corporate accountability'. Addressing corporate environmental and social responsibility and accountability, paragraph 17 of the *Johannesburg Plan of Implementation* called for actions to '[e]ncourage industry to improve social and environmental performance through voluntary initiatives, including environmental management systems, codes of conduct, certification and public reporting on environmental and social issues, taking into account such initiatives as the International Organisation for Standardisation (ISO) standards and Global Reporting Initiative guidelines on sustainability reporting'. And, while the WSSD did not result in the creation of a convention on corporate accountability, ISO did start a process to develop a new international standard on 'Social Responsibility'. This process is set to deliver a guidance standard by 2007. While nominated experts participating in the ISO process have agreed that the new standard will not be a management system standard, both industry and labour representatives participating remain sceptical about what each fear would be a new standard that is either too demanding or too superficial.

Like the 'S' in CSR, 'social responsibility' is meant to cover all dimensions or pillars of sustainable development. Most probably 'societal' would have been a better term to use. Ongoing discussions on the societal role of business reflect a growing awareness that the distinction between what happens within and outside of the factory gate is no longer clear-cut. What is viewed as a social cause or external event today may easily turn out to be a business question related to internal operations tomorrow. This awareness of shifting boundaries in rights and responsibilities applies not only to business but to all societal actors, governmental and non-governmental, as we develop a better comprehension of the complexity of environmental and social problems that are systemic, transnational and occurring globally.[4]

The 2000 Millennium Declaration listed targets for the next 20 years related to, for example, income, hunger, schooling, gender equality, child mortality, HIV/AIDS and access to safe drinking water. The 2002 *Johannesburg Plan of Implementation* also listed targets related to sanitation, harmful chemicals and endangered fish stocks. State-of-the-world databases such as the *Global Environment Outlook* (GEO) of UNEP, Human Development Index of the UNDP, the World Bank's World Development Indicators, FAOSTAT of the Food and Agriculture Organisation (FAO) and EarthTrends of the World Resources Institute (WRI) remind us of worrying trends and challenges that still face us. The *GEO-3 Report* (UNEP 2002a: 327) noted that the realisation that individual states cannot shield themselves from environmental change is changing the basis of geopolitics and global governance. It is clear that proactivism is required of all, governmental and non-governmental role players. In this respect the role of business and industry as part of the solution is critical. We most likely will not engage the private sector by threats and doomsday theories. The way to attract the business mind and to spur innovation is to present these global problems as challenges. In addition, much of the task ahead lies in the change in attitudes of management, both management in the public and private sector. This reminds us again of the importance of the values and principles that underpin organisational vision and leadership.

14.2 Core principles of the GC and the GRI

The GC challenges companies to integrate into their operations a set of core values in the areas of human rights, labour standards, the environment and anti-corruption. These values are embodied in ten principles that have been taken from existing intergovernmental agreements. The three environmental principles have been taken from the 1992 Rio Declaration. They require business to:

- Support a precautionary approach to environmental challenges

- Undertake initiatives to promote greater environmental responsibility

- Encourage the development and diffusion of environmentally friendly technologies

Compared to the human rights, labour and anti-corruption principles which are fundamental, the three environmental principles are aspirational. They are fundamental in the sense that certain minimum requirements must be met, yet aspirational in the sense that there is always room for improvement. We all know that a principle such as precaution is complex, which is why it is all the more valuable for participants in the

---

4   A process launched in the UN system to internalise the Global Compact principles, begun in 2004, showed UN agencies how much can be done if UN agencies were to start incorporating social responsibility principles in activities such as public procurement, investment (UN Pension Fund) and facilities management (environmental management systems).

GC to share their experiences in its implementation. A workshop on precaution during the 2003 GC Learning Forum in Belo Horizonte, Brazil, highlighted company experiences in dealing with technology matters such as leaded petrol and electromagnetic waves. Discussion focused on steps companies take to avoid possible harm to environment or human health in the face of insufficient scientific evidence. It confirmed that both the private and public sector face the difficult question of how to manage risk under conditions of imperfect scientific knowledge and that precaution can symbolise a new, co-operative approach in decision-making on health and environmental issues.

The role of four of the core UN agencies involved in the GC is to act as guardians of the ten principles, making sure that their interpretation and implementation follow current consensus on what constitutes acceptable or best practice. These agencies are the Office of the High Commissioner for Human Rights (OHCHR), the International Labour Organisation (ILO), the UN Office on Drugs and Crime (UNODC) and UNEP.

In sum, the GC provides a voluntary values-based platform and framework for advancing corporate citizenship and corporate contributions to sustainable development. Complementing this initiative, the GRI provides a natural link. The GRI offers a voluntary accountability framework for measuring and communicating progress toward implementation of the GC principles.

The mission of the GRI is to develop and disseminate globally applicable sustainability reporting guidelines.[5] The aim is to elevate the quality of reporting to a higher level of comparability, consistency and utility. The guidelines can be used by any organisation—corporate, governmental and non-governmental. Early pioneers among public authorities in using the GRI Guidelines for reporting include local authorities, national government departments and international institutions such as the World Bank. The GRI process as a matter of principle is about sustainability (covering the triple bottom line), transparency, accountability and stakeholder engagement. In the third revision of the GRI Guidelines during 2005, 'stakeholder engagement' emerged as a central reporting principle. Four years earlier, participants in the second revision process agreed on 11 principles that are essential to producing a balanced and reasonable report on an organisation's economic, environmental and social performance. These principles, listed in the 2002 (second) version of the Guidelines, relate to the framework of the report, what to report on, the quality and reliability of the report, and accessibility of the report. The 11 reporting principles are:

- Transparency

- Inclusiveness (stakeholder engagement)

- Auditability (assurability)

- Completeness

- Relevance (materiality)

- Sustainability context

- Accuracy

---

5   See www.globalreporting.org.

- Neutrality (balance)

- Comparability

- Clarity

- Timeliness

The essence of the above relate to (i) what information a report should provide and (ii) the quality of the information in a report. With respect to what an organisation should report on, key considerations relate to stakeholder opinion, completeness, relevance or materiality, and sustainability context. The last principle is of key importance to an international organisation such as UNEP. It requires the organisation to present its performance in macro-level context by referring to broader sustainable development conditions and goals. Its application is highly relevant when examining the contribution of business to goals of the Millennium Declaration and the Johannesburg Plan of Implementation.

The GRI Guidelines indicate that its reporting principles define a compact between the reporting organisation and the report user, ensuring that both parties share a common understanding of the underpinnings of a GRI-based report (GRI 2002: 22). They were designed with the long term in mind, with the conviction that new knowledge and learning will continue to advance performance measurement. Again, a key principle in discussion of the state of the world and global governance is sustainability context, which underlines that sustainability reporting draws significant meaning from the larger context of how performance at the organisational level affects economic, environmental and social capital formation and depletion at a local, regional or global level.

14.3 From commitment to action

The most general of the three environmental principles under the UNGC is the one requiring business to promote greater environmental responsibility. What steps should the company take if it wishes to promote environmental responsibility? Key steps would include the following (see Barbut and Van der Lugt 2005):

- **Redefine company vision, policies and strategies to include the 'triple bottom line' of sustainable development:** economic prosperity, environmental quality and social equity

- **Develop sustainability targets and indicators** (economic, environmental, social)

- **Establish a sustainable production and consumption programme**[6] with clear performance objectives to take the organisation beyond compliance in the long term

---

6   On sustainable production and consumption, see www.unep.fr/en/branches/pc.htm. Before the arrival of the sustainable consumption debate in the 1990s, the focus of UNEP and its partners since the 1980s was on cleaner production and eco-efficiency.

- **Work with suppliers, other business partners, designers and consumers to improve environmental and value chain performance**, extending responsibility up the supply chain and down the product chain

- **Adopt voluntary charters, codes of conduct, codes of practice** in global and sectoral initiatives to confirm acceptable behaviour and performance

- **Measure, track and communicate progress in incorporating sustainability principles into business practices**, including reporting against global operating standards

- **Ensure transparency, unbiased dialogue and systematic engagement** with stakeholders

In doing the above, the existence of appropriate management systems is crucial in helping the company to meet the organisational challenge. Essential environmental management tools for the company are those that provide for analysis (assessment tools), action (management tools) and communications (engagement and reporting tools). A key example of a reporting tool is the GRI Guidelines.[7]

Good practices undertaken by a proactive company—from its vision through appropriate management systems to its self-evaluation—need to include reporting as a means of measuring and communicating its achievements. Increasingly the emphasis is on not only financial and environmental reporting but 'sustainability reporting' as foreseen under the GRI. It is estimated that corporate environmental reports have increased in number from less than 200 in 1990 to more than 2,000 by the end of the 1990s. Yet much remains to be done. From an overview UNEP did with industry associations for the WSSD of progress made in various industry sectors since 1992, it was clear that environmental or sustainability reporting is still a minority practice in many industries and countries (see UNEP 2002b). This is particularly the case where legal frameworks or public pressure is weak, and where mainstream investors—as opposed to socially responsible investors—are showing limited interest.[8] The weaknesses have been addressed more directly in the last three years, with more reporting requirements or incentives being introduced either by regulation or voluntarily by, for example, stock exchanges such as the Johannesburg JSE and the São Paulo BOVESPA. The GC Leaders Summit in June 2004 presented a finance package with statements and reports from stock exchanges, financial analysts and investors about applying the GC principles and sustainability criteria in their services (see UNEP FI 2004; UNGC 2004).

---

7   A practical tool for stakeholder engagement by companies is the *Stakeholder Engagement Manual* by AccountAbility, SRA and UNEP (2005). The organisation AccountAbility has also issued a voluntary standard for stakeholder engagement, as part of its AA1000 series.

8   In 2002 it was estimated that less than 1% of all listed companies on the New York and London Stock Exchanges report on social performance, with only about a third of the FTSE 350 companies producing environmental and social reports. The May 2002 edition of *Environmental Finance* therefore reported that the UK Environment Minister is looking with interest at the new mandatory approach in France, where all publicly quoted firms are required since 2002 to include environmental and social data in their annual reports. Today, the Operating and Financial Review (OFR) in the UK has similar requirements with respect to environmental and social risks.

14.4 Dialogue, learning and communicating progress

Most companies still have much to learn about reporting, what to report on, how to report and how to link reporting with stakeholder engagement and strategic planning (cf. AccountAbility/SRA/UNEP 2005). Many large companies are still taking only the first steps towards integrating reporting with other information management systems. Feeding reporting via multi-stakeholder dialogue back into vision and management is central in the 'Performance Model' that has been developed under the GC. The model has been presented along with related tools, internationally recognised and available for companies in the publication *Raising the Bar* (Fussler *et al.* 2004). The development of the Performance Model, building on the example of total quality management, was initiated by a group of experts participating in the 2002 Compact Policy Dialogue on Business and Sustainable Development. The model is highly relevant in ISO discussions to design a new international standard in social responsibility.

Multi-stakeholder policy dialogues and learning forums have been two key activities under the GC since its launch. The emphasis on learning is an important one, one in which openly communicating and reporting progress is a natural ingredient. It implies an approach that focuses on proactivism and leadership, rather than reactive follow-up on those that have not followed a set of rules. The emphasis here is on leading by example, rather than naming and shaming. The GC therefore follows a learning model. Not being a regulatory instrument or legally binding code does not imply being a 'safe harbour' for companies to 'sign on' without demonstrating real involvement and results. In addition to being a proactive learning model, the GC is based on a worldwide network open for any company or stakeholder organisation to join (see Nelson 2002: 137-40; UNGC with GPPi 2005: 53-54).

The initial approach followed with the GC Learning Forum was to require participating companies to submit annually case studies or examples of their implementation of one or more of the Compact principles. These submissions were put on the GC website for public comment. During the pilot phase of the Learning Forum in 2001, an initial 30 case studies were submitted by companies. Analysis of the submissions noted that they showed a strong bias towards the extraction and manufacturing sectors, while other industries are either under-represented or absent. Of the initial submissions, there were 14 case studies on environmental issues; 5 on health; 4 on labour rights; 3 on infrastructure; 2 on corruption; and 2 on education.

Some key themes emerged from a review of the initial submissions. To start with, it was clear that implementation of the principles requires a substantial degree of organisational change. Important organisational and managerial factors appeared to be training, change management and leadership. The case study submissions also demonstrated that many businesses faced difficulties assessing the priority of corporate citizenship responsibilities relative to other profit-seeking business activities (see McIntosh and Thomas 2004).

Following the pilot phase during the first year of companies' submitting 'case studies', it was agreed that companies could submit shorter 'examples' in which they indicate sources for further information, sources such as annual financial or sustainability reports. The link to reporting is important, coinciding with an announcement by the GC and the GRI on 28 November 2001 of a 'co-operative framework' according to which company sustainability reporting along the GRI Guidelines can also be considered as submissions fulfilling the participation requirements of the GC. At the inauguration of the GRI in New York on 4 April 2002, Secretary-General Annan referred to the GRI as an 'important complement' to the GC.

The initial idea of annual submissions of case studies and examples was that these would form the basis of a learning bank on the GC website where, through transparent public commentary and analysis, best practices would be identified. This approach has shown its shortcomings over the first two years, due to the absence of an analytical framework, lack of capacity, language barriers, and lack of resources on the part of participants to comment and analyse. As a result, it was agreed by the GC Advisory Council in January 2003 that companies would no longer be required to submit examples annually as a precondition for participation. Rather, it was agreed, companies will be asked to indicate in their annual financial and sustainability reports what steps they have taken to implement the GC principles. Companies were asked to issue annual 'Communications on Progress' (COPs), which may or may not involve submitting their sustainability or CSR reports. In addition, the development and analysis of case studies has been decentralised with the involvement of business schools that work with participants to present their analysis at the annual Compact meetings.

Companies were asked to issue COPs within two years of joining the GC. The first deadline for companies participating for two years was set as June 2005. By this time, only 38% of the 977 implied companies submitted COPs.[9] It should be noted, however, that 98% of the FT Global 500 companies involved did submit COPs, and that the uptake of COPs has been quicker under companies who joined more recently. As was expected, COPs in the form of reports were less common among small and medium-sized company (SME) participants. Aware of the resource constraints SMEs face, national Compact networks such as the United Kingdom network developed a simple template that small companies can use to report their activities related to the ten principles. Working with the GRI and others, the GC Office (2005) also published a *Practical Guide to Communication on Progress* to explain the procedure in simple terms. In its response to SME needs, the GRI (2004) itself published its *High 5!* guide targeted at SMEs. The guide explains how to introduce sustainability reporting using the GRI Guidelines. In the Compact guidance note on COPs, companies were encouraged to use performance indicators such as those appearing in the GRI Guidelines. A table listing the ten Compact principles and a brief selection of GRI core indicators relevant to each has been posted on the GC website since 2003. This provided a simple and practical indication of the types of activities companies can report on.[10] As more COPs are collected today, debate is growing on the role that national GC networks can play in supporting quality control, validation and verification.

9   UNGC press release, 15 July 2005.
10 The table lists core indicators of the GRI Guidelines against each of the ten principles. It lists, for example, 16 environmental indicators next to principle 8 and the following reporting element against principle 7: 'Explanation of whether and how the precautionary approach or principle is addressed by the organisation'.

14.5 Walking the talk: giving new meaning to performance

At the GC China Summit in late 2005, UNEP and the GC Office are launching a publication entitled *Talking the Walk* (UNEP *et al.* 2005). Transposing the title of the WBCSD/Greenleaf publication *Walking the Talk* (Holliday *et al.* 2002), this was done particularly with the role of responsible advertising in mind. As an output of the 2004 GC Policy Dialogue on 'Sustainable Consumption: Marketing and Communications', the publication examined challenges companies have in promoting sustainable consumption in all regions. At the 2004 Dialogue in Paris, a representative of the Worldwatch Institute reminded participants that the relative share of people who belong to the so-called 'global consumer class' is still very low in, for example, China and India. As a result, there is further demand for growth and the prospect of increased social and environmental stress on the planet.

While focusing on 'talking' *à la* 'marketing and communications', the debate showed how the seeds of a successful strategy ultimately goes back to core operations and product design. Examples of approaches followed by companies range from a minimalist approach (greenwashing) or niche strategy with one or more product lines, to an advanced or integrated strategy which implies changing the entire mode of production (for example, an oil company transforming itself into an energy company). The debate also showed how vulnerable intangible assets such as corporate reputation can be. Specific risks, which range from environmental issues, human and labour rights, health and safety, to corporate governance issues, affect these assets. Still, it is difficult for financial analysts to evaluate these risks. The relative importance of these assets in how the company creates value and how they are defined and measured varies from industry sector to industry sector. A sustainable growth policy can help to mitigate these risks. Analysts expect from companies a clear and coherent strategy with continuity in its main objectives. They are also very attentive to how the budget is allocated and to its vulnerability to economically adverse situations. Both quantitative and qualitative indicators are therefore needed. This is where the value of a harmonised set of indicators available in the GRI Guidelines is again so evident.

Behind the debate on 'walking the talk' and corporate reputation lies the issues of credibility and trust. If it is so complicated to 'walk the talk', why do companies join voluntary efforts such as the GC in support of corporate citizenship and sustainable development? What we have been seeing is a growing trend that departs from the traditional reductionist view of 'the business of business being business'. Many companies become involved because of trigger events such as bad experiences of criticism of their practices. But increasingly companies are also becoming involved as a result of positive inducements, taking note of the growing business case for sustainable development. Many companies today view proactive corporate citizenship as good business, helping to advance their overall performance, profitability and corporate image (see SustainAbility/UNEP 2001; SustainAbility *et al.* 2002). As the body of research on the so-called 'business case' grows, leading companies today focus more on the combination of core values and strategic business models.

A source of encouragement is regular reporting by a growing number of companies, using the GRI Guidelines to undertake reporting both as (i) a means to display accountability and transparency, and (ii) a means to improve their management systems. The latest KPMG (2005) survey of 1,600 international company reports concluded that corporate responsibility reporting in industrialised countries has clearly entered the mainstream, adding that there has been a dramatic change from purely environmental reporting up until 1999 to sustainability reporting in 2005, encompassing social, ethical, environmental and economic indicators. Companies undertaking annual reporting on their sustainability performance are responding to various drivers for disclosure, coming from shareholders and other stakeholders. In a globalising world, major companies increasingly need to think in terms of shareholders and consumers abroad.[11] This poses multinational companies with at times complicated decisions on the boundaries of their responsibilities. The Internet has brought the world more-connected and more-informed consumers. As a result, companies are often challenged to display principled behaviour with respect to activities that fall beyond their ownership or what they perceive to be their sphere of significant influence. Behind this lies greater focus on significant environmental and social risk, which sets the scene for new partnership approaches in supply chain management. Subcontracting or outsourcing does not allow one to simply pass the buck.

Both the UNGC and the GRI offer valuable and internationally recognised approaches to organisations wanting to display responsibility in the way they conduct business. Both initiatives also offer involvement in a global multi-stakeholder process and partnering with UN agencies in displaying societal responsibility. Core competencies that the UN offers under the GC include the power of the principles, the power to convene, and the capacity to network. Out of these competencies must flow the ability to advance integration. This refers to both questions of substance (sustainability) and organisation (complementarity). The GC and GRI support action to mainstream and integrate key principles into core business operations. Ultimately, the strength of the business case will lie in its display of integration between the economic, social and environmental. In addition, the strength of the GC and GRI in supporting global governance for sustainability will lie in its ability to complement and inspire other global voluntary initiatives, showing how open learning and communicating progress can make a difference in performance.

References

AccountAbility/SRA (Stakeholder Research Associates Canada)/UNEP (United Nations Environment Programme) (2005) *The Stakeholder Engagement Manual* (2 vols.; London/Cobourg/Paris: AccountAbility/SRA/UNEP DTIE).

Barbut, M., and C.T. van der Lugt (2005) 'Corporate Responsibility: The UNEP Experience', in S. Tully *et al.* (eds.), *Corporate Liability and Responsibility* (London: London School of Economics/Elgar Publications).

Fussler, C., A. Cramer and S. van der Vegt (2004) *Raising the Bar: Creating Value with the UN Global Compact* (Sheffield, UK: Greenleaf Publishing).

11 Consider, for example, that some 40% of the value of the Paris Bourse is held abroad, and some leading French companies derive more than 75% of their turnover from international sales.

GRI (Global Reporting Initiative) (2002) *Sustainability Reporting Guidelines* (Boston, MA: GRI Secretariat).

—— (2004) *High 5! Communicating Your Business Success through Sustainability Reporting* (Amsterdam: GRI Secretariat).

Holliday, C.O., Jr, S. Schmidheiny and P. Watts (2002) *Walking the Talk: The Business Case for Sustainable Development* (Sheffield, UK: Greenleaf Publishing).

KPMG Global Sustainability Services and University of Amsterdam (2005) *KPMG International Survey of Corporate Responsibility Reporting 2005* (Amsterdam: KPMG/Amsterdam Graduate Business School).

McIntosh, M., and R. Thomas (2004) 'Learning from Company Engagement with the Global Compact', in M. McIntosh, S. Waddock and G. Kell (eds.), *Learning to Talk: Corporate Citizenship and the Development of the UN Global Compact* (Sheffield, UK: Greenleaf Publishing): 205-12.

Nelson, J. (2002) *Building Partnerships: Co-operation between the United Nations System and the Private Sector* (New York/London: United Nations Department of Public Information/International Business Leaders Forum).

SustainAbility/UNEP (United Nations Environment Programme) (2001) *Buried Treasure: Uncovering the Business Case for Corporate Sustainability* (London/Paris: SustainAbility Ltd/UNEP DTIE).

——/—— (2002) *Trust Us: The Global Reporters 2002 Survey of Corporate Sustainability Reporting* (London/Paris: SustainAbility Ltd/UNEP DTIE).

——/—— (2004) *Risk and Opportunity: The Global Reporters 2004 Survey of Corporate Sustainability Reporting* (London/Paris: SustainAbility Ltd/UNEP DTIE).

——, International Finance Corporation (IFC) and Ethos Institute (2002) *Developing Value: The Business Case for Sustainability in Emerging Markets* (London/Washington/São Paulo: Sustainability Ltd/IFC/Instituto Ethos).

UNEP (United Nations Environment Programme) (2000) 'Private Sector and Environment: Preparing for the Twenty-first Century' (discussion paper UNEP/GCSS.VI/4; Paris: UNEP DTIE).

—— (2002a) *Global Environment Outlook 3 (GEO-3)* (Nairobi/London: UNEP/Earthscan Publications).

—— (2002b) *Industry as a Partner for Sustainable Development. Ten Years after Rio: The UNEP Assessment* (Paris: UNEP DTIE).

——, United Nations Global Compact and Utopies (2005) *Talking the Walk* (Paris/New York: UNEP DTIE/UNGC Office/Utopies Ltd).

UNEP FI (United Nations Environment Programme Finance Initiative) (2004) *The Materiality of Social, Environmental and Corporate Governance Issues to Equity Pricing* (Geneva: UNEP FI).

UNGA (United Nations General Assembly) (2001) 'Cooperation between the United Nations and all Relevant Partners, in Particular the Private Sector. Report of the Secretary-General' (A/56/323; UNGA, 28 August 2001).

UNGC (United Nations Global Compact) (2004) *Who Cares Wins: Connecting Financial Markets to a Changing World* (New York: UNGC Office).

—— (2005) *A Practical Guide to Communication on Progress* (New York: UNGC Office).

—— with GPPi (Global Public Policy Institute) (2005) *Business UNusual: Facilitating United Nations Reform through Partnerships* (New York: United Nations).

WBCSD (World Business Council for Sustainable Development) (2002) *Sustainable Development Reporting: Striking the Balance* (prepared by Deloitte Touche Tohmatsu, Rabobank Group and STMicroelectronics; Geneva: WBCSD).

15
Global governance
CHALLENGES FOR CIVIL SOCIETY AND DEMOCRACY

Nicola Bullard

Focus on the Global South*

The Rio de Janeiro UN Conference on Environment and Development in 1992 was the first in a decade of United Nations mega-summits.[1] It was launched in a climate of tremendous optimism, after the collapse of the Berlin Wall and the disintegration of the Soviet Union, at a time when many thought it would be possible to create a 'new world order'. It was also a time when the state was no longer seen as the sole repository of political power. This sentiment emerged out of complex and contradictory forces including the anti-state and pro-market ideology of neoliberalism, the apparent (and in some cases actual) failure of the state to fulfil its responsibilities and the inability of traditional institutions, such as trade unions and the Church, to respond effectively to emerging social concerns such as feminism and the environment. The response to this complex situation was a new 'multi-stakeholder' approach to politics that brought non-state actors, such as NGOs (non-governmental organisations) and the private sector, into decision-making processes. In many respects, the UN environment summit was the first attempt to create international norms and mechanisms for global governance *in a globalising world.* But, as we shall see, it was doomed from the start because of the fundamental contradictions between environmental sustainability and human development on the one hand and global capitalism on the other and the unequal power relations between the various stakeholders.

The outcomes of Rio were ambitious, extensive and in many respects positive. But even at the time critics saw in Agenda 21 the seeds of further environmental destruc-

---

* Focus on the Global South is a policy analysis, research and activist NGO based in Bangkok, Thailand (focusweb.org).

1 The list is long: World Summit for Children (1990); World Conference for Education (1990); United Nations Conference on Environment and Development (1992); World, Conference on Human Rights (1993); International Conference on Population and Development (1994); Fourth World Conference on Women (1995); World Summit for Social Development (1995); UN Conference on Human Settlements (1996); World Food Summit (1996); World Conference against Racism, Racial Discrimination, Xenophobia and Related Intolerance (2001); plus a string of '+5' and '+10' follow-up conferences (see van Rooy 2004: 20).

tion because it failed to address two key obstacles to sustainable human development: the capitalist model of consumption and production which had proved so environmentally destructive and the destabilising (and environmentally disastrous) inequality between the South and the North. In the Rio framework, economic growth was seen as an essential component of sustainable development but, over time, environmental sustainability has been reduced to profit sustainability. What's more, by 2002, the business sector had woken up to the full marketing potential of 'greening' its image and the UN had realised the benefits of 'public–private partnerships' and corporate sponsorship.

At the time, though, Rio was seen by many as a breakthrough and in the wake of this success, a series of multi-stakeholder UN summits took place: including the Vienna conference on human rights in 1993, the Cairo population summit in 1994 and, in 1995, the Beijing women's conference and the Copenhagen World Summit on Social Development. Each was preceded by long preparatory processes involving government, NGOs and the business sector. During the summits themselves, NGOs and business representatives were often members of official government delegations, especially, but not exclusively, on delegations from the North. With all these opportunities for international diplomacy, NGO representatives soon became adept at 'engaging' the system and learned to be skilful diplomats and expert negotiators. More often than not, NGO caucuses focused on proposing 'language' to be inserted in the official declarations and, in between, worked the corridors pushing the NGO agenda. Over time, the distance between the increasingly bureaucratised, professionalised and mainly Northern NGOs and those they often claimed to represent—the (mainly Southern) social movements and marginalised groups—has widened.

The UN system of accreditation, preparatory conferences, consultations and so on conferred legitimacy on the bureaucratic and professional NGOs who engaged (constructively) in the process, while those who stayed outside the system and protested were marginalised, delegitimised and (post 11 September 2001) even criminalised.

15.1 Ten years later

After a decade of NGO involvement in UN summits, what do we have to show? Very little, I would argue, other than having learned a great deal about the limits of reformism and the tremendous capacity of the dominant powers to ignore or undermine global norms and institutions that do not serve their interests.

This was crystal clear in Johannesburg at the World Summit on Sustainable Development (WSSD). After a decade of mega-summits and +5 evaluations, people were already sceptical. We had seen the results of the Geneva summit on social development where the United Nations signed on to the 'Washington Consensus' (see Bullard 2000). We had seen the outcome of the Monterrey conference on finance for development where the fundamental problems of debt and financial markets were swept under the carpet. We had seen the UN-sponsored 'Global Compact' which gave corporations a free public relations makeover by allowing them to sign up to non-binding, non-enforceable and non-monitorable human rights commitments. Long before Johannesburg, there was a growing consensus among activists—and not only the radicals—that the UN was being used to legitimise the globalisation project. History did not indicate a favourable outcome for Rio +10.

In May, at the fourth preparatory meeting in Bali ('prepcom') there was a feeling of pessimism among the movements and organisations concerned with sustainable development and environment: the draft declarations gave pre-eminence to trade liberalisation, financial market liberalisation and the private sector as engines of 'sustainable development' while institutions such as the WTO (World Trade Organisation) were characterised as environment-friendly. The mood did not change in Johannesburg and, in contrast to Rio, which was an enormous fiesta of civil society and alternatives, people stayed away in droves, assessing that it was a waste of time, effort and greenhouse gases.

What we witnessed in Johannesburg was a deep crisis of the UN system of multilateralism. In the past years, and especially since the Bush administration, US unilateralism has been used to threaten and undermine the effectiveness and legitimacy of the UN. The track record of the Bush administration is appalling: withdrawal from the Kyoto Protocol, repudiation of the ABM (Anti-Ballistic Missile) treaty, rejecting the International Criminal Court and now riding roughshod over international law in its efforts to secure its imperial ambitions in Iraq.[2] Who knows what will be next? The UN has responded to the contempt of the US by becoming even more obsequious and accommodating to the point that it often appears that the UN's sole objective is to keep the US at the negotiating table. The consequence of this in Johannesburg was that the agenda of environmental sustainability was rendered invisible and replaced by the agenda of sustainable growth (read 'sustainable profits').

The corporate world had a field day in Johannesburg. The great German company BMW held sole rights to the main foyer of the official conference centre which itself is located in the most elite and opulent commercial building in the richest suburb of Johannesburg. The city's expressways were lined with billboards advertising the Summit with images of smiling people from the developing world and captions extolling the joys of fresh water, solar energy or sustainable agriculture. Not at all discretely, in the bottom left corner, a cluster of giant corporate logos implied that all this happiness was somehow a result of their largesse and vision. The extent to which corporations have penetrated the halls of power in the UN is astonishing (despite the outcry in response to the UN Global Compact) and shows just how radically *our* institutions of global governance are being transformed in line with the interests of power and capital.

15.2 Where did the optimism go?

So, how did we get from 1992 to 2002? How did everything change from optimism and engagement to pessimism and dissent?

---

2   This chapter was written before the US illegal invasion and occupation of Iraq. The trajectory of US foreign policy and engagement with the UN continues to be characterised by unilateralism and arrogance.

Over the past decade, the promises of globalisation have been revealed as lies. Financial crises have ricocheted around the world, the number of people living in poverty has grown, corporations are raking in enormous profits and workers around the world are paying the price. The Cold War dividend has never been paid and rather than building a multi-polar world we see the emergence of a new imperialism built on United States military and corporate interests. The world is unstable, divided and discontented.

What's more, global *economic* integration has highlighted the weaknesses and biases of the existing global *political* institutions and the paucity of democratic spaces at the international level. For example, it is now virtually uncontested that the institutions enforcing the rules of neoliberal globalisation—the World Bank, the International Monetary Fund (IMF) and the World Trade Organisation—are undemocratic and that their policies exacerbate poverty and inequality and promote the interests of the market and the rich countries.

In this context, the global elite no longer talks of sustainable development; they talk of sustainable growth as if it were the same thing. The 'new' paradigm is poverty alleviation and the logic of this paradigm is dangerously simple: poverty alleviation is the outcome of economic growth and economic growth is the outcome of integration into the global market through the expansion of exports and the opening of trade and financial markets. The Utopian idea of sustainable development has been downgraded to the much more limited objective of poverty alleviation and even this seems like a faraway dream with the UN's unambitious and probably unreachable targets of merely *halving* human deprivation by 2015.

This emerging world order of inequality, marginalisation and domination has created tremendous opposition and resistance, particularly on the national level, as unemployment rises, as the incomes of small farmers dwindle below subsistence, as landlessness increases and as people are denied their basic rights to food, water, health and education, simply because they cannot afford to pay.

Social fragmentation and marginalisation caused by economic integration, though, is not the only process that has emerged in the past ten years. There has been a highly visible counter-trend of radicalisation, mobilisation and convergence of social movements resisting *this* form of globalisation. The rise of the anti-globalisation movement has been an extremely important element in changing the discourse on globalisation by making the processes, interests and institutions driving neoliberal globalisation visible: the G8, corporations, the military, the IMF and World Bank and the WTO, and all the other moving parts of the neoliberal machine are now uncovered. The movement has also made visible the victims of globalisation: laid-off workers, impoverished farmers, entire communities displaced by dams, the women of the *maquiladoras*, landless peasants and unemployed youth. In addition, campaigns on specific issues, such as intellectual property rights, genetically modified organisms, financial markets and debt have linked forces with mass organisations and social movements to develop common perspectives and common demands.

In Johannesburg, this emerging international movement was both inside and outside the WSSD and the official processes. There were three main groupings but with a great deal of overlap and interaction between the three and with layers of complication due to the local political context. The strongest critique of the WSSD came from the Social Movements Indaba and the Landless Peoples Movement who were completely outside the WSSD. Next was the Global Peoples Forum, the official NGO event and, finally, the processes inside the WSSD where many NGOs were members of government delegations and actively lobbied in the halls of power. However, unlike the Rio Summit, the insiders' sole purpose was damage control, the 'official' NGO forum was a damp squib and the events organised by the Social Movements Indaba, the Landless Peoples Movement and dozens of other unaffiliated and autonomous events were the most lively, the most radical and the best attended. The simplest measure of this radicalisation is that the 'official' march drew less than 5,000 while the Social Movements United demonstration was 30,000-plus strong. (Domestic politics played a large part in this. The official march was supported by the African National Congress [ANC], so the Social Movements United march was a double rejection, both of the WSSD and of the neoliberal policies of the ANC. That this happened in post-apartheid South Africa speaks volumes about the extent to which neoliberal policies are being rejected in every part of the world.)

15.3 A new internationalism?

Although this may seem like a picture of fragmentation and a sign that the 'international movement' is a fiction, I see the situation quite differently. The WSSD was, in my assessment, the end of an era. It was the last gasp of the failed experiment in UN-sponsored multi-stakeholder attempts to build international norms legitimising neoliberal thinking and an undemocratic world order. According to those activists inside the process, their best assessment was that the absolute worst didn't happen (for example, the multilateral environment agreements were not *explicitly* subordinated to the WTO agreements). On the other side, the success of the Social Movement United march was not that it opposed the ANC's neoliberal policies (although that was important locally) but that the leaders and participants identified their local struggles with the international justice movement. This was a decisive factor in overcoming local differences and creating the unity of the protest. This political process has been repeated in many parts of the world as national coalitions are formed by groups who were previously antagonists, under a common project of resistance to neoliberalism, imperialism and militarism (for example, in the construction of the European Social Forum, and national social forums in many countries) and under the common call 'Another World is Possible'.

The most dramatic and positive manifestation of this new movement is the World Social Forum (WSF)[3] which has been held for the past two (and soon to be three) years in Porto Alegre, Brazil. The WSF is a huge tent accommodating a tremendous diversity of groups and organisational structures, perspectives, concerns and demands. The thread that binds the WSF together is a common rejection of neoliberalism, militarism and domination by the market and a common purpose of social justice, equity and freedom. There is a strong consensus on many demands, such as debt cancellation, land reform, regulation of corporations and financial markets, a dramatic reduction in the powers of the international institutions such as the IMF and the WTO and the end of

---

3 See www.forumsocialmundial.org.br, which contains a wealth of material documenting the evolution of the World Social Forums.

superpower domination. The demands are clear and there are many positive proposals about alternatives, democratising governance and re-balancing power relations within and between countries.

But there is no place to put these demands. We have many forums of 'global governance' but most of them have lost their legitimacy in the eyes of the people (the UN included). At the national level, we are faced with a political void: the people have no trust in political parties (Brazil notwithstanding), the market is beyond our control and governments are increasingly deaf to the voices of the people. Internationally, the institutions protect the interests of the powerful and an increasingly dominating US rides roughshod across all. At every level, it seems, there is no effective counterpart, no place, no forum, no process, where the concerns and demands of the people and of the movements can be placed, heard, and debated with sincerity and operationalised.

In short, we have a real and deep crisis of legitimacy in the system and a highly polarised dynamic between a growing and increasingly radicalised, informed and co-ordinated international movement and an increasingly detached, arrogant and unresponsive international elite.

Is it possible to find a bridge between these seemingly unbridgeable worlds or can they even co-exist? I am very pleased to hear that Shell has had a Copernican revolution in its thinking and now puts society at the centre of its world-view (see Chapter 13 in this volume), but this is not enough because Shell still envisages a society shaped by the market. We need to go further and replace the market as the driving determinant of economic, environmental and social outcomes because the market cannot deliver environmental sustainability, human rights, gender equity and peace. The only way we can guarantee these outcomes, which are themselves vital for the future of a humane humanity, is to re-embed people's sovereignty and freedom in our society, in our markets, in our political and cultural institutions and in our international governance. It is not enough simply to *negotiate* interests because the power differentials between South and North, between men and women, rich and poor, labour and capital, are simply too great. We have had enough of this crazy ideological cult of neoliberalism because its values of individualism and competition are antithetical to sustainability. In its place, we need to realise our common values of respect for individual and collective sovereignty and freedom, for justice and equality and to build, at every level, social/political/economic/cultural institutions and processes that take decisions out of the invisible hands of the market and put them into the *visible* hands of the people.

References

Bullard, N. (2000) 'United Nations Shows its True Colours', *Focus on Trade* 52 (August 2000), www.focusweb.org/publications/FOT%20pdf/fot52.pdf.

Van Rooy, A. (2004) *The Global Legitimacy Game: Civil Society, Globalisation and Protest* (London: Palgrave).

16

Civil society plus global governance
WHAT CAN WE EXPECT?*

Dieter Rucht

Social Science Research Centre (WZB), Germany

16.1 Opening question

Just as in the mid-1970s, when political science spoke of 'political overload', 'failure of the state' and 'ungovernability' (Offe 1979), limits to policy-making or, to be more precise, limits to the state are currently being discussed. While the earlier discourse focused on the containment of an 'inflation of demands' induced by dynamics of the welfare state in the face of scarce governmental budgets, the current discourse focuses on limitations of the state's ability to govern. The current discourse does not address notoriously scarce financial resources but an inability observable in many policy fields to make and implement decisions that are:

- **Adequate**: that is, solve or ameliorate the problems at hand as well as consider and address important consequences of the decision itself

- **Considered legitimate**: that is, they are widely respected or at least do not raise open dissent

This problem of government action is even more evident at the level of international regimes, which are considered to be 'global domestic policy without a global government' (Habermas 1998: 165). The number and complexity of the problems in this regard have increased. On the other hand, decision-making processes are sluggish, often only a policy of the lowest common denominator is feasible and the possibilities for implementing decisions once they have been made and to sanction rule breaches are limited (Zürn 1998). In addition, international policy is less and less the arcane sphere of diplomacy and is facing demands towards more transparency and participa-

---

* Some of this text was presented at the 31st congress of the German Sociologists' Association (Deutsche Gesellschaft für Soziologie) in October 2002 and was published in the congress proceedings (Rucht 2003b).

tion (Berndt and Sack 2001; Brunnengräber *et al*. 2001; Grote and Gbikpi 2002). Such demands are especially visible in the context of international institutions' summits (World Bank and IMF [International Monetary Fund], WTO [World Trade Organisation], G8, EU), which frequently face broad 'negative coalitions' of non-governmental organisations (NGOs) and global justice movements (Fues and Hamm 2001; Pianta 2001; Rucht 2002). These protests reach back to 1980s, but during the last few years they have grown broader and more radical; the protesters increasingly define themselves in opposition to a globalising neoliberalism (Ayres 2002; Rucht 2003a) and claim to speak in the name of the global civil society.[1]

At first, governments and international institutions basically ignored the protests and the growth of transnational and civil-society groups, which received relatively little media interest. Yet they now realise that they are under increasing pressure to react. For now, symbolic policy and rhetoric dominate the reactions, but partially procedural and material changes can be observed, even more so as the outlines of alliances between civil-society groups and a number of governments emerge: for example, the Scandinavian countries, some of the poorest countries as well as a number of small island states (the AOSIS group).

Lack of political control and legitimacy at the local and national level is countered by participation of civil-society groups in advisory committees, by public–private partnerships as well as the delegation of formerly public tasks to QUANGOs (quasi-autonomous non-governmental organisations) or private institutions. Similar developments are taking place at the international level. NGO representatives are granted observer status at conferences and they are being included in international delegations and groups of experts (starting at Rio in 1992). NGOs perform as initiators and executive bodies in a multitude of projects of international administrations; in official statements, for example by the Secretary-General of the UN and by the European Commission, participation of civil society in the field of international policy is considered indispensable.

In this way, two ideas are being propagated and at least sometimes actively promoted, which, in combination, are hoped to contribute significantly to the amelioration of problems in international policy. On the one hand, increased importance is placed on the term and concept of civil society by governmental as well as non-governmental actors. On the other hand, the outlines of a policy of partial inclusion of non-governmental actors within a concept of *(global) governance* becomes evident.[2] This includes a renunciation of purely governmental control mechanisms. Besides the state (primary medium: power) and business (primary medium: money), civil society not only puts its capacity for self-regulation beyond the state and business into effect, according to its traditional self-conception, but also claims the right to participate in world policy. This is happening with increasing self-confidence and to the applause of

---

1　Since the campaign against the WTO conference in Seattle 1999, global justice groups increasingly present themselves as the representatives of (global) civil society. This self-image was especially clear at the World Social Forum meetings in Porto Alegre, Brazil (2001 and 2002), as well as at the first European Social Forum meeting in Florence in 2002. Meanwhile, the World Social Forum has established an International Council comprising representatives of social movements and citizen associations from all parts of the world.

2　It would usually be more appropriate to speak of 'international' instead of 'global' governance. The area addressed does not always encompass the whole of the world.

the liberal media. I will try to show that some expectations in this context go beyond what reality has to offer.

16.2 Civil society, NGOs and global governance: concepts and problem constellations

The attractiveness of concepts such as modernisation and sustainable development as well as civil society and global governance arises from problem constellations where traditional structures, ways of thinking and approaches to problem-solving do not seem to hold appropriate solutions any longer. In any case, these concepts have a normative core; they refer to unfinished projects and because of their indeterminacy they offer a common ground to a multitude of groups and join representatives with heterogeneous interests. At the same time, this makes the concepts suspicious to some observers and they inevitably become the object of criticism with regard to their ideological aspects. Yet, before problems can be pointed out and an assessment can take place, the concepts need to be clarified.

16.2.1 Civil society

Discussion about civil society can only make sense if it includes a specification of society or a relevant part of it. We can speak of civil society to the extent that major parts of this society fulfil the criteria of 'civility'. 'Civil' as an adjective has at least two meanings. On the one hand, it refers to a non-governmental or non-military phenomenon. This meaning is reflected in words such as civilian service or civilian. On the other hand side, the adjective 'civil' is synonymous for moderated, tolerant, civilised and peaceful. This meaning again is reflected in terms such as civil disobedience or civil behaviour. Another ambiguity stems from the combination of a descriptive statement (civil society does exist) with a normative statement (civil society as an idea, an unfinished project). We have grown used to thinking that civil society is something that exists yet at the same time we have to admit that every society that we may address as a civil society also contains uncivil elements (Dubiel 2001). The reports of, for example, Amnesty International and Human Rights Watch have a lot to say in this matter.

How can civil society be defined as a social sciences concept? In my opinion, there are two fundamentally different definition strategies. The first and most common follows a 'domain logic'. Following this logic yet depending on the scope of the perspective, civil society would be the sphere of the non-governmental or the sector beyond state and the economy. While there is a consensus to exclude the state from the definition, the exclusion of the economy is a matter of fierce dispute; liberal theorists, especially the Scottish moral philosophers Adam Smith and Adam Ferguson, understand the economy, namely the market, as a genuine part of civil society. Not surprisingly, today's business representatives claim to be a natural part of civil society. This is evident in terms such as corporate citizenship and the public relations strategies of leading corporations.

Another definition strategy, which I prefer, follows an 'interaction logic'. Here, spheres of society are being identified that show a prevailing but not exclusively valid principle of interaction and integration. In the context of sociological thinking, these notions were expressed by Talcott Parsons (1980), among others. With regard to modern societies, he defines four essential interaction principles (interaction media) and their respective domains (Table 16.1).

Medium	Domain
Power	State, bureaucracy
Money, exchange	Economy, market
Solidarity	Community, family
Recognition, respect	Civil society

TABLE 16.1 Media of social interaction and domains

Following this interaction logic approach, civil society does not consist of a fixed institutional and actor-related domain. Rather, civil society is a *relational* term. It comes into effect by the measure in which its mode of interaction prevails over other and competing modes of interaction. As a consequence, there are civil-society actors or actions in spheres usually attributed to the state, the economy or communities or families but where a different action logic prevails. For example, contracts have an important role in the economy which is not exclusively based on the medium of money but also on mutual trust and, in the case of a breach of contract, on sanctions by the state.

Likewise, civil society's mode of interaction can play a complementary role in other domains without suspending or replacing the dominant mode of interaction in the domain in question. This is true, for example, for large and abstract communities such as nations. Other than intimately small groups, which are integrated through direct interaction, a nation relies on imagined similarities, which nevertheless have real consequences for individual behaviour (Anderson 1983). At the same time, a nation is mainly based on interaction among strangers in the mode of recognition (and not exclusively solidarity). But, while even large communities such as nations (just like the state) rely on territorial, legal and symbolic demarcations, civil society does not have such boundaries. Similar to the economy, civil society is in principle an open system so that there is no sense in talking of French, European or Asian civil society.[3] Behavioural principles and not territorial boundaries mark the ambit of civil society. The boundary to the uncivil cuts across countries and continents.

Another important aspect of this conception of civil society is that no identity of interests can be assumed for the persons concerned, not even for those in pursuit of the common good. It is also not being assumed that, in order to establish a civil society, all or most of the groups need an orientation towards the common good or, like commu-

3   Accordingly, Dahrendorf (1999: 29) calls civil societies 'imperfect' as long as they confine themselves to national boundaries (similar: Gellner 1994).

nities, have to be connected via mutual solidarity. Rather it is sufficient that certain interaction principles are valid: respecting that others are different; respecting fundamental human and civil rights—this includes to abstain from violence as a means of solving conflicts, to respect that conflicting interests of others may well be legitimate or even more legitimate than one's own interests; respecting the principle that conflicts should be solved fairly and that a compromise is a solution that has to be accepted.

16.2.2 Non-governmental organisations (NGOs)

NGOs are often perceived as the core of civil society (Warren 2001). Their participation is constitutive for the global governance idea. The term 'NGO' was created in the historical context of the United Nations after the Second World War and is mentioned in article 71 of the Charter of the United Nations. The term became necessary in order to address all those groups and organisations that governments sometimes had to deal with but who do not possess the legal status of governments, such as the Red Cross and labour unions (Willetts 1982: 11ff.).

Yet the term 'NGO' was created only as a kind of linguistic garbage can wherein all non-state actors easily fit: the Catholic Church and the Mafia, IBM and the small plumber's firm, the Socialist International and Scientology. So it appears not completely unjustified for Egon Bahr to qualify al-Qaeda, in an ironic but at the same time consistent manner, as an NGO (according to Kraushaar 2001: 23). In the light of this and similar consequences I have proposed to eliminate the term 'NGO' from the language of academia (Rucht 1996: 31) although I was quite aware that the use of certain words cannot be controlled by appeals.

From this use of the term 'NGO' as a kind of large 'container', a narrower and increasingly popular application of the term is to be distinguished. Here, the term 'NGO' (or 'INGO') refers to groups and associations oriented towards the public interest and not towards profits (public-interest groups). This narrower term again holds definition problems, which it shares with the term 'third sector' (referring to a sector beyond the market and the state, sometimes beyond the market, the state and the family) (Salamon and Anheier 1996). To give just one example: does the Car Drivers' Party really pursue the Swiss public interest? Are there any criteria to distinguish public and private interests, even though all actors in political conflicts claim some kind of link to the public interest? Regardless of this need for clarification, it would be appropriate to introduce a special term for NGOs in the narrower sense of the word (or, for a lack of better alternatives, to continue using the term 'public-interest group')—a term to address the specific differences compared with other NGOs.

In addition, I perceive the necessity to introduce an even narrower category with regard to movement-like transnational NGOs. For those, the term 'TSMO' ('transnational social movement organisation' [Smith 1996]) has been proposed, given that they are transnational actors. This is only a subset of the associations organised by, for example, the Union of International Associations. Yet along with the term 'TSMO' a need for clarification is incurred with regard to social movements, which will not be addressed on this occasion.[4]

---

4 Social movements are efforts of networks of groups and organisations, who, based on a sense of collective identity, are trying to accomplish or prevent social change mainly by collective and public interest.

16.2.3 International governance

Since the UN conference in Rio in 1992, the term 'sustainable development' has become common knowledge. Soon after Rio, so it is said in a critical essay, global governance became the new buzzword (Hierlmeier 2002: 127) to be spread with 'categorial roar' (Lothar Hack). The Commission on Global Governance, initiated by Willy Brandt, played an important role in the diffusion of the term.[5] Most often, the term is normatively interpreted to mean 'good governance' (Falk 1995). This is for example evident in proposals to interpret global governance—for which there is no satisfactory equivalent in the German language—as 'rule of international law and global responsibility ethics' (Messner and Nuscheler 1996: 19) or to ascribe global governance the function to establish 'globalisation with a human face' (UNDP 1999). Many of those who say 'global governance' and mean 'good governance' envision a kind of rule that is open to participation, holds comparatively little lust for power and is oriented towards the common good.[6] In contrast with this view, there is a proposal from the periphery of the German Green Party dating back to the 1980s to translate the term quite sombrely as 'global (or international) structural policy'. I think that both proposals miss the semantic core that has evolved in this debate which is that governance refers to a mode of governing that includes non-governmental actors. These semantics are not so much inherent in the term governance itself[7] but have to be borne in mind in the context of this new application. These connotations are the whole point of using the term 'governance' instead of 'governance, policy, etc.'. This new meaning is expressed in the following quotation:

> As a matter of fact, global governance does not refer to government action, but to the co-operation of governments, international and supranational institutions, economic and other non-governmental actors in a network of formal and informal relationships. In addition, global governance encompasses the linkage of different policy levels, namely the international, national and local levels (Brand et al. 2000: 13).

5   The commission ('an independent group of 28 public figures') was established in February 1993 and presented its first report in 1995, the 50th anniversary of the UN. A second report followed in the run-up to the Millennium Round. Its Terms of Reference state: 'Together with the world-wide movement towards participatory democracy, there has been greater attention to the rights of individuals and of minorities, and to the role of civil society and its voluntary organisations in advancing the people's interest. The Commission will be concerned with the protection of these rights. It will consider how individuals, peoples and nations can be empowered to exercise greater control over their fate and how democratic accountability can be fostered at all levels, from local to global' (www.cgg.ch/tor.htm). In a way, the commission is a follow-up to the North–South Commission chaired by Willy Brandt. This institution was founded by World Bank president Robert McNamara in 1977. In its 1980 report (*A Program for Survival*), the commission proposed a tax on weapons spending and transfer to finance development programmes.

6   Similar is the conception of the European Commission: 'The term "governance" points to rules, procedures and actions describing the manner of how authority is exerted at the European level, in particular with regard to openness, participation, responsibility, effectiveness and coherence' (European Commission 2001: 11).

7   The *Oxford English Reference Dictionary* (1996 edition) describes governance as: '1. the act or manner of governing. 2. the office or function of governing. 3. sway, control.' The first meaning is exactly the same as that of government as 'the act or manner of governing' (*ibid.*).

Of course, the idea that rulership—at any level whatsoever—should not be left to elected or nominated political specialists is not entirely new. During the late 1960s and early 1970s, the idea was quite fashionable at the local and national level in the context of the debate on participation. Yet, until now, the field of international regimes was clearly the domain of government representatives. This is true notwithstanding the inclusion of NGOs in bodies of the UN since the Second World War; only since the 1980s has there been a debate and an increasing number of occurrences to suggest that acknowledgement of NGOs goes beyond symbolic gestures.

The willingness to let non-governmental actors participate can be attributed to three factors:

- The aforementioned lack of democratic control and the related problematic legitimacy of international policy-making

- The increasingly urgent demands for participation by national and transnational NGOs; these are at last the delayed results of the 'participatory revolution' (Max Kaase) at the transnational level

- The increase in numbers, resources and mobilising capacity of national and transnational NGOs

Growing factual urgency of problems and growing external political pressure—not political wisdom—led institutions of international policy to not only court civil-society actors but also to grant them participation opportunities in political processes. This is taking place in a rather differentiated manner and, as will be shown, to a rather moderate extent.

16.3 What practical experience with the concept of global governance is available and what are the limitations?

There are no civil societies at the local, national and international level in a *pure* form, nor is there, despite all claims to the contrary, any such thing as global governance—at least not if you take the concept's normative elements seriously. Even with the programmatic impetus of global governance, international policy is still power policy and the powerless will be given the opportunity to participate only in symbolic or marginal issues. This is true *cum grano salis* for the governments of economically unimportant countries; this is also true for civil society in general and certain parts of civil society in particular.

This fact should not be covered up by the self-perception of many civil-society groups or the rhetoric of international institutions, most notably the United Nations and its subsidiary organisations. There are tremendous differences concerning the role of civil-society actors between and within distinct policy fields which I am going to discuss later on.

However, there is generally speaking a trend towards paying more attention to civil-society actors and sometimes even giving them more influence. This is attributable to a number of factors that have already been mentioned:

1. The increase in transborder problems requires increased international co-operation and negotiation. This increases the importance and perceived importance of international policy, which is less and less the domain of diplomacy and secret negotiations among states and instead becomes a matter of public forms of politics.

2. The growing urgency of problems to states and state associations is not offset by an increased problem-solving competence at the level of governmental bodies. This amounts to a lack of political control concerning the governmental bodies, rendered more severe by opportunities for blockade politics and resulting in 'lowest common denominator' politics. At the international level, the pressure is growing because decision-makers are relatively uninformed with regard to concrete regional and local problems.

3. Civil-society actors pour into this gap performing varying objective functions, especially as problem indicators, critics and accusers, as allies in case of conflicting interests between and within governments; they lend legitimacy in the context of making and implementing decisions and finally as sources of advice, as helper and executor in the implementation of sectoral policies. These very different functions probably explain why civil-society actors are being scolded and embraced at the same time—often by the same governmental actors.

4. The availability of modern information and communication devices facilitates cross-border co-operation and mobilisation for civil-society actors and thus enlarges the opportunities even for groups with very limited resources.

5. Civil-society actors command increasingly professional expertise on fundraising and some of them have even begun to employ commercial service providers for acquiring members and donations.

6. Finally, some of the civil-society actors benefit from affectionate media coverage and thus reach mass audiences.

The real gain in importance of civil-society actors in the context of international governance is far overestimated by the public and many civil-society actors. Minor successes serve as evidence for general tendencies, not least to boost one's own morale; some civil-society actors already perceive the fact that they are being invited, listened to and flattered as a significant breakthrough, with no heed for the possibility that they might be just a decoration in a game on which they are allowed to comment but not exert an influence. This pattern was to be observed, for example, at the Johannesburg summit in August/September 2002, when NGOs, as Type II groups, were separated from the real wielders of power (Type I) and thus had next to no influence at all on what was happening.[8]

---

8 Young participants invited by governments to the preparation conference and the summit itself were not allowed to wear T-shirts with political slogans.

Some civil-society actors also overlook the fact that they are pawns in a strategy of 'divide and rule'. The well-meaning actors with modest demands and agreeable manners are offered favours and get invited to talks and delegations while the radicals, the system changers, are being stigmatised and become the object of police action (Wahl 1997).

This differentiated treatment of civil-society actors by public bodies correlates with their different roles and importance in other policy fields. Just as feminists had to realise that their presence in national institutions grew at the same measure as these institutions themselves faced a loss in power (e.g. parliaments in their relation to governments), in the field of international policy-making civil-society actors are most likely to be listened to and to participate where questions of power play a minor role.

It is quite instructive to take a look from this perspective at policy fields that are to a varying degree accommodating to the participatory thinking within the global governance discourse with regard to their respective inherent logic and actor constellations: human rights policy, climate policy and international debt regimes. With regard to these three policy fields I propose that the opportunities for the realisation of civil-society participation in international politics depend on three parameters:

- The relative importance of economic issues and questions of political power within the policy field

- The amount of control and/or legitimacy problems

- The power of civil-society mobilisation

The impact of NGOs tends to be significant on policy issues, which the economically leading countries perceive to be marginally important. This is quite evident with regard to the International Whaling Commission (Stoett 1995: ch. 5), the London Dumping Convention (Stairs and Taylor 1992) and the anti-landmine campaign (Price 1998). In these areas it was easy for NGOs to attain opportunities for participation and even co-determination and also easy to achieve some kind of success. Within the core business of power politics, the situation is quite the opposite: namely, questions of armament and military strategy, international finance including global debt regimes or issues in global energy supply. Here, I see no or at best a symbolic right to a say in the matter and no or only symbolic influence of public-interest groups.

In between the extremes of soft and hard issues lie areas with a contingency to the amount of inclusion and exclusion of public-interest groups. In this context, policy-specific actor and problem constellations can decide the issue one way or the other. While, for example, a hard and exclusive strategy prevails concerning patent rights on seeds, there are other fields that show tendencies towards a softened stance of the political elites. The debate on major conventional, technical projects, which has been going on for decades, not only led to a few withdrawals of international lenders such as the World Bank from projects of this kind (e.g. the Narmada project in India) but also led to the World Bank applying more demanding criteria with regard to social and environmental effects for such projects. In addition, a commission with a number of seats assigned to representatives of public-interest groups was established, the International Commission on Large Dams, which has proposed a remarkable change of direction. This is even more noteworthy because of the fact that industry representatives participated in the proceedings. A limited success was also achieved by the international campaign of a number of NGOs against the pharmaceutical industry, even considering that they did not reach general institutional arrangements. After 41 corporation had filed lawsuits against South Africa because it intended to facilitate access of its citizens to cheap imitations (generic pharmaceuticals) of patented AIDS drugs, the firms faced so much public pressure in advance of the AIDS summit in Durban that they abandoned the suit in April 2002.[9]

Other examples of limited influence of public-interest groups and transnational movement organisations on the course of single decision-making processes or on structures could be found, but a comprehensive account would still be likely to show a negative bottom line. Intervention opportunities and even more so actual influence of civil-society actors in the process of international governance are quite humble. Maybe my scepticism is too harsh because I perceive too much rhetoric from governmental actors at the same time, and civil-society actors who are too starry-eyed and overestimate their abilities.[10] I am quite aware of the impressive transnational mobilisation which has received a lot of attention since Seattle and in the meantime caused reactions from some representatives of national and international governments. Cases in point are the statement of high-ranking politicians at the World Economic Forum in Washington, DC in January 2002 as well as initiatives to establish dialogues, to improve on transparency and to respect sustainability criteria within the World Bank, the International Monetary Fund and the WTO.

Anyway, I remain sceptically attendant on future development. The disposition to move from exclusive rulership to structures and processes of inclusive global governance are not so much a question of understanding and better arguments but of political pressure from those who are still outsiders and spectators. Many observers, feminists among them, are quite right in their criticism that the concept of global governance is oblivious to power (Brand 2001), insofar as the global circumstances should not be mistaken for a global civil society. There is no such thing (Roth 2001; Heins 2002) even if global justice groups gathering in Porto Alegre or elsewhere pretend to be so very self-assured, even if social scientists excitedly praise transnational civil-society networks as the 'liberation of democracy from the confinement of the state' (Beck 1998: 13).

The opening question of what to expect from global governance and its emphatic relationship to civil society is for now to be answered rather sceptically. Global governance is an action programme and not reality. For now, there is more of a side-by-side than a true dialogue of a multitude of actors.[11] Whether more inclusion of civil-society groups solves the problems ahead remains to be seen. I think it is quite probable that such attempts at solutions are usually better than attempts from governments alone; I also feel that this inclusion is desirable from a democratic perspective.

---

9   *Die Tageszeitung*, 8 October 2002: 9.
10   For example, Naomi Klein (2001: 430) claims that the international co-ordination of corporation critics is 'good and devastating to its opponents'.
11   The UN conference on Financing for Development in Monterrey in March 2002 was symptomatic in this regard. There were three forums: the round of political leaders, the Business Forum and the Global NGO Forum with very little going on between them.

References

Anderson, B. (1983) *Imagined Communities: Reflections on the Origin and Spread of Nationalism* (London: Verso).

Ayres, J.M. (2002) 'Transnational Political Processes and Contention against the Global Economy', in J. Smith and H. Johnston (eds.), *Globalization and Resistance: Transnational Dimensions of Social Movements* (Lanham, MD: Rowman & Littlefield): 191-205.

Beck, U. (1998) 'Wie wird Demokratie im Zeitalter der Globalisierung möglich? Eine Einleitung', in U. Beck (ed.), *Politik der Globalisierung* (Frankfurt am Main: Suhrkamp): 7-67.

Berndt, M., and D. Sack (2001) *Global Governance: Voraussetzungen und Formen demokratischer Beteiligung im Zeichen der Globalisierung* (Wiesbaden, Germany: Westdeutscher Verlag).

Brand, U. (2001) 'Ordnung und Gestaltung. Global Governance als hegemonialer Diskurs postfordistischer Politik?', in M. Berndt and D. Sack (eds.), *Global Governance? Voraussetzungen und Formen demokratischer Beteiligung im Zeichen der Globalisierung* (Wiesbaden, Germany: Westdeutscher Verlag): 93-110.

——, A. Brunnengräber, L. Schrader, C. Stock and P. Wahl (2000) *Global Governance: Alternative zur neoliberalen Globalisierung?* (Münster, Germany: Westfälisches Dampfboot).

Brunnengräber, A., A. Klein and H. Walk (eds.) (2001) *NGOs als Legitimationsressource: Zivilgesellschaftliche Partizipationsformen im Globalisierungsprozess* (Opladen, Germany: Leske & Budrich).

Dahrendorf, R. (1999) 'Die Bürgergesellschaft', in A. Pongs (ed.), *In welcher Gesellschaft leben wir eigentlich? Gesellschaftskonzepte im Vergleich* (Munich: Dilemma): 87-104.

Dubiel, H. (2001) 'Unzivile Gesellschaften', *Soziale Welt* 52.1: 133-50.

European Commission (2001) *Europäisches Regieren: Weissbuch* (Luxemburg: Europäische Gemeinschaften).

Falk, R. (1995) *On Humane Governance: Toward a New Global Politics* (Pennsylvania, PA: Pennsylvania University Press).

Fues, T., and B.I. Hamm (eds.) (2001) *Die Weltkonferenzen der 90er Jahre: Baustellen für Global Governance* (Bonn, Germany: Dietz).

Gellner, E. (1994) *Conditions of Liberty: Civil Society and its Rivals* (London: Hamish Hamilton).

Grote, J.R., and B. Gbikpi (eds.) (2002) *Participatory Governance: Political and Societal Implications* (Opladen, Germany: Leske & Budrich).

Habermas, J. (1998) *Die postnationale Konstellation* (Frankfurt am Main: Suhrkamp).

Heins, V. (2002) 'Der Mythos der globalen Zivilgesellschaft', in C. Frantz and A. Zimmer (eds.), *Zivilgesellschaft international: Alte und neue Global Players* (Opladen, Germany: Leske & Budrich): 83-101.

Hierlmeier, J. (Moe) (2002) *Internationalismus. Eine Einführung in die Ideengeschichte des Internationalismus: von Vietnam bis Genua* (Stuttgart, Germany: Schmetterling Verlag).

Klein, N. (2001) 'Abschied vom "Ende der Geschichte": Organisation und Vision in konzernkritischen Bewegungen', in J. Mander and E. Goldsmith (eds.), *Schwarzbuch Globalisierung: Eine fatale Entwicklung mit vielen Verlierern und wenigen Gewinnern* (Munich: Riemann): 421-42.

Kraushaar, W. (2001) 'Die Grenzen der Anti-Globalisierungsbewegung', *Mittelweg* 36.6: 4-23.

Messner, D., and F. Nuscheler (eds.) (1996) *Weltkonferenzen und Weltberichte: Ein Wegweiser durch die internationale Diskussion* (Bonn, Germany: Dietz).

Offe, C. (1979) 'Unregierbarkeit: Zur Renaissance konservativer Krisentheorien', in J. Habermas (ed.), *Stichworte zur 'Geistigen Situation der Zeit'* (vol. 1; Frankfurt am Main: Suhrkamp): 294-318.

Parsons, T. (1980) *Zur Theorie der sozialen Interaktionsmedien* (edited and with a foreword by Stefan Jensen; Opladen, Germany: Westdeutscher Verlag).

Pianta, M. (2001) 'Parallel Summits of Global Civil Society', in H. Anheier, M. Glasius and M. Kaldor (eds.), *Global Civil Society 2001* (Oxford, UK: University of Oxford Press): 169-94.

Price, R. (1998) 'Reversing the Gun Sights: Transnational Civil Society Targets Land Mines', *International Organization* 52.3: 613-44.

Roth, R. (2001) 'NGO und transnationale soziale Bewegungen: Akteure einer 'Weltzivilgesellschaft'?', in U. Brand, A. Demirovic, C. Görg and J. Hirsch (eds.), *Nichtregierungsorganisationen in der Transformation des Staates* (Münster, Germany: Westfälisches Dampfboot): 43-63.

Rucht, D. (1996) 'Multinationale Bewegungsorganisationen: Bedeutung, Bedingungen, Perspektiven', *Forschungsjournal Neue Soziale Bewegungen* 9.2: 30-41.

—— (2001) 'Transnationaler politischer Protest im historischen Längsschnitt', in A. Klein, R. Koopmans and H. Geiling (eds.), *Globalisierung, Partizipation, Protest* (Opladen, Germany: Leske & Budrich): 77-96.

—— (2002) 'Rückblicke und Ausblicke auf die globalisierungskritischen Bewegungen', in H. Walk and N. Boehme (eds.), *Globaler Widerstand: Internationale Netzwerke auf der Suche nach Alternativen im globalen Kapitalismus* (Münster, Germany: Westfälisches Dampfboot): 57-82.

—— (2003a) 'Global Governance: Eine Antwort auf Steuerungsprobleme internationalen Regierens?', in J. Allemendinger (ed.), *Entstaatlichung und Soziale Sicherheit: Verhandlungen des 31. Kongresses der Deutschen Gesellschaft für Soziologie in Leipzig 2002* (Opladen, Germany: Leske & Budrich).

—— (2003b) 'Social Movements Challenging Neo-liberal Globalization', in P. Ibarra (ed.), *Social Movements and Democracy* (New York: Palgrave Macmillan): 211-28.

Salamon, L.M., and H.K. Anheier (eds.) (1996) *Defining the Nonprofit Sector* (Manchester, UK: Manchester University Press).

Smith, J. (1996) 'Characteristics of the Modern Transnational Social Movement Sector', in J. Smith, C. Chatfield and R. Pagnucco (eds.), *Transnational Social Movements and Global Politics* (Syracuse, NY: Syracuse University Press): 42-58.

Stairs, K., and P. Taylor (1992) 'Non-governmental Organizations and Legal Protection of the Oceans: A Case Study', in A. Hurrell and B. Kingsbury (eds.), *The International Politics of the Environment: Actors, Interests, and Institutions* (Oxford, UK: Clarendon Press): 110-41.

Stoett, P.J. (1995) *Atoms, Whales, and Rivers: Global Environmental Security and International Organization* (Commack, NY: Nova Science).

UNDP (United Nations Development Programme) (1999) *Globalization with a Human Face: Human Development Report* (Oxford, UK: Oxford University Press).

Wahl, P. (1997) 'Mythos und Realität internationaler Zivilgesellschaft', in E. Altvater, A. Brunnengräber, M. Haake and H. Walk (eds.), *Vernetzt und verstrickt: Nicht-Regierungsorganisationen als gesellschaftliche Produktivkraft* (Münster, Germany: Westfälisches Dampfboot): 293-314.

Warren, M.E. (2001) *Democracy and Association* (Princeton, NJ: Princeton University Press).

Willetts, P. (1982) 'Pressure Groups as Transnational Actors', in P. Willetts (ed.), *Pressure Groups in the Global System: The Transnational Relations of Issue-orientated Non-governmental Organizations* (New York: St Martin's Press): 1-27.

Zürn, M. (1998) *Regieren jenseits des Nationalstaates* (Frankfurt am Main: Suhrkamp).

Abbreviations

ABM	Anti-Ballistic Missile
AIDS	acquired immuno-deficiency syndrome
ANC	African National Congress
AOSIS	Alliance of Small Island States
BMBF	Bundesministeriums für Bildung und Forschung (German Federal Ministry for Education and Research)
BMU	Bundesumweltministerium für Umwelt, Naturschutz und Reaktorsicherheit (German Federal Ministry for the Environment, Nature Conservation and Nuclear Safety)
BOVESPA	Bolsa de Valores de São Paulo (São Paulo stock exchange)
BSE	bovine spongiform encephalopathy
CFC	chlorofluorocarbon
CGG	Commission on Global Governance
CO_2	carbon dioxide
COP	Communication on Progress (UNGC)
CPR	common pool resources
CSR	corporate social responsibility
DAWN	Development Alternatives with Women for a New Era
EC	European Commission
EIA	environmental impact assessment
EMAS	Eco-management and Audit Scheme (EU)
EO	Evaluation Office (UNDP)
EU	European Union
EWL	European Women's Lobby
FAO	Food and Agriculture Organisation (UN)
FDI	foreign direct investment
FSC	Forest Stewardship Council
FT	*Financial Times*
FTSE	*Financial Times* Stock Exchange
GAD	gender and development
GATS	General Agreement on Trade in Services
GATT	General Agreement on Tariffs and Trade
GC	Global Compact (UN)
GEO	Global Environment Outlook
GMEF	Global Ministerial Environment Forum
GMO	genetically modified organism
GNP	gross national product
GRI	Global Reporting Initiative
GWP	Global Water Partnership

HIPC	heavily indebted poor country
HIV	human immunodeficiency virus
HSE	health, safety and environment
ICC	International Chamber of Commerce
IFI	international financial institution
IGO	intergovernmental organisation
IGO	international governmental organisation
ILO	International Labour Organisation
IMF	International Monetary Fund
INGO	international non-governmental organisation
IÖW	Institut für ökologische Wirtschaftsforschung (Institute for Ecological Economic Research, Germany)
IPP	integrated product policy
IPRs	intellectual property rights
ISO	International Organisation for Standardisation
IT	information technology
JSE	Johannesburg Stock Exchange
KPI	key performance indicator
LA21	Local Agenda 21
LCA	life-cycle assessment
LDC	less/least developed country
LTCM	Long-Term Capital Management
MDGs	Millennium Development Goals
MFN	most favoured nation
NGO	non-governmental organisation
NIMBY	not in my back yard
ODA	official development assistance
OECD	Organisation for Economic Co-operation and Development
OED	Operation Evaluation Department (World Bank)
OFR	Operating and Financial Review
OHCHR	Office of the High Commissioner for Human Rights
PRSP	poverty reduction strategy paper
PTA	participatory technology assessment
PVC	polyvinyl chloride
QUANGO	quasi-autonomous non-governmental organisation
R&D	research and development
RBM	Roll Back Malaria Initiative
RTB	race to the bottom
S&T	science and technology
SIA	sustainability impact assessment
SME	small or medium-sized enterprise
SO_2	sulphur dioxide
SOA	sphere of authority
SÖF	Sozial-ökologische Forschung (Socio-ecological Research, BMBF)
SPRU	Science and Policy Research Unit, University of Sussex
STI	science, technology and innovation
TNC	transnational corporation

TRIMs	Trade-Related Investment Measures
TRIPS	Trade-Related Aspects of Intellectual Property Rights
TSMO	transnational social movement organisation
UN	United Nations
UNCED	UN Conference on Environment and Development
UNCTAD	UN Conference on Trade and Development
UNDP	UN Development Programme
UNEP	UN Environment Programme
UNGC	UN Global Compact
UNICEF	UN Children's Fund
UNIFEM	UN Fund for Women
UNODC	UN Office on Drugs and Crime
WBCSD	World Business Council for Sustainable Development
WCD	World Commission on Dams
WHO	World Health Organisation
WID	women in development
WRI	World Resources Institute
WSF	World Social Forum
WSSD	World Summit on Sustainable Development
WTO	World Trade Organisation
WWF	Formerly World Wildlife Fund and World Wide Fund for Nature

About the contributors

Thorsten Benner is Associate Director of the Global Public Policy Institute (GPPi), Berlin. He studied political science, history and sociology at the University of Siegen (Germany), the University of York (UK) and the University of California at Berkeley. From 2001 to 2003 he was a McCloy Scholar at the Kennedy School of Government, Harvard University, where he received a Master in Public Administration (MPA). Prior to co-founding the Global Public Policy Institute in 2003, he was a Policy Analyst at the Office of Development Studies, United Nations Development Programme, New York; a Research Fellow with the German Council on Foreign Relations (DGAP), Berlin; and a Research Associate with the Global Public Policy Project, Washington, DC.

Nicola Bullard has worked with trade unions, women's organisations, human rights groups and development agencies for more than 20 years, in Australia, Thailand and Cambodia. She has also worked as a journalist and editor and has studied geography and international relations. Since 1997, Nicola has been with Focus on the Global South, an international policy research and advocacy organisation based in Bangkok, Thailand, researching, campaigning and writing on the political economy of neoliberal globalisation and alternatives. She edits the monthly electronic newsletter *Focus on Trade* and is active in the international 'movement of movements' for another globalisation.

Dr **Jens Clausen** has a diploma in engineering and from 1991 to 2005 has been undertaking research as a member of the Institute for Ecological Economic Research (IÖW) in the field of environmental management. Before joining the IÖW, he worked in the research and development department of the Continental Corporation in Hannover. In 2004 he completed his dissertation on sustainable entrepreneurship at the University of Bremen. Since 2005 he has been a partner of the Borderstep Institute for Innovation and Sustainability, Berlin and Hannover. His activities focus on entrepreneurship, innovation, sustainable markets, sustainability reporting and CSR.

Prof. Dr **Martin Jänicke** studied sociology, political science, economics and history at the Freie Universität Berlin. In 1970, he habilitated in political science and has been a professor for Comparative Politics at the Department of Political Science since 1971. In addition, he has been head of the Environmental Policy Research Centre (FFU) since 1986. Between 1974 and 1976, he was adviser to the planning staff of the Bundeskanzleramt and from 1981 to 1983 Member of the Berlin State Parliament. Since April 1999, Martin Jänicke has been member of the German Advisory Council for the Environment (SRU) and was its vice-chairman from 2000 to 2004. He has been involved in numerous scientific boards and advisory committees, including the German UNESCO Commission (1991–96) and the National Research Committee for Global Environmental Change (1996–98). He is member of the Board of Advisors of the Deutsche Bundesstiftung Umwelt (DBU). In 1998, he received the Environmental Award by the Berlin Foundation for Nature Protection (Stiftung Naturschutz Berlin).

Martin Khor is the Director of the International Secretariat of the Third World Network. He has also been a member of the Board of the South Centre (1996–2002) and was formerly a vice-chairman of the Expert Group on the Right to Development of the UN Commission on Human Rights. He is a member of and consultant to the Consultative Group on Globalisation established under the National Economic Action Council in the Prime Minister's Department in Malaysia. He has also been a consultant to UNCTAD, UNDP, UNEP and the UN University, and has conducted studies and written papers for these agencies. Recently he co-ordinated a report of the Third World Network for UNDP on *The Multilateral Trading System: A Development Perspective*, which was published by UNDP in January 2002. He is the author of the book *Globalisation and the South*, which was a report he wrote for UNCTAD and distributed at the South Summit in Havana in 2000, and has written several other books and papers on trade and WTO issues, and on environment and development issues, including the book on *Intellectual Property, Biodiversity and Sustainable Development*. An economist trained at Cambridge University, UK, he has lectured in Economics at the Science University of Malaysia.

Angela Liberatore works in the Directorate General for Research of the European Commission on issues of governance, citizenship, conflicts and security, and was involved in the preparation of the Commission's White Paper on Governance. She holds a PhD in Political and Social Sciences (European University Institute) and a degree in Philosophy (University of Bologna). Her publications include: *The Management of Uncertainty: Learning from Chernobyl* (Gordon & Breach, 1999); the editing of a special issue of *Science and Public Policy* (Vol. 30 No. 3 [June 2003]) on 'Democratising Expertise, Expertising Democracy', with Silvio Funtowicz; and various articles on science–policy relations, risk management, environmental policy, European integration and governance issues. Her most recent work relates to the relations between security policies, democracy and expertise.

Ulrich Petschow is an economist and taught at the Berlin School of Economics during the 1980s. Since 1989, he has been senior researcher and since 1992 head of the unit environmental economics and politics at the Institute for Ecological Economic Research (IÖW). He has participated in the publication of several books as an author as well as an editor and is member of several councils. His general research area is sustainability and globalisation; more specific research interests include economic ecological valuation, analysis of new technologies (nanotechnologies, bionics, etc.) as well as firm strategies.

James N. Rosenau is University Professor of International Affairs at The George Washington University. A former president of the International Studies Association, he is the author of a number of articles and books, three of which retrospectively amount to a trilogy: *Turbulence in World Politics: A Theory of Change and Continuity* (Princeton University Press, 1990), *Along the Domestic–Foreign Frontier: Exploring Governance in a Turbulent World* (Cambridge University Press, 1997) and *Distant Proximities: Dynamics beyond Globalization* (Princeton University Press, 2003).

Dr **Frieder Rubik** studied national economics at the University of Heidelberg. He has worked for a number of environmental economics research institutes since 1982. He is currently senior researcher at the Institute for Ecological Economy Research (IÖW) and head of the Ecological Product Policy department. His key publications deal with product information schemes/eco-labelling, integrated product policy and life-cycle assessment (LCA); these include: *Integrierte Produktpolitik* (Metropolis), *LCA in Business and Industry: Adoption Patterns, Applications and Implications* (with Paolo Frankl; Springer, 1999) and *Product Policy in Europe: New Environmental Perspectives* (with F. Oosterhuis and G. Scholl; Kluwer, 1996).

Dieter Rucht is Honorary Professor of Sociology at the Free University of Berlin and co-director of the research group 'Civil Society, Citizenship and Political Mobilisation in Europe' at the Social Science Research Centre, Berlin. His research interests include political participation, social movements and political protest. Among his recent books are: *Women's Movements Facing the Reconfigured State* (edited with Lee Ann Banaszak and Karen Beckwith; Cambridge University Press, 2003); and *Cyberprotest: New Media, Citizens and Social Movements* (edited with Wim van de Donk, Brian D. Loader and Paul Nixon; Routledge, 2004). Currently, Rucht is involved in several research projects, among these the EU-funded project on 'Democracy in Europe and the Mobilisation of Society'.

Dr **Bernd Siebenhüner** is assistant professor of ecological economics and head of the GELENA research group on social learning and sustainability at Carl von Ossietzky University of Oldenburg (www.gelena. net). He is also deputy leader of the Global Governance Project (www.glogov.org). Bernd Siebenhüner holds a PhD in Economics and masters' degrees in Economics and Political Science. His research interests cover social learning, sustainability, corporate environmental management, organisational learning, linking social and natural sciences, and studies of human behaviour.

Charlotte Streck is Director of Climate Focus BV, Rotterdam. Climate Focus is a consultancy company that provides services to public and private entities active in the international carbon market. Before founding Climate Focus, Charlotte worked for five years as Senior Counsel with the World Bank in Washington, DC. In her work at the World Bank she specialised in providing advice on emissions trading operations and on questions related to the UNFCCC/Kyoto Protocol. She was educated in both Law and Biology at the Universities of Berlin, Regensburg and Freiburg, Germany, and Cordoba, Spain. Before she joined the World Bank in 2000, she co-operated with the Global Public Policy Project, which provided strategic advice for the Secretary-General of the UN. She is a founding and Board member of the Global Public Policy Institute and authored and co-authored several books and a series of articles on environmental governance, law and policy.

A South African by birth (1967), **Cornis van der Lugt** is based in Paris at the Division of Technology, Industry and Economics (DTIE) of the United Nations Environment Programme (UNEP), where he is responsible for corporate responsibility (CESR), the UN Global Compact (GC) and the Global Reporting Initiative (GRI). In recent years he has represented UNEP and the GC at various international conferences and in GRI expert working groups. He is also GC-nominated expert in the ISO process to develop a standard on social responsibility, building on his close involvement in promoting UNEP–business partnership and accountability. He has undertaken long-standing research in the field of International Political Economy, focusing on the environment and the role of business and industry. He received his PhD in International Relations at the University of Stellenbosch in 1998. His doctoral studies involved research at the Albert-Ludwigs-Universität Freiburg (Germany) and the Rijksuniversiteit Leiden (Netherlands), following which he gained experience as multilateral diplomat in international negotiations under the UN agreements on climate change and ozone depletion.

Dr **Claudia von Braunmühl**, born in 1944, studied political science at the Free University of Berlin and lectured in International Relations at the Department of Social Sciences of the University of Frankfurt from 1968 to 1979 with a one-year (1976/77) period as guest professor at the Department of Politics of the University of Edinburgh. Following the years 1980–84, when she was posted in Jamaica as country director of German Development Service, she did and still does consultancy work in development and lectured at various universities. Since 1996 she has been Honorary Professor in International Relations at the Free University of Berlin. From 2002 to 2005 she was acting chair in development sociology/ development politics at the Faculty of Sociology of the University of Bielefeld.

Dr **Ernst Ulrich von Weizsäcker** has held positions as Founding President of the University of Kassel, Director of the United Nations Centre for Science and Technology for Development, Director of the Institute for European Environmental Policy, and President of the Wuppertal Institute for Climate, Environment and Energy. From 1998 to 2005 he was Member of the Bundestag (German Parliament), SPD, for Stuttgart, and Chairman, Bundestag Environment Committee, from 2002 to 2005. In 1989 he received the Italian Premio De Natura and in October 1996 the Duke of Edinburgh Gold Medal of WWF International. Among his publications is *Factor Four: Doubling Wealth, Halving Resource Use* (Earthscan Publications, 1997; available in 12 languages). From 2006 he has been Dean, Donald Bren School for Environmental Science and Management, UCSB, Santa Barbara, California, USA.

Dr **Mark Wade** joined Shell in 1979 as a research biochemist in support of the Chemicals business. Since then he has served in a variety of posts, including Technical Graduate Recruitment manager for Shell

International and Head of External Affairs for Shell Chemicals. In 1997 he moved to the Corporate Centre of Shell International as a founder member of the Sustainable Development Group. Mark relinquished his position as Head of Sustainable Development Policy, Strategy and Reporting early 2003 on moving to Shell Learning's Leadership Development group. He leads the Sustainable Development Learning activity charged with bringing about a step change in sustainable development awareness, understanding and capacity in Shell people. Mark is Shell's Liaison Delegate to the World Business Council for Sustainable Development and Chairman of the Business Network of the European Academy of Business in Society. He also serves on the Advisory Boards of the student organisations AIESEC and OIKOS.

Matthias Weber joined ARC systems research as Head of Department Technology Policy at the end of 2000. He is a trained Process Engineer (Dipl.-Ing.) and Political Scientist (Magister Artium), and holds a PhD in Innovation Economics from the University of Stuttgart. Before joining systems research, he had been working for several years at the European Commission's Institute for Prospective Technological Studies (IPTS) in Seville on research projects and policy analyses in the fields of transport and mobility innovations, European competitiveness, enlargement, and the impact of regulation and innovation in the energy and transport sectors. His current research interests address on the one hand issues of science, technology and innovation policy from a multi-level governance perspective, in particular in relation to foresight, priority-setting and policy strategies. On the other hand he has been working extensively on innovation and sustainability, with a particular interest in system innovations and the governance of transition processes in ICT, transport and production.

Jan Martin Witte is a co-founder and Associate Director of the Global Public Policy Institute (GPPi). Jan Martin holds degrees from Johns Hopkins University/SAIS and the University of Potsdam. He is currently completing a PhD thesis at Johns Hopkins University. His work experience includes consulting and research assignments at the Brookings Institution (Washington, DC), the Corporate Strategy Group of the World Bank (Washington, DC), the Office of Development Studies of the United Nations Development Programme (UNDP), and the Private Sector Partnership Unit of the United Nations Office for Project Services (UNOPS), New York. From June 1999 to June 2001 he served as a Research Associate with the Global Public Policy Project, Washington, DC.

Index